ONE
OF THE
BOYS

ONE OF THE BOYS

Beatrix von Watzdorf

ANDRE DEUTSCH

First published in Great Britain in 1995 by
André Deutsch Limited
106 Great Russell Street
London WC1B 3LJ

What Makes a Man a Man (John Pizer) © 1971 EMI
Catalogue Partnership/EMI Unart Catalog Inc. USA
Reprinted by permission of CPP/Belwin Europe, Surrey, England.

ISBN 0 233 98925 0

Cataloguing-in-Publication data available for this title
from the British Library

Printed in Great Britain by
St Edmundsbury Press
Bury St Edmunds, Suffolk

To the 'girls'

Cast of Characters

All Aboard

Principals:
Becka
Misha
Carla
Queen Bea
G-stringed boys:
José
Marcia (Mark)
Jamie
Barbettes:
Marcie
Pepper
Tanya (replaced by Barbie)
Tevita
Director/Choreographer:
Ruby Venezuela/Jason
Dresser:
Daisy (replaced by Claire)

Back to Havana

Principals:
Misha
Carla
Queen Bea
Teddi
G-stringed boys:
Alexander
Craig (later Zach)
Marcelle
Barbettes:
Barbie
Marcie
Mitzi
Sugar
Director/Choreographer:
Pablo
Dresser:
Claire

Forty Years a Queen

Principals:
Misha
Queen Bea
Ruby Venezuela (Brian)
Venus ManTrap (Jason)
G-stringed boys:
Zach
Marcia
Steve
Barbettes:
Barbie
Marcie
Mitzi
Mo (replaced by Amber)
Director/Choreographer:
Ruby Venezuela/Jason
Dresser:
Claire

Far from Reality

Principals:
Misha
Queen Bea
Ruby Venezuela
Venus ManTrap
G-stringed boys:
Ada
Jake
Steve
Barbettes:
Amber
Angel
Marcie
Mitzi
Director/Choreographer
Ruby Venezuela/Jason
Dresser:
Michael

Acknowledgements

I am indebted to all the colourful characters on the scene who generously shared their thoughts and experiences with me, in particular 'the gang' at JoJo's, my fabulous interviewees and our Ruby in the rough.

A heartfelt thanks to my literary agent, Patrick Walsh, for leading me through the maelstrom of an unconventional first, high-risk book; Zoë Ross, editor extraordinaire; and various individuals at Christopher Little and André Deutsch.

Also, to my dear friends for their constant encouragement and support – you know who you are. Most crucially, to Peter, Francis and Hazel, who gave me the courage to throw caution to the wind in the first place.

And finally, all my love and gratitude to my family, who have swallowed hard at my often unpalatable decisions but stood by me nevertheless.

Contents

Introduction

One of the most frequent misconceptions I have encountered is that drag equals transvestism. It does not. Drag is an art form in itself and, whether finding expression in Kabuki or Pantomime, it remains a profession. Anyone can be a transvestite, man or woman, hairdresser or accountant. As women, our cross-dressing is legitimised and has been since Marlene Dietrich shocked the world in a tuxedo; these days the impact has been reduced to a mere issue of fashion. This is sadly not applicable to male transvestites who, as a rule, carry their secret around with an air of guilt that could not be further removed from drag's unapologetic and cynically perverse nature. We had only one transvestite doubling as a drag queen in our 'Spectacular', which was to place him in a unique position that was further emphasised by his heterosexuality. Although drag has less to do with being gay than being camp, I can number the 'straight' queens of my acquaintance on one hand. Likewise, I am unaware of any growing trend towards drag among women. For over two years, I was the exception. A heterosexual, female drag queen.

The life of a drag queen is not pure glitz or Hollywood, as much as it may seek to impersonate the glamour in camp Bette Davis and Joan Crawford imagery. Drag is all too often Harvey Fierstein's *Torch Song Trilogy*, epitomised in the cry of a man's loneliness and frustration at pretending to be a woman but wanting to be loved by a man as a man. It frequently attracts bitchy, insecure egocentrics who would stomp over their own grandmother in stilettos to be noticed. Also charming, intelligent and kind human beings who can be contradictingly childlike and yet painfully wise. Equally, inhabitants of a genre that defies categorisation.

Many people have asked me the why, how and wherefore of living the peculiar existence I inherited at Madame JoJo's, Britain's most infamous drag club. Julie Andrews may have done similar in *Victor/Victoria* but, being comedy, it glossed over many dimensions of drag by presenting an acceptable face for conventional society. I was allowed to experience this unusual world from within, offering me an invaluable insight usually denied to anyone not gay, male and into drag. Not that I fully appreciated all of this as I originally hurled myself in the deep end.

When I first pulled up in front of Madame JoJo's Club Extraordinaire for my audition, I was terrified. Not only because I felt poised at the Gates of Hell in latterday Sodom & Gomorrah, but because I was starting to get desperate. I had graduated eighteen months earlier from the University of St Andrews, and promptly relegated my MA Honours degree to a back burner in the quest for theatrical stardom. After treading water in a BBC administrative position for what seemed like an eternity, I was fortunate enough to be cast as a lead in an Edinburgh Fringe production. The part and plot were about as challenging as watching paint dry, but we were nevertheless chosen for a BBC filming session on *Edinburgh Nights*. Fame and fortune at long last . . .

A rude reality check awaited in London, assuming the form of dodgy agents and any number of potential, non-Equity, topless cruises to Turkey. Therein lay my angst: I felt I had moved mountains to obtain a Provisional Equity card, only to stand in very real danger of losing it again. Both types of Equity, Actors' and Variety Performers', give a six-month deadline to produce qualifying work towards full union membership; otherwise, provisional acceptance runs out and the whole shebang starts from scratch all over again. I needed work that paid certain rates under specific conditions and *soon*. Istanbul really did not register on my map of procedure and, on top of that, the two-year deadline I had agreed on with my father was rearing its 'stable' head. Despite great parental support for all my dreams, an arrangement had been dealt and I had promised to consider other alternatives if I couldn't cut the stage as a career.

The major obstacle, therefore, was finding an opportunity to professionally perform, and it was with this outlook that I opened the hitherto useless *Stage* one day and discovered the advertisement: '*Girl Singer/Dancer Required*'. Simple and to the point. Listed under 'Madame JoJo seeks Drag Artists, "High Camp" artists and G-Stringed Boy Dancers', they may as well have added '*Do you dare?*'. Go straight to hell, do not pass Go, and you'll be lucky if we pay you £200. Initially, I was in a quandary. Part of me thought, 'What have you really got to lose at this stage? It's good experience, may be a laugh, and if I presume to think positively it would mean an Equity card.' The more rational part of my brain slammed on the brakes, contemplating this chance to send my star into orbit in light of what type of company I'd be keeping and what I would have to do.

Having been raised to think that nothing worth having comes easily, I was naturally sceptical about any once-in-a-lifetime career opportunity being listed under these circumstances. I had enough sense of family honour not to want to bring disgrace upon those I loved, and wasn't entirely certain how my similarly sheltered friends were going to react to *this* little gem. My final reservation, however, lay in the fact that my knowledge of drag was even less than my awareness of gay culture. I felt queasy at the prospect of being hauled up in front of a gay audience on charges of fraudulently posing as Sally Bowles' natural successor.

I suppose my ignorance was not entirely a drawback since it meant that I arrived with comparatively few prejudices. Preconceptions, yes . . . I expected to enter the club and find high exotica, only to discover a remarkably 'real' Ruby Venezuela, now parading under the more sober guise of Brian and accompanied by the no-nonsense Venus ManTrap, a.k.a. Jason. Considering that an initial worry about going for this audition had been my possible devolution into drug-addicted, prostitute go-go dancing, said development came as something of a relief. Nonetheless, I had been anticipating an explosion of excitement, degeneracy, worldliness and over-the-top behaviour, and the disillusionment was about as profound as seeing the *Mona Lisa* smiling and revealing a row of rotten teeth. In screaming contrast, *I* had gone to the extreme and dressed up totally out of character in fake fur, instant paralysis stilettos and the slinkiest black velvet lycra dress I could manage without giving myself a tourniquet of the waist. I was stomach-wrenchingly nervous and asked my friend Julie, fellow 'show girl' in Edinburgh, to join me in attacking a bottle of wine at the Soho Brasserie a few hours before auditions finished.

We were aiming for the last audition time, on the last day, and barely made it. I echoed an earlier exercise in ground reconnaissance (tracking my elusive fake fingernails in the brasserie toilets) by tripping while ascending the stage steps and falling flat on my face, bum high in the air. *Begin as you mean to continue* fortunately proved not to be my modus operandi, although in retrospect I would argue that being slightly sozzled was the best thing I could have done: I felt blasé and confident. As Ruby and Jason recounted, they were bowled over by the contrast. Apparently they'd had nothing but the usual audition types along for three days, including the obligatory stage school leavers. Finally, a job where not being a lovey was an advantage.

What followed was a total triumph of style over content. Mirrored in the blood red walls with fake gilt designs, I crooned through 'Diamonds are a Girl's Best Friend' and 'Life is a Cabaret'. My recall was set for the following week, and I was nothing short of amazed. Soaring out of the club in a state of euphoria, I never once asked myself who, or what, this Paul Raymond Organisation Ltd. was. It never occurred to me that I might soon be working for the King of Soho, in a club that was the polite face of his empire. I only knew that after the rejections and insecurity of constantly placing your self-esteem on a plate for some stranger either to accept or dismiss, somebody had finally acknowledged my talent. At the back of my mind also lurked a clichéd need to explore life's 'dark' side so, aged twenty-three, my new motto became *Carpe diem*. Let down your hair and take that walk on the wild side.

With hindsight, I regret nothing. I am as proud and glad of my choice now as I was during the club's heyday, and I feel a stronger and better person for all the tears of frustration and fulfilment. I have a wealth of knowledge and friendships to show for the experience, not to mention the opportunity perhaps to explain this curious world to those who would like an insight but haven't had the same opportunity I had.

I don't really know where I thought it would all lead. The idea to ultimately write a book didn't strike me as a serious option until about a month before my departure, and even now I would not classify myself as an authority on all things drag. My short-term goals, to begin with, were obviously to obtain that ever-elusive Equity card, which I achieved within the first six months. Why stay another year and a half?

There was always that big chance 'just around the corner', we were assured: that tour of Hong Kong; the amazing club in Palm Springs; an opening of Ruby's own truly chic drag venue. Nothing ever materialised of earth-shattering consequence and I suppose I ended up staying partly for the contentment of being a paid performer and partly out of laziness. The club became a comfortable companion and, although they frequently drove me crazy, my colleagues had also become my friends. It became a very seductive existence, until I realised one day how very easy it is to become over-contented and cease striving. I saw it with too many tired, ageing drag queens on the scene, and the thought of becoming a Miss Havisham of the drag world frightened me.

Add to this the very real demands made upon me as a woman and as a broadcaster, and I eventually threw out the stilettos and the make-up. I still can't bring myself to chuck the eyelashes for some reason. Perhaps I've peered out through the deceptively hazy, yet glittering, perspective for too long to cut off completely. While I initially may have felt out of place, the balance imperceptibly changed somewhere along route, the most telling sign being when I started to refer to myself as a drag queen. My experiences as part of what many narrow-minded people still consider a freak show have changed and formed the person I've become, to the extent that I mentally now inhabit an undefined world that is neither drag nor 'normal'. Then again, as Derek Jarman pointed out about our heterosexual world and behaviour, maybe 'it isn't normal, it's just common.'

At night I work in a strange bar, impersonating every star;
I'm quite deceiving . . .
The customers come in with doubt, and wonder what I'm all about,
but leave believing.
Each night the men look so surprised;
I change my sex before their eyes.
Tell me if you can, what makes a man, a man?

Around three o'clock I meet with friends to have a bite to eat
and conversation;
we talk and empty out our hearts, on every subject from the arts
to liberation.
We love to pull apart someone and spread some gossip just for fun,
or start a rumour;
we let our hair down, so to speak,
and mock ourselves with tongue and cheek
and inside humour.

So many times we have to pay, for having fun and being gay:
it's not amusing . . .
There's always those who spoil our games, by finding fault
and calling names,
always accusing.
They draw attention to themselves, at the expense of someone else:
it's so confusing.
Yet they make fun of how I talk, and imitate the way I walk;
Tell me if you can, what makes a man, a man?

My masquerade comes to an end, when I go home to bed again:
alone and friendless.
I shut my eyes, I think of him, I fantasise what might have been;
my dreams are endless . . .
We love each other, but it seems, the love lives only in my dreams:
it's so one-sided.
But in this life, I must confess, the search for love and happiness
is unrequited.

I ask myself 'What have I got?', what I am and what I'm not,
what am I giving?
Then answers come from those who make the rules that some of us
must break,
just to keep living . . .
I know my life is not a crime, I'm just a victim of my time;
I stand defenceless.
Nobody has the right to be, the judge of what is right for me.
Tell me if you can, what makes a man, a man?

What makes a man, a man?

('What Makes a Man, a Man?' John Pizer)

I

All Aboard

MADAME JOJO

Requires
for the new Late-Nite Cabaret Revue
Opening May at the

WORLD FAMOUS

MADAME JOJO

Club Extraordinaire

GOOD ALL ROUND PERFORMERS
DRAG ARTISTS
FEMALE IMPERSONATORS
'HIGH CAMP' ARTISTES
ATHLETIC GOOD LOOKING GUYS
EXPERIENCED GIRL SINGER/DANCER
(please bring backing tape if possible)

AUDITIONS
at Madame Jojo –
8–10 Brewer St., Soho, London W1
3pm.

Monday, 25th March 1991

I got the job.

I don't know whether to scream and tell everyone I know or keep quiet, seriously consider changing my name amd start wearing a fake beard. On one hand my parents are relaxed about most things, especially after having been transferred to the Indian sub-continent three years ago. But suddenly to get a phone call announcing that your daughter is going to start parading around in five inches of make up and stilettos, sequined gowns and feathers, pretending to be a man pretending to be a woman?

I don't think the 12.15am starting time of the show is going

1

to do much in the way of reassurance either, let alone tackling safety fears by pointing out that 'It's OK, because I'm working for the "King of Soho" Paul Raymond and he owns most of the area and its population.'

I wonder how the guys tell their families?

Oh, I also had the pleasure of meeting the 'Chief Executive' of this illustrious organisation, a South African lawyer by the name of Carl Snitcher, whom I instantly rechristened Schnitzel. Tough as nail varnish, discussing contracts and wages, which, if I wasn't so excited about my first 'properly' paid performing job, I would probably have dismissed out of hand. I mean *please* – £200 for six performances a week, no sick pay, no holidays, no accident insurance, high kicking around that ice-skating rink of a stage? You must be joking.

You really have to love this to do it. For me, I see a full Equity card dangling enticingly in the six-month distance, but as I look at my new 'colleague', Carl, a.k.a 'Carla', I can't help but wonder: what's in it for him? Is it, as he says, just a second job? That's the way Schnitzel is selling it to us. I can't believe that somehow: as a man, you are sacrificing *a lot* more. Your masculinity, for starters. The glamour, the performing, the adulation, are the only reasons I could imagine people like him going for it.

Saw some of his promo pictures: God, is he gorgeous. I don't have that kind of bone structure, let alone make-up skills, and he looks like Linda Evans. Unlike Ruby, our director 'extraordinaire' and star of the current show. I don't know what exactly I *was* expecting from this legendary cabaret figure – although a cross between Danny La Rue and Cinderella's step-mother does spring to mind, with perhaps a sprig of Quentin Crisp on the side. Certainly *not* a somberly dressed cherub which, combined with his very down-to-earth approachability, has completely defied my preconceptions. His decision in employing Carla and myself as the 'Gemini Twins' was explained (something to do with our mirroring each other in looks, attitude and presentation) and now Carla is already off and talking about us as '*sisters*'. Weird.

Monday, 29th April

Whoah-ho-ho!

Met my fellow principals today – *what* an eye-opener. For starters, one of them is a woman! And I thought I was going to be the only one. I don't know whether this is a comfort or an insult.

I, for one, cannot figure out why they would want one woman in a drag show, much less two. Call me narrow-minded, but I always thought drag equals men. Asking Jason, a.k.a Venus ManTrap and our new choreographer, I was rewarded with eyeball rolling and a 'God only *knows*'. The man is to encouragement what barbed wire is to the underwear industry, although he eventually deigned to inform me that it was all in the element of mystery. Keep them guessing.

I suppose it boils down to intrigue, as well as the fact that a woman probably provides an opportunity to assess how convincing the men are in their impersonation; a measuring stick, if you like.

I would imagine that our ability to sing well hardly hindered this decision. In the pre-women show days at JoJo's, musical talent was often sacrificed on the altar of finding a persuasive drag queen. After all, excessive pickiness has no place when you're seeking a man who can pull off a decent female impersonation, which often means having to forego vocal ability. As there are many more struggling musical actresses than convincing drag queens, having a woman in the show allowed them to deal with one of the show's major weaknesses.

My fellow female, Becka, is gargantuanly sized both in mass and ego by the sounds of it, and has got to be the biggest fag-hag in the universe. She was totally aloof with me, which is going to make six months together in a dressing room smaller than my closet a real joy. Madam works at the Piccadilly Theatre box office by day/early evening, and would appear to be the West End Fruit Fly of choice, to the extent that they know her of old and chose her to come in and replace Ruby.

It's just been made clear to me that Ruby et al. are off to New York for their big break. It is their singular misfortune that this is the name of a club in Manchester, but the departing cast appear to have done everything short of opening charge accounts at Bergdorf's in anticipation of the real thing. We were assured by Ruby that it is just a matter of time before she collects us, her 'babies', and whisks us off for a season in Palm Beach. Maybe we can fly on the pigs.

We appear to have had some problems choosing our fourth star. Apparently the amazing fellow who could play everything, including his armpit, was a bit too greedy for his unique services and has now been replaced by a very pretty guy called Misha. Who, it was clarified, is not gay but simply a transvestite. Clear as mud. He was a ballet dancer, then a 'Cagelle' when *La Cage Aux Folles* was staged in London, and is now a 'swing' on *Aspects of Love* which, as he explained, means an understudy dancer/actor for

3

several parts. Apparently some nights so many cast members are off that his coverage results in schizophrenic characters or, at the very least, some rather altered scenes. The other night, for example, he was supposed to cover two characters throwing a ball to one another and ended up standing centre-stage and juggling. And I thought my progression was interesting. I'll say one thing for him, he actually seems slightly sane. A relief, but also somewhat dubious.

We met for costume fittings first, with a lovely, maternal woman called Joan, who did not so much as bat an eyelash and in a comfort meaning way complimented me on my 'child-bearing hips'. I was not amused or encouraged. Apparently she's been doing this job since before I was in training bras, which considering I might as well still be is somewhat misleading. Suffice it to say, an old hand.

Ruby actually designs all the costumes and I gather she and Jason brainstorm show ideas over a traditionally drunken dinner, 'although we forget them all by the time we sober up.' The outfits are surprisingly brilliant in light of this: sequins galore, satin-style materials, and colours that defy being viewed without sunglasses.

Then on to Nigel, our music supplier extraordinaire. A Royal Academy of Music graduate who could pass for a Hare Krishna and of course lives in Camden, he has the unenviable task of taking all of Ruby's choices – largely old show tunes, some even music hall – and putting them into at least quarter tempo if not faster. This is especially fun with the slow romantic ones such as Carla's 'Ten Cents a Dance' which ends up coming out like something off the Smurf album. Thank God most of mine are from *Starlight Express*. Having tried on my first pair of five-inch heels, I think I'd prefer to go authentic and have the roller skates. Maybe they could glitter them.

Monday, 6th May

We are finally moving onto the meat of things. Perhaps I should rephrase that – I've just learned that this is a favoured expression for my new colleagues' preferred genitals. Everybody running around talking about meat and two veg and here I am, trying to figure out how they manage to stay rake thin. Lots of exercise.

Rehearsals started with a bit of a whimper, all of us sussing one another out. Wandering into JoJo's during the daytime is a rather surreal experience, on a par with seeing a candlelit Adonis the next morning hungover and washed-out. Sin pits do not generally translate well in the light of day, be it natural or, as in this case, floodlit.

I've only been down once at night so far, and the contrast is astounding. Walking through those famous portals, past a rather vicious doorstaff, one is promptly hurtled down a flight of scarlet stairs towards an imposing wall. Turn right and boom! The club explodes in front of your eyes. The Upper Bar, with cocktail waitressed tables and banquets, is surprisingly civilised in appearance. The entire gilted, blood-red room is geared towards the stage, which rises up from behind the Lower Bar. This verges on the dance floor, renowned for its sardine-like conditions during showtimes.

The stage itself is a miniscule affair and I cannot see how on earth we are going to manage to fit eleven stationary people on there, much less moving. Jason has apparently awarded me some rather optimistic dance moves across the 'bridges' that join the stage with the electronically powered centre, which similarly juts out across the bar. To top it all off, we're actually expected to run, skip and jump across the foot-wide bar itself as well! Not in this life, honey.

There are only two barbettes and two 'boys' from the previous show left, so this is an inexperienced cast in every sense of the word. I have no idea where they conjured up the word 'barbette' to describe our backing chorus 'girls', who double as cocktail waitresses during the rest of the night, but they wear the title as a badge of honour. The rest of us are anxiously eyeing each other and the stage plan up, in between a rousing 'pep' talk by Herr Jason, OberGruppenFührer and day-to-day director/choreographer.

Having just moved to Drury Lane, right behind *Miss Saigon*, I feel happily ensconced in my new *artiste* existence. I wish this feeling could transcend into this strange new world I've entered, with people I don't really understand or relate to.

I suppose that is a bit unfair as I can certainly sympathise with the desire for glamour and show business. It's just that they appear a pretty bizarre crew, with hides like calloused rhinoceroses. By comparison, I must seem a totally wet fish.

The collection is mind-boggling. We have the four principals, Carla, Misha, Becka, *et moi*. Then a fifth, who doubles as a G-stringed 'boy', Jamie, a short dark guy with stunning looks and a voice to match. The other two boys consist of Marcia (Mark), the perfect beach-boy blond with immaculate tan and teeth, and a very masculine José. As the name suggests, José is from España, and appears to have successfully retained his Iberian macho indifference towards irritating little details like punctuality and effort. Having said that, he is probably the most open and relaxed. They are all aiming for an Equity card in the long run.

In screaming contrast are our beautiful queens, the barbettes. They seem terribly shrewd and streetwise, but one can't help but wonder about their financial acumen. Who, in their right minds, would work for £125 a week, setting up the club at 9pm, working seven-hour shifts as cocktail waitresses and doing a nightly show? Their tips must be phenomenal, or they should all be certified.

The feisty and aptly named Pepper has been around longest, followed by Tevita, a Polynesian stunner who could have modelled for Gauguin. Our new girls are Marcie and Tanya. The latter I'm sure must have driven lorries before coming to work here; a mouthpiece that rains acid on any unfortunate causing displeasure, or for that matter breathing, she of course gets on with Becka like a witch on fire.

We received the proper show list and it looks like I have a fair bulk of the numbers, that is to say ten out of thirty-four. While some of these are mixed duets as well as numbers backed with 'dancing' barbettes or boys, my concern about solos and attendant dance routines was not assuaged by Jason's casual 'oh just wing it.' I already know I'll end up standing like a lobotomised rabbit in headlights on opening night.

I'm finding the concept of drag a rather hard one to wrap my head around. Obviously it's an exaggerated manner of self-expression that somehow has to give an outrageous impression; but *how*? I know it must sound absurd, but I've never had to camp it up as a woman before. Correction: a caricature of a woman.

It's easy for the guys, they have to stretch their imagination to womanhood anyway, so this is probably just a small leap further. Men have been dragging up for centuries now; everybody thought *Tootsie* was such a breakthrough and yet this has been going on since at least Shakespeare's time. As a 23-year-old woman, however, the prospect of impersonating Lady Bracknell sits uncomfortably with me. I have to create some kind of identity, but I don't know how or what. Carla has mentioned Bette Midler as an example of a woman pulling this sort of thing off, a camp virtuoso, but

the only film of hers I've ever seen is *The Rose*. I can't imagine impersonating a junkie rock star is the kind of thing I'm
supposed to be doing. I may have to extend some of my film
viewing.

Ruby and Jason seem to expect that we will all automatically
know what to do, and I feel like a child being flung into water
without instruction: sink or swim, babe. It's hard enough to make
this transition without the tremendous pressure we are all under
to be worthy successors to our fore-runners. As it is, I'm shy about
laying myself open to the cast, let alone several hundred strangers,
in what seems to me a crude and totally un-self-conscious mode of
behaviour that verges on vulgarity.

Otherwise, I'm pretty excited. The most amazing development
has been my status as a performer, and not just with friends
who appear delighted with their new eccentric and degenerate
drag queen of a mate. For the first time I can actually claim
performer on my employment records. What a high. One that I
can quite easily come down from as well, every time I look at my
pay packet.

Having slugged it out with Schnitzel, Carla and I have managed to
up our weekly salary by £20. I was only sacked for forty-five minutes,
while Carla had to sweat it out all weekend, which left me feeling
perversely valued. Realistically, however, I doubt that champagne
corks were flying all over my tax office at this phenomenal concession.

We have two weeks in which to prove ourselves. I feel sick.

Friday, 10th May

A new development.

Unfortunately, one that has left my stomach performing a passable
impersonation of a tumble-dryer on legs. I am due to take over
the infamous Baroness Izzy's part in the current show *Continental
Capers*. What can they be thinking? I am totally unprepared!

Izzy, as *femme fatale* of the last few shows, has had one-and-a-
half years to get used to doing this and has defined her role in the
present production for six months now. I'm already nervous enough
about the prospect of being compared to her, without handing the
critics an amateur example of her songs and routines on a plate. I
know I have got a week left before being flung in with the lions,
but this is ridiculous – I don't even know the show for starters, I

feel a complete imposter, and the very notion of my pulling off a professional drag performance with all the old pros is as improbable as a pigmy high-jumper.

Choice was about the only thing they did not hurl at me. I am at present submerged in a sea of costumes, with veteran and current star Jay smearing 4W panstick on my face by the trowel and flinging glitter on my trembling lips. They've told me more about the cause of my predecessor's sudden firing (a long-planned business trip to Sri Lanka which, in light of the delayed opening of our show, seems entirely excusable), than my numbers or routines. I'm continuously reminded of how *lucky* I am to be given a head start, how prepared I'll be for our big opening but, all in all, it's about as enticing as being boiled alive in athlete's foot lotion. Actually less, as my feet are in agony from these bloody heels.

Hearing the crowds pile in is absolutely terrifying. Apparently we have full capacity again tonight: in safety regulation theory, 250; in practice, cram in another hundred. I nervously quizzed Jay as to the types that constituted our 'loyal' clientele and he snorted, 'Every type, darling, but mostly those *dreadful* women.' Hello, what do you think you're talking to? I know I'm part of our little gang here, but some things cannot be overlooked; even if you are busy digging out tit-pads to fill out the costume for me.

He poured himself another vodka and groaned, 'You'll get used to it soon enough, these hen nights, Sharon and Tracy down from Essex in their white stilettos, dancing in a circle around their matching white handbags.' Lovely. 'Actually,' he added, 'we have a blend of men and women on weekends, these days more city types and secretaries. Weekdays it's more gay, but not like it used to be, sadly.' He rhapsodised about stars and I thanked my lucky ones that none were supposedly in tonight. That would be just too humiliating.

The current cast are all being very helpful which is a small relief, but the prospect of performing with both Ruby and Jason is petrifying. Jay is the one consolation – a very kind, sincere man who has got to be the sexiest woman I have ever met. He's taken me under his boa and psychologically – not to mention physically – prepared me for my first big trial. I could really fall for this guy. If I don't fall off stage first.

Sunday, 12th May

Prophetic words . . .

My first preview night was a revelation. My second, a disaster. Had I known the effect sobriety would have on my on-stage competence, I would have knocked them back both nights. As it was, I only indulged out of terror and then mistakenly judged myself ready for a sober head-on collision course with the audience tonight. My great pride in delivering a semi-competent performance inebriated led me to the conclusion that I would be even better thinking – BIG MISTAKE. I promptly flew five feet down into the bar during our glam 'Pearly Queen' finale while singing 'Boiled Beef and Carrots'. What a way to go.

Reflecting upon it, I was not totally to blame. Jay had instructed me to mirror all his movements, so when he cruised forwards for what turned out to be a solo I met him halfway. Major booboo. He hissed at me to return, which I promptly attempted to do without turning around. Lesson Number One: never go backwards over a ten-inch platform suspended over a bar while wearing five-inch heels. I have a vague recollection of my top ripping open as I flashed past the assorted audience, most of whom could have easily auditioned for the Village People, so this was not as traumatic or revealing as might be expected. Obviously a gayer, or more alternative, crowd in than usual.

The next sensation I experienced was kissing hard wood and floor as I dived into the bar. 'Ouch' does not even come near it. I think Ruby had a near coronary as somebody whispered blood: the prospect of killing off her new cast pre-opening night was a bit too much for her brandy-laden stomach to handle. They did their closing bit, everyone taking bows and yours truly waving a tiny pathetic hand from somewhere below the bar, and I was finally hoisted up and into the dressing-room. Whereupon which 'Mother' Ruby funnelled brandy down my shocked throat and cheerfully advised me to down as many aspirins as I could fit in my mouth. Betty Ford would have been proud.

Have decided to go by the stage name 'Queen Bea'.

Friday, 17th May

What a week.

Rehearsing by day, performing by night, drinking like a fish and eating an occasional apple. Needless to say, I am not on Joan's favourites list with costumes being taken in on a daily basis.

These are absolutely stunning, if bordering on kitsch, and I feel like a little girl finally being allowed to wear the gaudy dress that Mama always insisted was too tacky. They are also surprisingly puritanical, which I am sure owes more to maintaining the mystery rather than any false modesty; after all, the more we are covered up, the less people can spot the tell-tale differences. I think my favourite is the 'Hello Dolly' finale outfit: gold with scarlet ruffles and huge auburn wig, piled up high. God only knows how we're supposed to do Jason's kicks in a full-length, no-slit dress, balancing five pounds of hair on our heads.

Carla and I have 'cute', matching, purple sequinned slash dresses for that bloody stupid 'Other Side of the Tracks'. Leave it to Ruby – she wanted the Monroe/Russell 'Two Little Girls from Little Rock' scene and accidently chooses the Bruce Forsyth version instead. Of *all* things. Then there's 'Money, Money' from *Cabaret*, which sees Carla in complete Sally Bowles, thirties flapper gear, and yours truly in gold jacket, top hat and black leotard. Looks gorgeous, too bad about the fact that Carla still can't get the canto on the song right for love nor money. We've worn tracks into my living-room carpet rehearsing and still no joy.

Our babe is over the moon about her sleazebag 'Ten Cents a Dance' basque and boa; less so about the striped Jiminy Cricket get-up she has to sport during 'The Runaway Train'. Becka and Misha have fabulous outfits for their Tramp sequence, Becka starting off fur-draped in 'He's a Tramp', complete with two 'Girl-dog' barbettes. Misha ousts her in his Cruella de Ville gear, doing 'Lady is a Tramp', although he has expressed his interpretive preference for 'Slut'. His two G-stringed 'Boy-dogs' get to simulate some interesting doggie-mating techniques with the two barbettes, which should go down a real treat with any fetishists in the audience.

We all get to share Opening and Finale outfits for both acts, and I finally know what being born a quadruplet must feel like. Amazingly, Ruby keeps costs down by recycling old costumes and through general know-how. She's been doing this so long that she knows all the right people and places, even if it does mean that some of our costumes should theoretically be soaking in vats of disinfectant for a few years before their next reappearance.

I still haven't quite sussed out where the thought flow for *All Aboard* went. The poster boasts a smiling train, and we start off with a rather breathless rendition of 'He Whistled at Me' from

Starlight. This is wheezy thanks to Jason's insane choreography of having me thrown from one boy to another throughout the number, high kicking and attempting to gasp out rapid-fire words simultaneously. I think I would rather roller skate, if it meant slowing down the tempo somewhat. Then on to such numbers as Misha's 'Steam Heat', Becka's 'Fire Down Below', and Carla's 'My Baby Takes the Morning Train'; the last also bears the distinction of being our most contemporary number, incidentally.

The next half, however, starts off with Misha and Jamie's 'Money' duet from Abba. Misha happily flounces off stage in his green sequined dress-coat, rechristened 'The Swamp Fairy Look', only to be replaced by a less than impressed Becka, decked out in cleaning lady finery and accompanied by feather duster-wielding barbettes for 'Money, That's What I Want'. After our *Cabaret* number, it's on to Jamie and 'the girls' tap-dancing up and down huge cardboard coins to 'We're in the Money', a fallacy if ever there was. It's actually quite entertaining to watch these chain-smokers constantly remounting their gigantic coins, rather like a geriatric step-class.

Suddenly we're in that magical, mystical tequila-land 'South of the Border' with 'Speedy Gonzales', and then into my personal nightmare, 'Beat Out that Rhythm on a Drum', a lethal number which I am expected to sing true to the *Carmen Jones* operatic style, all the while running around in a pink leotard with a headdress of fluorescent skipping ropes tangled around my throbbing head, in UV lighting. Ma, I've finally made it. I think Becka shares these sentiments, coming on after me dressed as a huge tomato for 'Mister Don't Touch Me Tomatoes'. There is definitely an element of sadism in the planning of these shows.

It is inadvisable to fall asleep, or you'll be totally clueless when you wake up. We finish on 'Carnival', in the scratchiest gold dresses ever devised, topped off with massive boa-flowing headpieces that make Carmen Miranda's fashion sense look tame. These things are monsters. If anyone had told me that one day I'd be crooning 'Quando', I would have laughed in their faces, but not as much as hearing Misha and Carla wail incomprehensively through 'Brazil' first. Jason's off-stage directions ('Sing out Louiiise') have achieved little in the way of clarity and the two of them still sound like they could be singing an impassioned song about Brazilian Tupperware. The ones I really feel for are the barbettes in this: they have to sweat and dance under virtual duvets of boas and cloaks. Needless to say, this has dampened their ardour and hairstyles some what, and I marvel particularly at the latter because these wigs are normally lacquered enough to deflect small calibre bullets. Thank God it's the last number or I think they'd pass out from a combination of physical exhaustion and horror at their own appearance.

Saturday, 18th May

Night-times are going increasingly well and I must concede that I *am* better prepared for the Big Night on Tuesday than my co-stars. Which is not saying much, if Jason's 'psych-up' talk was anything to go by today, our last pre-dress rehearsal. I swear, I could see embryonic Fu Manchu whiskers sprouting. We were 'useless', he would be *so* embarrassed: pathetic, pathetic, *pathetic*. I mean, I didn't expect praise on high, but this seemed a bit harsh in light of everybody's efforts. In the end our technician Dave, better known as 'Mother Herb', came to the ego rescue alert and murmured some words of encouragement afterwards. Becka and I just went off and slammed Jason at a nearby wine bar.

I think I may have seriously underestimated her. Beneath that occasionally vicious exterior lies the heart of a very warm, talented woman. Admittedly, people close to Margaret Thatcher have been known to spout the same heady praise but I genuinely believe we will get on quite well. Especially as she doesn't hit on me.

This was a subsequent experience when we met up with Jason and a lesbian friend of his, whose siren call included suggesting a cucumber as a suitable alternative to male companionship and telling me to let her know any time I changed my mind. Becka's hard-fast heterosexuality came as a sudden comfort, as I found myself totally repulsed by this woman's extreme pick-up routine. I have had a few lesbian friends and must be fortunate because I never found them to be the usually preconceived man-haters. To me they were extremely beautiful, artistic and sensitive women, with whom I had meaningful conversations and who made me appreciate being a woman. A thing I am finding increasingly lacking in my predominantly gay male surroundings.

It is perverse, considering that we are all dressing up as women, to find phrases like 'fish' being bandied about. At first I wasn't entirely sure to what, or to whom, they were referring – until *I* was suddenly included in the coterie. Now *that* was a shock. Revealed to me in joke form by the ManTrap himself, this of course being his all time favourite, and goes something like this. 'Adam and Eve fuck in the garden of Eden. They finish off and Eve goes down to the river to wash. God pokes his head through the clouds, he and Adam say their hellos, and God enquires what they've been up to. "Oh, just fucking Eve, God" comes the reply. "So where's she now?" asks God. Adam answers, "She's gone down to the river to wash herself, God." God looks horrified and says, "Oh no, that's the last thing I wanted fish to smell of."

Charming. Makes me come warm all over.

I'm not sure whether it is insecurity or simply that they are interested in men because we are considered somehow unclean or unappealing. All I know is that it seems terribly insulting, and if I didn't like them so much I'd deck them.

Speaking of 'them', the cast has had its fair share of frictions this week. Little incidents like Pepper breaking a glass and holding it to José's jugular spring to mind, which admittedly could be down to hormones. I understand that Pepper and Tevita, the two most feminine of the barbettes, are trying to become transsexuals and are up for the 'chop'. Difficult to explain to most of my proud-to-be-male friends, let alone for this extremely men-are-the-best environment, but suffice it to say that while the rest of us are gender euphoric, they appear to be gender dysphoric. Fascinating stuff.

Thanks to my night-time work I am getting to know Jay of the old cast better, and I thank my stars. A true professional, who is a real mentor for me and a total inspiration. I'm a bit worried as I find myself drawn to him in a way that with hetero-sexuals I would describe as falling in love. I am attracted to him on an emotional level but, paradoxically, not on a physical one. It makes no sense to me that I feel this rush when I'm with him as a woman, and yet when he's dressed as a man I'm fairly indifferent. Not towards the person, mind you, but quite simply the sense of awe leaves me. I guess the closest it comes to is falling for your female teacher when you are a young girl. Part emulation and admiration, part neediness in defining your own identity.

I've also got to know the overseer of the club, George, who is a tough bird to figure out. On one hand gushing so obsequiously to Ruby that you half expect to see an oil slick forming on the floor and, by the same token, quite vicious to all and sundry when incurring his displeasure. I never want to get on his bad side, that much is for sure.

Otherwise, we are all 'one big happy family'. Sort of the Family

Von Trapp meets *Dynasty*. Tuesday night is going to be a real trip.

Wednesday, 22nd May

Well, let's see . . . where to start?

Saturday night, closing performance of the old show, was a gas. Everybody on a high, either literally or emotionally, with tears flowing like Niagara and a huge turnout. Ruby et al. ripping apart the dressing-room in a last ditch frenzy to organise all of us for the switch-over, and the party began.

My new colleagues were looking slightly putrid with sick antici-pation of our opening, while I was also trying to come to terms with our closing, thus sending my peripheral sensory system into confused overdrive. The disorientating mixture of relief at this nightmare scenario having finished, coupled with fear at what lay ahead and a sadness to be 'losing' my newfound friend Jay, had the effect of someone pulling a plug out of the soles of my feet. All energy seemed to drain out of me, and much faster than the pee was draining out of our perpetually hair-clogged sink.

If there is one thing I never thought I would have to get used to, it is our dressing-room scenario. Peeing in a sink and running around G-stringed in front of eleven guys is hardly the kind of stuff pubescent talks with mother are made of. I'll say one thing, though: lack of choice is a great teacher. Our only other backstage drain is a shower, packed with costumes. Considering that we are crammed in, three and five to two bathroom-sized rooms, with the three boys changing in the hallway, creates a need for improvisation of the sort they never teach you at drama school.

Then of course, there was the adjustment of Miss No Chest parading topless backstage. At first, I kept trying to maintain an artificial modesty, based less upon etiquette than embarrassment. When you grow up being teased about fried eggs on your chest, even by your own parents, there is definitely a slight leaning towards the paranoid and obsessive. If I had the body of the Venus de Milo I'm sure I would have ripped my double C bra off as soon as I walked into the club, but as it was I felt more of a brother to these guys than a sister. Let's face it, it is just too impractical to try and cover what little there is while attempting extensive one-minute costume changes, all the while ably assisted by our dresser Michael. If they don't care what you're sporting, why should you?

Anyway back to the party. Ruby, accompanied by toy boy del

14

momento and sporting a wig resembling a storm-damaged hay-stack, was busily bidding emotional farewells to countless admirers and promising never-ending, unconditional maternal love to all us babies. Jason, in turn, was demonstrating a seduction technique about as subtle as a bagpipe serenade and tongue wrestling a new found paramour at the lower bar. I think he passed out for a few moments under the bar but was well back into his tonsil-tennis when we spotted Schnitzel, who'd come along to bid adieus and give us a final rah-rah for opening night. He assured us that both he and Paul Raymond would be there to herald the new era – what a *great* comfort. At this stage it seemed about as reassuring as rearranging deckchairs on the *Titanic*.

The next two days were manic. Our two techies, Dave and Nick, worked around the clock dismantling a spectacular set and resurrecting a new one, again made by the tremendously talented Ruby. We, in turn, spent our last rehearsal opportunity sewing sequins, buttons and various paraphenalia onto our incomplete costumes. I gather this is a production weekend tradition, but I cannot imagine Patti LuPone having to trot in pre-opening with thimble in tow. Ruby, it transpired during our sew-athon, used to be the head window-dresser at Harrods a few decades ago, with a phenomenal budget at her disposal. Must make the transition to Soho-land all the more stark.

I never realised the kind of money it takes to put on one of these shows, let alone to maintain it: we are talking a good £10,000–15,000 for a six-month run, just to get the ball rolling. Small wonder PR (as he is called in the company) wants to extend them as long as possible. Apparently he started out as a music hall illusionist, which has obviously provided him with the appropriate background to create a lavish extravaganza based on next to nothing, at least when compared to West End shows.

And yet for cabaret, it is expensive. Even with a £10 per head cover charge and astronomical drink prices, the recession is starting to hit if punter numbers are anything to go by. I won't say the club's popularity is on the wane, but it seems like over-exposure is creating a new, straighter clientele which is more weekend-based. Good, I thought, maybe there will be fewer people on Tuesday.

Guess again. Opening night was invitation only, which translated into packed; intimidatingly enough, entirely by people either in or around show business, or people very familiar with the previous show's standards. That this did not assuage any of our inferiority complexes goes without saying. By the time Tuesday night rolled around, we were so behind schedule that no form of dress rehearsal had even occurred. Our nerves had hit an all-time high and backstage was witnessing more snapping, snarling and general bloodshed than a busy watering hole in the Serengeti.

Having said that, it all went off without too many major hitches. Even if it was simply adrenalin born of terror, everyone pulled through with amazing grace under fire.

PR, resembling a tanned Club Med aficionado, was downright gallant to me, kissing my hand, complimenting me and then redirecting his attentions precisely two-and-a-half milliseconds later. Made me uneasy, somehow. Then of course there was the usual 'Darling you were the best in the show, it was *faaaabulous*', coupled with the equally expected sotto voce 'Well it's not the old show, is it?' bitching. But all in all, I felt pretty damn proud. And fairly well dead by the end of it.

All this working hard and playing hard is a novel excitement after the lethargy and frustration of trying to break into the business, but how to maintain it? I'm embracing all these feelings like a sponge on one hand, but I feel a million miles away from the person I was a month ago and I know I'm going to have to reconcile the two at some stage. You can't be a drag queen both day and night. Especially if you're a woman.

Sunday, 2nd June

Weird things a-happenin'.

A case of two planets colliding, the old and the new. While *All Aboard* seems to be settling into a comfortable pace, albeit with a fairly different clientele, my encounters with Jay are becoming increasingly bizarre. I've met up with him continuously, getting helpful tips and general exposure to 'the scene', and falling for him more and more. I just don't get it.

Take last night, for example. After the show, he suggested returning to his council flat near the LA, a leather-n'-chains gay bar that fairly oozes testosterone. A *place d'infamie* and no doubt frequented by the majority of my colleagues. Not to mention one of my new flatmates, whose joy at finding a built-in fag-hag has led to many a 5am post-Heaven Club tears at my bedside. As he tells it, the LA is definitely not your bring-a-first-date kind of joint, unless, of course, you plan on handcuffing them to the bar and taking them from behind, as one well-known pop star was reported to be enjoying on his last visit.

Anyway, Jay and I cruise off, accompanied by two of his transvestite friends, Bunty and Arthur (says it all, really) and some nameless, sad little Puerto Rican character who obviously had our two guests in a real lustful spin. I expected at least a fun night after a mad Saturday show, a chance to unwind with the person I'm growing increasingly attached to.

Maybe I should have been a little more on the ball, but this naïvety cost me in terms of respect, both self and for Jay. After downing as much vodka as your average Russian army contingent could handle, in a rather dire atmosphere to boot, I watched both Bunty and Arthur disappear with this Guido in turns. Then Jay went. My heart nearly broke, not because of his desire but simply because of the pathetic seediness of it all. It was somehow so desperate. To cap it all off, this obnoxious little twerp comes in and starts launching into a major charm offensive, trying to chat me up. Piss off, amigo.

I was totally miserable, not to mention disgusted, and couldn't fathom what the hell I was doing there. It was all so *tacky*. God, if my parents could have seen me . . .

I'm told that not all gay/trannie encounters are handled in this way, although I've discovered from the barbettes that the bulk are the old check-into-a-hotel-room-and-don't-take-off-your-makeup routine. It's just coming from Jay, beautiful talented Jay, that it was a sad discovery. A handsome, sexy guy I could understand, but all of them were going off with a character who seemed content only when resembling an especially naff San Juan pimp. I wanted to cry.

Carla assures me that real gay relationships are meaningful, married and much classier than my unfortunate experience. I don't know what to believe, from a guy who lies to his family about being gay and refuses to have public photos taken of him at work to ensure they don't find out. Not to mention one whose emotional stability has more in common with a turbo-injected seesaw. On a daily basis he is fairly calm and secure, but give him a few drinks and Ms Hyde comes into her own. Then the dear love suddenly only has two modes, bile and fawn. He calls his aggressive bitching 'playing with my sister'. I call it jumping on my head, which appears to be one of his favourite past-times when loaded and not just with me. The other version we are treated to is Saint Carla, which can be most easily compared to a chipmunk on Ecstasy; at times like these, she'd make a great understudy for Glinda, the good witch of the North.

In the meantime, we've all learned to run like hell whenever Carla gets going on her 'I have a soul' spiel and, by now, these little speeches have taken on a predictability that is about as flat as a 2am Open University transmission. I am fortunate to have Becka as the third member of our cosy dressing-room trio, but not as lucky as Misha, who gets to sit in the backroom with the four barbettes. OK, he has to do most of his own changes, whereas we have a dresser, but that will seem a small sacrifice when Becka and I get hauled in for premeditated homicide. I wonder if you would call it homo-cide? I'm going bananas already, and it's only two weeks into the show.

Actually, we do have quite a bit of fun, which is maximised by our new dresser Daisy, a.k.a David. Daisy replaced Michael, who has now gone back to concentrating full-time on dressing at *Miss Saigon*. Daisy is absolutely unbelievable! This babe knows her stuff.

I suppose I should clarify the 'she' business: everybody here is a she, a queen in some mutation or other. Becka and I are the only butch men here besides José and Jamie, who cling onto their masculinity in a very major way, to the extent that the latter has taken to licking my neck. Five seconds later one of the barbettes is in for the same treat, and I now think he's the only glimmer of a bisexual we have in this place.

Daisy, by contrast, came sailing in self-proclaiming the arrival of 'Dolores del Argo, the slut from Chicago.' She has been Wardrobe Mistress on more shows than I've had hummus which, with my new found fetish for the stuff, is really saying something; especially when I arrive home at 4am, ravenous and definitely the worse for wear, only to pour granola into the dip because there's no other food in the house. My flatmates, whose food this usually involves, are understandably starting to get a little annoyed with my early morning munch-athons. Basically, you can kiss anything that isn't stapled down goodbye.

To combat this late night bingeing I have increased my aerobics with a vengeance, but I am getting slightly concerned as my periods appear to have pretty much ceased – which makes me feel even more like a man. Combining this with my rather unhealthy, stressed lifestyle is making me worried about long-term effects. One month and I'm already contemplating rehab – what a wildchild. You can take the girl out of her upbringing, but you can't take the upbringing out of the girl. Or the hypochondriac for that matter.

At least that's one thing I have in common with Carla, who

has already started freaking about the possibility of red lip glitter causing cancer. If the old saying that you are only a true performer when you start shitting glitter has any truth in it, then we are all certified professionals by now.

Saturday, 8th June

Pretty uneventful, if expensive, week.

If I'd realised how much keeping myself in make-up and tights would cost, I would not only have moaned at my salary but already started planning my eventual tax exile in Bolivia. I must be single-handedly keeping Charles Fox and Theatre Zoo in business! Our tights are less of a prestige matter – 30 denier at Littlewoods, capri tan. I'm queuing with all the fat Middle Eastern ladies in chadoris, clutching onto our identical purchases and praying that nobody will think that I actually buy these as some kind of fashion statement. They are, sadly, the only tights without gusset lines and, as I wear two together per night and snag them on a regular basis, this is becoming a routine, joyous outing. My own personal contribution to international bonding.

My social life is in a bit of a whirl at present, which is not helping my financial stability. As a new figure on the scene I seem to be in increasing demand, and it is quite a bizarre sensation to have people recognise me when I go into Soho restaurants and cafés. I went into Kettners the other day, which admittedly is leased by PR, and was astounded to be greeted by at least three people whom I didn't even know. It is unusual, as I generally feel like my double life allows me to lead a fairly low-key existence during the day-times. I mean, how many people are going to actually recognise you without your drag face on, especially when the bulk of them expect to see a man?

My friends are having a whale of a time and getting a lot of mileage, if not kudos, out of my new found 'fame'. I think they find it terribly amusing and exciting to have me suddenly on the degenerate inside. The fact is that most of my university friends left St Andrews and were immediately swallowed by the yuppie move-ment. We're talking accountants, management consultants, the odd solicitor or doctor, and a smattering of Public Relations agents. Those that branched out into more 'daring' territories became runners and eventually producers for television or film companies, but generally my 'conversion' was the one that left the 'phone lines burning and the dinner invitations flying.

19

It is inevitable that as soon as I arrive at a place, I get the usual grace period for cocktail chit chat and then someone pulls the old drag rabbit out of the hat and off we go on a non-stop barrage of questions until I whizz off to work. The most common query is also the most basic – 'Where do they put it?' Between their legs, darlings, well strapped down with two pairs of tights and tourniquet-style jock straps to hold it all in. Outsiders' wild speculations about seedy backstage activities can be squashed right away: most of the time the guys can't even feel anything until the blood starts painfully flowing back. Breasts are easily taken care of, that is to say tit-pads to the rescue. Most of the queens go for body shaves, although some prefer waxing, and real masochists like Tevita, Pepper and Misha go for facial electrolysis. Whoever said suffer to be beautiful should have seen this.

People's fascination with this taboo territory is normal, I guess. I can certainly understand the intrigue, as well as the desperate desire for some real thrills, but it feels odd to be the supplier of everybody's fantasies. People can't seem to grasp that as much as I enjoy work, it is a job. They come to the club, get drunk and have a wild time and assume that every night must be a party for me. Sometimes it is but, more often than not, it's just a job.

I would be lying if I said that I don't derive a lot of personal pleasure and excitement out of JoJo's, of course I do. But I think anyone who has ever worked in the service or entertainment industry will understand that one man's relaxation is another's hard work. Especially when they are shoulder to grindstone with someone who is having a hard time adjusting the politics of the club to his advantage. George has only been here for three months and consequently felt forced to kowtow to Ruby. Now we're all more or less new and, thanks to our director and choreographer pissing off to Manchester, we are left without an acting head and pretty much at his mercy. In theory, the floor and the show are two entirely distinct productions, but in practice he makes sure that we all know who calls the shots.

The old cast have now been demonised beyond recognition by both management and office, to the extent that Jason is officially barred from the club for not paying his drinks bill. This surprises no one but he claims that the office still owes him money for his choreographing, so it sounds like a convenient excuse to cut the strings, which they are quite good at if the eponymous hostess's case is anything to go by.

JoJo, the previous hostess and effective manager of the club, decided to go solo about three months ago. She left asking for nothing but her freedom and the use of her name. PR, naturally, was none too thrilled about this development and announced that he had named the club first and she/he had adjusted her name accordingly. She's now working at the Limelight Club up the road, and the case is in full swing. I'm told she will be lucky if she survives professionally intact. I get the distinct impression that where PR burns, no grass grows.

On a lighter, if still economical, note, punters have fortunately been buying me drinks at the club. At £2.50 a beer, £3.00 per shot, this is not to be underrated. It's unbelievable how much easier dull people are to tolerate when they're paying for your booze. Terrible if you think of it as selling yourself for liquor, but I've never had a problem twisting this logic to my advantage; it's a courtesy, a 'thank you for the show'. If they're too unbearable I usually, sob, sniff, don't accept.

Ditto in the Piano Bar, a nice opportunity to wind down after the show, before our joint 3am closing. It took a few days before I cottoned on to the fact that the Piano Bar and club function individually and yet as a joint enterprise. The separate entrance next to ours, that leads into the street-level bar, initially fooled me into assuming it was a totally separate venture.

The Piano Bar is tiny, with similar decor to ours downstairs, but with the pleasant alternative of a drag 'hostess' compering the evening to live piano. Certain punters get up and sing which, depending upon your luck, can be a joy or an ear-shattering agony. The latter usually depends upon how much of a regular they are and how tolerant the audience is feeling. Jimmy Trollette is on most nights, she of 'Trollette Sisters' fame, and insists we give a post-performance croon along with visiting West End musical stars. A real ego high, even if more often than not we are the chopped liver to the vocal pâté.

Now I'm off to Jay's for an Italian night. We have been going around the culinary world as of late – last time we visited Mexico, sitting on the roof of my apartment building and swigging Dos Equis. He's started talking about extending this to real travel, in the shape of New York, and has decided that the ideal situation would be our living in my family's house in New Jersey, with my working in NY and his playing housewife. Get a grip boy. I don't think so somehow.

Sunday, 23rd June

Jay is starting to get on my nerves.

21

His constant harping about moving to New York, especially in light of my only just started career here, seems rather calculating and manipulative. I've started to get the impression that all he wants is to lounge around, when not being a prima donna of course, and live a cushy lifestyle drinking vodka gimlets and watching soap re-runs. Not that I am so terribly far removed in my ambitions, but he seems to think he's owed it.

Add to that another sordid night spent at his place and I'm feeling rather turned off. This time *I* got to play pimp, encouraging our G-stringed *wunderkind* Jamie to come back to Jay's. The idea was to unwind and check out the video of one of the previous shows for 'inspiration'. While I knew that Jay fancied Jamie, I didn't quite expect him to jump his passed-out bones later on. Fortunately I was not aware of this at the time.

It started out all chummy, with both guys keeping me company as I jacuzzied my way into some semblance of post-show cleanliness. It's amazing how much we sweat out during performances; I'm sure it must be 95% Smirnoff anyway, but those lights and costumes make me feel like a baco-foiled chicken. Add to that the fact that the management has a lovely little habit of turning off the air-conditioning during sweltering summer weather to 'encourage' punters to buy drinks and you have a club hot enough to melt formica.

We sat down to a buddy viewing session, Jamie getting very drunk and Jay fast-forwarding continuously to himself. I tell you, it was about as sad as taking a bow every time the fridge light goes on. We move Jamie to Jay's bed, I settle down on the couch in the living-room, and Jay makes a great pretence of staying in the spare room. That is, of course, until I get early morning beckons to bring the two lovebirds a cup of tea.

I felt like a total schmuck. Here Jamie had been reluctant to come, I had convinced him that this was just a fun, harmless outing, and off he goes walking bow-legged for the rest of the day. Having said that, he is turning out to be quite the tart, so my guilt pangs have abated as their fling continues. In a way I even feel sorry for Jay; he so desperately wants to fall in love with someone. I can't help but think this is going to end in drama.

In pleasant contrast, last night turned out to be a howl. Becka and Marcie came over for dinner, Becka insisting on taxis to and from the club since the seven-minute walk might have meant exercise. Marcie, one of the new barbettes, is a riot, especially once she has a few litres of Bull's Blood in her. Used to be a hairdresser (who wasn't? is my attitude now), and has launched into her new androgynous lifestyle by copying the Sinead O'Connor fashion approach. The three of us had a marvellous time, whereupon Becka and I dragged up and out to show the *Rocky Horror Show* last-night party at the Piccadilly what transvestism is really all about. Can you believe it? A few months ago the thought of rubbing elbows with Richard O'Brien was the stuff that *Twilight Zone* episodes are made of, whereas now I can happily flirt with Adrian Edmondson from behind two-inch spider lashes and ogle Tony Hall without a canister of Gold Blend.

It's not quite a case of becoming a household name – I'd probably have more success changing my surname to Windolene or Ajax – but what a psych-up, especially sashaying through Soho, not to mention in and out of the party, in our garb. People just stand there gob-smacked at these two walking explosions in a paint factory and either start clapping or trying to take pictures. Which considering they're not allowed to in the club is probably their only chance. You can just imagine tourists taking their shots back home – totally redefines 'Why don't you come over and see our holiday snaps?'

Tanya was chosen to join the gang in Manchester and has raced off to her rightful place in the spotlight. She's been replaced by a lanky brunette called Barbie, who seems so nice and well-adjusted that I keep expecting to find out she's really a homicidal drug addict.

Am off to Richmond now for a day's normality with my friends Rita and Fiona: Sunday paper reading, pink champagne and homecooked Thai food. My chance to stop orbiting the Forbidden Planet and come back to earth for twenty-four hours. Which I will definitely need with the coming week's craziness.

We are scheduled to appear at Gay Pride next Saturday. Talk about an initiation – 50,000 gays from around the country all marching through London and converging in Kennington for a mega-party. We seem to be sandwiched between two bands, the former which I keep forgetting and followed by Björn Again. Don't you just love it?

Sunday, 30th June

Oooooh, my poor head.

I have never, repeat never, experienced anything like yesterday. I feel like I've just played Wembley naked for want of a better comparison, and not only survived but triumphed, which we were none too sure of doing by the time we hit Kennington.

Having only had two mini-rehearsals with tapes we put together

ourselves, Misha, Becka, Carla and I were feeling none too confident. Not least of all thanks to our no-show boys, who decided to
put in an appearance late Saturday afternoon just in case we weren't
paranoid enough. Daisy came along with an interesting assortment
of 'costumes', more a case of running amok in a frillies shop. Misha
was of course thrilled, this line of clothing being right up his alley.
Thank God he has at least progressed to another eyeshadow colour
besides blue. The dime store transvestite is slowly but surely developing taste.

Off we leap into two taxis with our bin liners of boas and
captured, bondaged boys. We contemplated locking José in the
trunk and nearly lost him during a traffic jam in Trafalgar Square.
As it was the grans and grandads at the bus stop made no pretence
of swallowing their dentures in amazement.

Arriving at the park we were lead to our snazzy dressing-room,
a trailer which would make the Black Hole of Calcutta look like the
Hilton. Which, I was informed, we were sharing with Lily Savage and
Regina Fong. Whoopee. It could have been Queen Elizabeth for all
I cared. All I knew was that we were nowhere near as prepared as
would have been required for the club, and once I discovered that
we were indeed going on that immense stage in twenty minutes I
grabbed the first alcoholic beverage in sight. I would have drunk
straight ether if it had been within swigging distance.

Wandered around behind the erected stage, where people kept
trying to talk to us from behind the gates and even offered us dope
in one instance. I expected a joint and suddenly had a lump shoved
into my palm, which promptly disappeared down a hyperventilating
José's throat. His mini-hysteria actually had the effect of calming me
down. He seemed to relax somewhat, judging by his buckled knees,
and especially when we bumped into Steve, previous boy at the club
and now also in Manchester.

I *adore* Steve, and not least of all for offering to join us on stage. Our
three monosyllabic G-stringed vegetables took this as a great boost
and suddenly made a new show of semi-enthusiastic commitment.
Even José. Despite intimidating surroundings, the Spanish spirit
showed through and, thankfully, he still went periodically beserk.
At least he was still alive.

The band was pounding away some indistinguishable but deafening
number as we crawled up the ladders to backstage. I say 'backstage'
– these were the wings, where we were also doing our two-second
changes. Peering out through cracks at this sea of people was enough

to make me vow to become an accountant. If I survive this, dear God . . . The one comfort was probably the performing band, who managed to create enough butchered melodies and massacred lyrics to produce some pretty impressive atrocities. My fear, however, was based more upon the contrast and our lack of preparation. I mean, we had the reputation of the club to uphold, we were the epitome of Soho scandal, and we were starting out with a poxy tape and limited costumes against a set that looked like it had been designed in the throes of a migraine.

Time to go on. Carla and I marched out in total silence, two tiny figures on this HUGE stage. The announcer did the whole hoopla, 'World-renowned Madame JoJo's blah blah', as a gentle roar started emanating from the crowd. By the time 'Big Spender' started blaring across the loudspeakers we had somehow found our voices, and we were off. What a rush. There is just nothing that equals it.

Whatever petty squabbles we may have, we were a team that day. I will never forget it. Even potentially touchy subjects, like my singing 'Dance 10, Looks 3' in Misha's baby-girl teddy and silicone boob bra, went down a treat. I had been warned that this might antagonise the lesbians, to which I thought great, one *more* thing to worry about. I was already visualising having bottles surgically removed from my head. My rationale was 'I'm a woman singing it, what would they find offensive about that?' Now if it were Misha or Carla, I could understand. The drawback of being a female drag queen, I guess. Nobody knows.

Misha was leaping across the stage like a rebel without a corset to the strains of 'Great Balls of Fire', and then Becka launched into her 'Don't tell Mama' from *Cabaret* with Carla and myself slinking around helicopter-blading our boas behind her. For me, though, the most moving moment was watching Carla, standing all alone in the middle of the stage in a beautiful long sequined green dress and Daryl Hannah hair, clutching a single red rose and singing – appropriately enough – 'The Rose'. If it didn't sound so corny . . . well, I'll say it, it nearly brought tears to my eyes.

Doing the club show that night seemed the easiest and best show we have ever done. I think our high transcended to the audience, some of whom were Pride-ers anyway, and I felt completely and utterly happy.

Unlike now, with a splitting hangover and a mother and seven-year-old sister due in at Heathrow for a week's stay. Somehow I don't feel the megastar I did last night.

Sunday, 14th July

A dizzying two weeks have passed, during which I swung in and out of drag queen mode faster than I change tampons. Which I'm having a rough time remembering as I still haven't managed to develop my 'punctuation', as my little sister keeps calling it.

Spent a blissful week with Mama and el bebe, both as dutiful daughter and wise older sibling. Puts a lot of things in perspective, as touching base with home always seems to do for me. Perhaps that's why I'm having my late 'rebellion' now – I enjoyed my family too much growing up to ever go through the usual pubescent revolt. We moved every two to three years, being transferred by my father's work, so family life has really been my one true nucleus, almost a sort of nationality.

Being born in America with a US passport, but to a German heritage and citizenship right as well, has always left me feeling a bit of a foreigner wherever I settle. It used to cause me great angst while seeking my 'identity', but I have grown not only to tolerate it but also to enjoy it. Another reason why my sexually isolated status at the club is not really that much of an adjustment. Any uniqueness stems more from the fact that my parents and I have an unusually open and understanding relationship.

My mother took to the club like a duck to water. She came down with two very dear friends of mine, one of whom, Hazel, is considerably older and functions as my surrogate mother here. Both Hazel and my mother are very cosmopolitan women and have lived an international high-life that has exposed them to more than the club could probably fling during a week of performances.

Whether they were terribly impressed by the Brewer Street entrance to the club is another matter. Somehow it's hard to maintain an image of crème de la crème drag when you pass 'Girls, Girls, Girls' and sex shops left, right and centre. Some of these places even make the Paul Raymond Revue Bar look a class act. While our notorious Red Light District only extends a few streets, and has been pretty much sanitised, I still prayed for a taxi with shaded windows.

They cut their swathe through the crowded floor to the rather optimistically titled 'Royal Box', were plied with drinks by a surprisingly kind George and thoroughly enjoyed the show. My other friend Peter looked quite proud, especially with barbettes comparing dear

Mama to Lee Remick in her sexy Karl Lagerfeld outfit. Pretty hard not to enjoy yourself, really. Final verdict: 'Well, schatz, having seen the Folies Bergère (aged eighteen), it's a lot of fun but really quite tame.' You'd think she had G-stringed staff running around the house in Karachi from her unflappability.

Becka was to encounter a similarly relaxed mother the following week, so I guess for us it's pretty easy. Working in a drag club with our respective degrees and backgrounds may cause our parents to swallow deeply, but it's not really any sexual indictment. There is none of the 'no grandchildren' gnashing of teeth, or 'where did we go wrong?' wringing of hands. It's more a case of 'our crazy kids are desperate to "make it", so let's support them rather than add to the difficulties.'

Went today with Becka and Daisy to see our friend Michael playing piano at the Limelight's Sunday Lunch. Well that was the legitimate excuse, as JoJo was also hostessing. The office has been very strict about us being in the same vicinity as 'that person', let alone – God forbid – being in the same photo. While I can understand that this is definitely bad press during the trial, they seem to have gone slightly overboard, to the extent that even talking to JoJo is now viewed in the same light as medieval priests regarded consorting with the devil.

Whatever the problems, the office's attitude of 'you are no longer any use so we don't know you anymore' is a bit worrying if you're not planning on dragging til death do you part. I saw it first with the old cast, now with JoJo, and in both instances the parties in question had dedicated a lot to helping create the now very popular club. Their only crime is in wanting to expand beyond the very real constraints of their jobs, and it seems somehow ungrateful, not to mention unchivalrous, to treat them in such a fashion.

Speaking of which, we saw Ruby and Co. afterwards at the Soho Festival. Made her feel good and guilty too for leaving us to fend for ourselves in shark-infested waters. I really miss them, they were such a breath of fresh air, plus they actually seemed so confident in knowing what they were doing. God only knows why, on one hand. Apparently Manchester is not turning out to be the promised land after all. They are practically squatting in a nearby flat, bills for the club appear to be unpaid, and now Ruby has been manipulated into becoming the licensee for all this bankrupt joy. Must make JoJo's look like paradise.

Schnitzel was doing a decent impersonation of a small moving bush with sunglasses, and checking out the scene. I had to laugh. First they claim that no way in hell should the old cast come back, and yet they have to be up on all their movements. I think they could probably give MI5 a run for their money.

It doesn't make me feel any more secure in my job prospects to know that they probably would accept them back into the fold, albeit after a lot of grovelling. Ruby is an international name after all, with a lot of pulling power. And yet I'm not too sure she actually wants to return. She's always wanted to open her own club and has now lifted her raddled nostrils to the entrepreneurial breeze and detected the faint possibility of becoming her own boss. Even if it is in a debt-ridden northern hellhole.

Sunday, 21st July

Saw *In Bed with Madonna* last night, whom my flatmate and I have rechristened Madge, and about the only positive development to emerge from this culture-fest was our subsequent backstage discussion of Madge's blow-job technique, as demonstrated with a bottle during the film. I confessed to my exceedingly experienced colleagues that I've always doubted my abilities in said department and requested their council. Pepper exhibited hitherto undisplayed tutorial skills and immediately proceeded to demonstrate the fine art with her hairbrush. I don't think I'll ever be able to borrow it again without wiping the handle first.

By the time George meandered in, advice was being flung from all corners: 'Open your mouth wider; head back further; try to open throat a bit more.' Four barbettes and two G-stringed boys, choking on hair and blusher brushes, was enough to convince him we should all be locked up.

Also went to see a chiropodist at Carla's instigation for a painful callous under my foot. Mr Foot Man chopped and dealt, all the while chatting to Carla, who had come along for moral support, and me. I now have a nicely bandaged sole, which is a real treat in stilettos.

He ended up being much more than I bargained for and this on two counts. As podiatrist at Covent Garden Pineapple he is used to handling the dancers' butchered feet, but also proceeded to tell us about his treks to King's Cross to soothe and realign the stubbly toes of the area's major attraction. Be it Soho's Queens of the Evening, or King's Cross's Ladies, he has seen it all. He showed us some pretty revolting pictures of deformed Bangladeshi feet, which I assume must be reliable podiatrist hard-sell tactics, because it instantly manipulated me into agreeing to a bit of elementary reflexology at his knowledgeable hands.

Agony. Total pain. I'd rather not give birth, flashed through my mind as my new-found guru assured me that, deity-like, he would give me back my period. He warned me that I would feel like death immediately afterwards, but I couldn't imagine feeling any worse than I currently did. The next day, however, it would be vive la difference! Tap dancing and bleeding my way to the club, no doubt.

No, no, it would take two weeks for that to develop, and after that he would be able to tell me exactly when I could best get pregnant. Great. Considering that I have been without a long-term beau for over a year now, I didn't think this was going to be a major drive just yet. To which he informed me that he used to be able to give his ex-girlfriend an orgasm through her feet; unfortunately, we skipped that part of the treatment.

Went Dolly Parton of the Lone Cactus Saloon-style to a Kinky Gerlinky 'Western' theme party with my friend Peter, who was warned outside by some macho derelicts to 'be careful – do you know that's a guy you're with?' The hysterical part is that they were serious.

Thursday, 25th July

The day after my totally exuberant birthday.

I was spoilt rotten at the club, embarrassed beyond belief, and drunk as a skunk, thanks partially to a day's worth of parties thrown from all angles of my life, starting at breakfast. By the time Rita and Fiona's surprise dinner rolled around, I was very merry indeed. They set up a picnic in my room, which I considered quite bizarre in light of our beautiful roof-top until I heard a small meowing from behind the door. Only to find a tiny kitten and basket, my real present. Wonderful.

Don't get me wrong, it was a lovely thought and who could not melt at this tiny little bundle. Even if, like myself, they happen to detest cats. I mean, I am the person *101 Things to Do with a Dead Cat* was written for; I am totally rah-rah canines. And yet it did tug at my heartstrings. And my blankets, and my clothes, and my curtains.

I smiled with weak gratitude and promptly nearly stepped on

it. Omelette, as we subsequently champagne baptised it, seemed to revel in the challenge and promptly leaped onto my head and abseiled his way back down. Oh joy, rapture. For the first time I wished I had my eighteen-year-old sister's convenient excuse of feline allergies.

We left Omelette eventually with my cooing flatmates, and went on to the party at the club. I received more diamante earrings than I would probably use in a lifetime of coronations, plus on-stage presentations of flowers, cake, champers, etc. I loved every minute. The barbettes went up to do their 'I'm Too Sexy' catwalk routine after the show, and as I minced around with them pouting and posing I felt about as happy as a pig in mud.

Until I got home that is, and had to deal single-handedly with . . . THE OMELETTE. Just when you thought it was safe . . . Crawling all over me throughout the night, to the point where I couldn't even sleep because I was terrified of rolling over and squashing it. Let's hope maternal instincts come to me better than this.

Sunday, 28th July

Gave the cat away. Hallelujah.

Saturday, 3rd August

I am exhausted. Physically, mentally and emotionally.

Have been doing some day-time word processing this week for extra cash. When Schnitzel talked about the club as a second job, he could not have meant in addition to a nine-to-five first one. It's been OK for a few days, but crawling out of bed four hours after a post-show collapse can be nothing but a short-term option. I only want to hear morning birds once per day, thank you very much.

The only positive aspect is that I at least miss the 9am antics of next door's little terrors. All sixty of them, at regular 45-minute intervals, although by the sheer volume you'd be understandably mistaken in estimating closer to 600. I stupidly figured that the back room of a fourth floor flat would ensure some morning peace. Guess again. I brilliantly managed to choose the only remaining roof-top school playground in the whole of the Borough of Westminster to plop my tired corpse next to nightly. The first time I nearly fell out of bed, anticipating some kind of Reckoning in my befuddled state; the next day went marginally better, thanks to my new purchase of some shooting earplugs. If that hadn't worked I would have been seriously tempted to get the gun as well.

Add to all of this last night's saga. Without sounding too much like the voice of doom, I just knew Jay and Jamie's affair was going to be a trauma. Not least of all for me.

Apparently Jamie told Jay after the show that he couldn't handle sleeping with a drag queen anymore. I would imagine having a few other logs on the fire didn't help, in that he just doesn't need Jay as much as he is needed in return and as a 'straight' gay man as versus a 'dragging' gay man has more options open to him.

This was explained to me by a tearful Jay in a semi-suicidal 4.30am phone call, along with a plea to mini-cab it over and save him from himself. I figured that the intermittent crunching between slugs of vodka was his nice little candy dish of valiums and opted for the Good Samaritan routine.

Jay already had *Torch Song Trilogy* in the video upon my arrival and, after a great deal of wailing and chest-beating, we settled down to watch Harvey Fierstein explain it considerably more eloquently. I was really moved, actually, at the tragic hopelessness of it all. I never realised how difficult it must be for a gay man to dress as a woman and still attract one of their own. Especially in view of the very feminine nature of most drag queens and their desire for a complementary masculine man.

A gay man by definition is not sexually interested in women, let alone the extreme caricatures cooked up by the drag world. They may enjoy the performance, but the attraction tends to fall into what has been labelled 'trannie-fucker' territory. Trannie-fuckers are generally men who are either bisexual or afraid to come out of the closet, but sexually want the hardness of a man. Needless to say, this does not always appeal to your average gay guy who happens to dress in drag as a job.

Jay's predicament is a sad, if common one. He meets a man at the club when he is dressed as a woman, and falls head over heels and vice versa. They agree to meet, but when Jay shows up at the appropriate venue the person in question walks straight past him because he is looking for a woman and not a man. Alternatively, he meets a guy as himself, starts having an affair, and is treated à la hot potato when the beloved comes to the club and sees him dragged up as a woman. Damned if you do, damned if you don't. The drag queen's catch 22, I guess. It's all so hopelessly sad and lonely. My tenderer instincts can't help but pity his weakness which, after all, is based on a very fundamental human need to be loved. Certainly that is something we all can understand.

What I hope never to share is this schizophrenic attitude towards his 'identities'. So far I've found 'Queen Bea' less of an alter ego than a performance that I've created, that I'm in control of, and consequently have not had a problem locking the character away at the end of the night. Then again, I'm not a gay man trying to attract another 'regular' gay man into a deep and meaningful relationship. For 'regular', read one that isn't a trannie-fucker or an attention-seeker but the average homosexual who desires a similarly masculine man. Certainly not the caricature of a woman.

I find it equally sad that Jay is not able to create a career life for himself outside of JoJo's. God help me if I ever end up that way. There's definitely a lesson to be learned here, although fortunately I can perform as a woman in any number of circumstances and venues. Jay's star would appear to have come and gone, as though he is nothing without the support and display case of the club. I find it very hard to accept that someone as talented as Jay could not get at least drag pub work, although I suppose that's just the point. He doesn't want to go back to drag, and if he did he certainly wouldn't leave the pinnacle to filter around in grotty pubs again. Talk about a spiralling descent.

Sunday, 11th August

CRISIS, big time. The catchword for the latter part of this absolutely dreadful week.

Becka has developed some kind of glandular infection and the night before my last temping date had to call in sick. This is firstly not a joy for her as the time when you most need money is when you're ill and the office is not about to win any humanitarian awards in the sick-pay department. From my rather selfish point of view, however, it was a total nightmare.

The words 'understudy' or 'swing', while familiar in most proper theatres, have no place in a Paul Raymond institution. That translates into everybody running around manically trying to find Becka's sheet music and take in her costumes accordingly.

It was my happy lot to discover this development at 11.15pm from a bemused doorstaff. Now a few words about our esteemed front of house. Tina, our cashier and coat lady, used to scare the hell out of me, and I distinctly remember telling Ruby on one of my first nights that 'that dragon has got to go.' She seems to have accepted me as one of her crew now, and is an absolute delight to me, whereas with Carla and Becka . . . Well, let's just say that their skirmishes are always of great interest to those who enjoy combats in which the weapons are invisible but the hits palpable.

The motley gang surrounding her are fronted by Rod, who is constantly trying to power grip me into a corner. What a smooth operator. There is definitely something about him that makes me uneasy. To illustrate: Carla had some row with a friend, rare phenomenon, and was bitching about it at the door. To which Mr Ever Ready asks her how much. Now underneath it all, Carla is a lot of bark and preciously little bite and consequently gave him one of her usual blank stares. He repeated his 'offer' and proceeded to inform her that £500 could break a few limbs, but if she wanted a more 'permanent' solution we were looking into quadruple digits. It's written off as a joke but I still wouldn't ever want to irritate him, say with the heinous offence of smiling, and find myself cement stilettoed at the bottom of the Thames.

The other two are quite sweet by comparison. Hell, they're Mother Teresa. Ronnie's primary fault from my point of view is intermittently attempting to shove his tongue down my throat, but at least he doesn't try and break my arm in the process. With the total uninterest downstairs, this nightly experience feels like passing through the Mecca of testosterone. Rounding off the trio is James, whose attentions are totally directed at his barman boyfriend. He seems almost pathologically polite after a run in with the other two. A genuine relief to encounter this cuddly penguin.

Anyway, back to Nightmare on Brewer Street. I arrive at the club to discover the developments and am promptly informed that I am to take over the bulk of Becka's numbers. Thank *you*. Daisy, lovingly rechristened the Welsh Witch, has gone into a human Singer machine frenzy and is attempting to alter Becka's costumes. Mother Herb runs back with a makeshift copy of her songs and I get to add eight numbers onto my already rather laden programme.

We might as well have renamed it 'The Bea Show' and had my costume changes on stage. I must have lost at least half a stone, and that was before I even trod the boards. On average I had one number on, one off, in this whirlwind of a substitute show, and to have pulled it off with such flair, if I do say so myself, can only be attributed to a healthy bit of professionalism. Man did we feel like we'd earned our Equity by the end of it.

This state of events was to last throughout the remainder of the week, but just to keep things from becoming dull, a twist was flung in the following night.

For my going away drink from my temp job, I went out with a gorgeous South African called Mark. A gorgeous, *married* South African. The first time I have ever been tempted to help someone break his nuptial vows.

Anyway, after a beer in one watering hole we proceeded to a newly discovered mutual friend's pub in Covent Garden. As manager, he very kindly showed complete attentiveness to our drinking needs despite a huge crowd of people. I wisely enough decided to pace myself, and had a Diet Coke between beers, which amounted to approximately four in total.

While admittedly four beers can get you a very nice buzz, this was over the course of five hours so I felt fairly safe. Guess again. I walked out of there, or maybe that should be staggered, and somehow managed to wind up at the club. Totally and utterly pissed, with breath you could set fire to. I just couldn't understand it.

They all gave me disbelieving looks when I slurred out something about 'unly fuh beahs', and managed to somehow get me together for the show. All I was concerned about was not throwing up on stage. Or passing out.

Daisy even started laughing and remembering Ruby in days of yore. Nights of such wastedness that they had to lay her down horizontally to pull her costumes on and prop her up on stage. I tell you, I was following mother's footsteps that night, to the extent of having my shoes buckled for me. Sad.

The worst thing was, I knew I was telling the truth. And I also know how much liquor I can hold. I just couldn't explain my state, and as much as I tried to counter that they were all confusing the process with smoking crack, and that I felt totally different, they just shook their heads knowingly.

Until Carla went upstairs to the Piano Bar. She met our Covent Garden pub manager there, who was laughing riotously and asking her what she thought of my performance. He then expounded on the fine art of Mickey Finn making, i.e. slipping double vodkas into every one of my 'sobering' Diet Cokes. The amount of alcohol I must have had flowing through my veins would have been enough to pickle an elephant.

Carla was livid with him, but not nearly as much as I and no amount of subsequent floral arrangements could mitigate my fury. The asshole. I'm sorry, but you just don't do that to someone, and especially not if they have to perform anything beyond hugging a toilet seat.

The rest of the week passed into routine and I'm off to visit Becka and do the condolence bit. It's taken me this long to get rid of my coyote-spit mouth and feel semi-human again, but I think a self-congratulatory drink is in order at least. Sunday is the only night where you can indulge without worrying about doing a show afterwards, so my liver doesn't end up having that religious day of rest unfortunately. Today I feel like I've deserved it.

Thursday, 15th August

Had an extremely sobering experience today.

Went with Tevita and one of the barmen, Brian, to Charing Cross Hospital to visit Auntie Bob.

Auntie Bob was the glass collector/washer upstairs in the Piano Bar and, after many strong years of hauling crates, suddenly collapsed with exhaustion last week, totally out of the blue.

Although he must be in his late fifties this guy was as sturdy as they come, and consequently quite perplexed as to this sudden development. They took him to the hospital only to discover that he had full-blown AIDS and must have been HIV positive for quite some time. What a shock. I've never known anyone who has died of AIDS, let alone seen the full-blown stages. The impact of my deflowering in this matter was unforgettable in terms of sheer horror.

We trouped through the wing trying to find him and getting totally lost. This was not aided by Tevita's attempt to scope out the sex change section, where she eventually plans on staying herself. Brian was turning whiter and whiter, and I have to give him full credit for guts. He has been labelled HIV positive as well, and in the tragic position of having his lover commit suicide by jumping off Kew Bridge and mailing his jewellery and farewell note previously. We made an odd trio.

We finally found Auntie Bob and it was all I could do not to gasp and turn away. He had become a wraith of a figure, this skeleton spread out on a bed, hollow-cheeked and incapable of moving. The worst of it was he was cheerier and more entertaining than we, his supposed spirit-lifting squad, could have ever hoped to be. We were stunned.

Thankfully some other people joined us, bearing ice-cream, and one of the big strong guys lifted Auntie Bob up with practically one arm to feed him. We told a few more tales and beat a hasty retreat into the sunshine outside. I don't think I was the only one feeling ice cold.

On the way back Tevita launched into her immediate desire to have a relationship, which Brian and I rightfully countered as a rather difficult ambition. I mean on an obvious level, any man who falls for her now, with penis, is not going to want a woman in six months' time. And vice versa. She just mused about how well the speech therapy and psychological counselling were going and speculated on how many more thousands she was going to have to accumulate to pay for the operation.

Brian was in a similar, if not equal, quandary. Short of lying, his position is somewhat hopeless unless he finds a really understanding guy who can live with the prospect of visiting a future Auntie Bob. I will never complain of the hardships of finding a decent relationship again.

Interview with Isabelle
On Madame JoJo's from an Outsider's Point of View

Met up with my eighteen-year-old sister, Isabelle (she of feline allergy fame), on the balcony of the Opera Terrace. Our get-togethers unfortunately have become somewhat erratic since we last sat there with Jay a few months ago, leaving a lot of experiences to cover. Then, Jay had been enlightening her about the curious world her older sister had been sucked into; now we sat bathed in glorious sunshine, a bit bright for my night owl eyes, as I recounted the horrors of the Omelette saga.

I've always fancied playing the reporter and I have decided to start compiling interviews on the subject. It would certainly help me understand my relatively 'new life' better. Deciding that the club was as good a starting point as any, I asked her for her developed impressions of the club.

I was lucky in that I came down with Jay, so I wasn't standing in queues, and understood a bit what the people and routines were about. Having said that, I was more familiar with the names than the place, so I really had more anticipation of seeing faceless names than the actual place itself.

What do you ascribe the attraction of JoJo's to?

I think the appeal boils down to this: I thought the whole concept was bizarre, that you actually go underground to this whole new place; almost as though reality stops at street level.

The girl at the door was 'normal', the bouncers looked 'normal', and everything was like a regular club. Then you go down the stairs and see nothing, just a wall, then turn right and – *sudden exposure*. It's almost as though they are, I don't know if you want to call them drag queens or transvestites, totally different at night. They transform themselves. It's a place where everybody is being what they want to be, which reality prohibits, or scorns, whatever.

What would you say is the reaction of an outsider to this rather strange world?

From a woman's point of view, it's *very* intimidating, on the basis that you have these 'women', who have almost no concerns or concept of what it means to be a real woman, i.e. the metabolic rates, the way a woman's body works: weight gain, water retention, periods . . .

The way I think they perceive women is through the external factors, which please the eye: the ability to disguise the true self with the clothing, the make-up, the hair, and the raunchiness which a woman can allow herself. Like the seductiveness, the way a woman moves, the using of the body in a way that a man cannot normally do: to seduce the *mind* into wanting more.

The way a man would seduce a woman, from my point of view, is through his effeminate qualities surfacing; it's like a drop of all machismo. They become emotionally and intellectually sensitive, and I think that's the appeal. It's allowing this to come out, by disguising themselves as a woman, in whom these qualities are accepted.

So how convincing do you think they are?

They come across as the perfect woman: they have these fabulous bodies, which they don't feel intimidated to expose. There's more self-confidence in their bodies as women than a real woman has in her own.

Would you ever act that way?

No, and I think that's the appeal of it. As a woman, you want to strut your stuff, have the men ogle you, but would never dare to. Because if you were to act upon it in the normal world, 'reality', you would be classified as sleazy.

Do you find the atmosphere of the club sleazy?

No, because it's the norm. That is what the club is there for, that's what people come to see.

I came down with a conservative friend, and the reason he came was as a dare, to prove a point to a mutual friend. We're talking about a BIG guy here, with an elbow-padded cardigan and *highly* sceptical about believing that these drag queens would make convincing women. Once he'd set eyes on them, however, he could not be persuaded otherwise.

Tevita, for example, he categorically denied was a man. And he was basically saying, 'A man could not pull something like this off.' I think he was thinking of *himself* not being able to pull it off.

All my male friends who have come down say the same thing and leave in awe. The women leave feeling ugly, fat and very simple. You go in thinking 'I'm looking good,' and end up sitting there thinking 'Oh my God, I'm overweight, my make-up is horrible, and I want to cover myself up.'

On the other hand though, you leave very aware that you are a woman and they are not. Because everything is so over the top. The make-up, the eyelashes, the dresses, are so wanting to please, wanting to seduce you into believing they are women. Yet a real woman knows she can go around wearing men's clothing and no make-up, but that everybody's still aware that she is a woman. We may enjoy dressing in men's clothing because it's more relaxed and casual, but not because we want to *be* men or appear as men. More men want to become women than vice versa, and the club just underlines that.

Was there any one feature that particularly struck you?

Yes, it was always really dimly lit; maybe so you couldn't see the stubble up close. On stage it was so brightly lit, that you couldn't see it there either.

I also didn't like going down with men, because of the constant fear that someone will hit upon the guy you're with. You have these very sexy, raunchy 'women' flaunting themselves, which may be what some men wish women were more like, and you're sitting there in baggy clothes. The only difference is that you don't have a penis. It's as simple as that.

What more is there to say, really?

Wednesday, 28th August

Last week was fairly normal, which made a pleasant contrast to the craziness of the Notting Hill Carnival. Ariba! Went with my dear old friend Sophie afterwards to see her boyfriend Tom, drummer in the jazz band 'Uncle Fish Fry', performing on the South Bank. They've offered to play with me at some stage which is a fairly exhilarating thought. The oom-pah-pah of the nightly backing tape is fine, but in light of the fantastic professional performances I witnessed I would like to try something a little more avant garde. This coming from a drag queen sounds quite amusing, I know.

New temping job started today and fortunately one that allows me to occasionally use my brain. Not that it is always engaged at 9am, but I am helping a very competent woman write this year's textbook for the Association of Corporate Treasurers. Talk about a night and day existence. Both sets of my colleagues seem to think it's a howl.

Following this vein of thought, who the hell do some of our punters think they are? Or we are, for that matter? Bad enough having them constantly staring at our crotches on stage but last night someone on the balcony actually clutched me during 'Barbette Express' and tried to grab me between the legs. I was *furious*. And mortified, perversely at having been felt and found out. Of course our competent bouncers, ever ready to abuse and throw out our friends, did sweet FA.

On a lighter note, we have been inundated with jewellery, sadly of the faux variety, by a rather strange little man called Derek. He claims to have been one of the finest jewellers at Garrard's, purveyors to Her Majesty, and has decided independently to create rhinestone tiaras, necklaces, brooches, and so forth. Apparently the mere pleasure of seeing us wearing his concoctions is payment enough, so we are happy glittering little campers. God knows, he is saving us a fortune. I alone must have already received about £250 worth of stones, so if you multiply that by about eight . . . Suffice it to say, we are always very happy to see him and his Polish wife Marge hauling in their goody crate.

The only request he had of us was to make Marge up for a surprise weekend he was planning to Paris. Misha, of all people, was awarded this special task and, at Derek's instigation, made her over into a creature that would make *Vogue* beauty technicians gasp. With horror. A forty-year-old unconvincing drag face departed with a glowing Derek, and once again I pondered the strangeness of some people. Poor Marge, she is mad about her husband and would do anything to please him, even to the extent of becoming a parody. For me, the idea of someone falling 'in love' with me as a drag queen is an absolute nightmare. God forbid.

For us, at least something interesting was happening at work. The weekday crowds have been tapering off, to the point that the cast outnumbered the clients on one night. In Equity circumstances that would be enough to cancel a show, but the office seems to regard this as conceding some sort of defeat, even though theatres are going dark all over the West End. Now our gay public seems to be on the decline, with an increasing number of tacky trannie-fuckers and lowlife characters, to the extent that on some nights the club gives the impression of being sheltered accommodation for deviants with chronically retarded dress sense.

Marcie managed to fly off the stage one night and pretended to fall into a coma, a sort of a spirited attempt to make contact with our remaining audience, I guess. She ended up pinching a nerve, which is especially serious with regard to long-term damage, and is off for the week. I'm already seeing an osteopath for a back complaint which he is convinced originated from my fall, and which without accident insurance is becoming quite costly.

Am looking for a new place to live as my current flat is no longer ideal, and Dave's non-stop replay of 'Gypsy Woman' is not making me feel any happier. 'She's homeless' all right. For that matter, I wish we could get some new songs into these continuous show reels before and during the show intermission. I can already tell how many minutes to count down and what stage of my make-up I should be at just by whether Doris is yelping 'Sugar in the Morning' or the assorted cast of *Annie* is welcoming punters with the nauseous refrain of 'We hope you're gonna like it here'. At least someone seems interested, because most of us just want to get the show over with and get out of the club's lame week-night atmosphere.

Sunday, 8th September

Our second backstage departure. Boo hoo.

Daisy has been offered a touring job and, having finished dressing

41

The Fabulous Singlettes at the Duke of York has decided to chuck in the loyalty-inspiring £125 weekly club pay in favour of some real moolah. A real shame.

We now have, wait for it, another *woman*. We are slowly inundating the place. After all, the club only added a woman to the show about two years ago and that was seen as a major concession. Now we have two performing and another dressing, although we were assured that this is only because she was Daisy's chosen successor. The Welsh Witch is planning to return in two months' time, so this temporary arrangement doesn't bother the office too much either way. I'm curious as to how this all-time first will affect the guys, having myself gone through the adjustment of a gay man dressing me.

When dresser Michael first started whipping frocks on and off my body, I must confess to having felt somewhat unnerved. It's odd, but there's an inexplicable comfort in a straight man seeing you naked or helping you change, in that they're at least likely to find your physique attractive; failing that, and excluding deformations, they won't be repulsed. Paradoxically, I felt less embarrassed, whereas with a gay man there's always the awareness that they don't find the female body all that appealing or beautiful. If they do, it's usually in an aesthetic 'art form' way as opposed to breathing, pulsing imperfections. Initially I almost felt like I was inflicting mental torture on this poor guy, who was job-bound to touch my body every two minutes. These days I don't give a damn, but I do wonder whether the guys will be put off by a straight woman's hands all over their naked parts. Not that there's a guaranteed attraction, but at least in my case I knew that there was absolutely nothing sexual in it. It quickly became more like being dressed by a particularly efficient nanny with an alcohol problem.

Claire, our newest addition, is also a dresser at *Joseph and his Amazing Technicolour Dreamcoat*. Lots of interesting stories, especially about Jason Donovan who, according to her, is getting a lot of unfair flack from the press. For this reason he is not planning on visiting the club except perhaps with major secrecy and in disguise. I'm sure we could dig up a Groucho nose and glasses set for him somewhere.

She seems a nice enough person, if slightly emotionally warped from her recent divorce. Should blend right in, and at least she has wonderfully warm fingers.

Sunday, 15th September

Am preparing to move out of Drury Lane to my own pad near Victoria. Expensive, but worth it considering that the few hours I have between temping and work are ones in which I want to unwind without a million people traipsing about.

Bad timing on one hand. This week could not have been more hectic if I had planned it. Looking back upon my recent comment about women taking over the club, I feel like some latter-day Oracle.

Carla is definitely in the office's bad books, having had her boyfriend call in on Thursday to announce that she was in dying throes after chomping a bad prawn spring roll at the Chinese near work. No, she most certainly was not up to moving from the flat for any purpose short of meeting the big Maître'd in the sky, which at this stage was almost a foregone conclusion. Schnitzel tried to call back, with no answer which, with his suspicious mind, resulted in a two-day BT telethon to Carla's flat. We were no more trusting, even going to the lengths of checking out the Chinese and discovering that they didn't even sell said delicacy.

We probably would not have gone to this extreme if Carla hadn't mentioned a potential free trip to Paris a few weeks ago, coincidentally on the same days as her fateful encounter with the Spring Roll of Doom.

So, show goes into backup mode again. Except this time with a beautiful addition. Misha pirouettes across the stage on Thursday night and manages to twist his ankle. Being the hardened pro that he is, he decided to continue the show but by the end of the night his foot was so swollen that he could barely fit it into his stiletto. Considering that he would already be in enough trouble with *Aspects* for missing shows due to JoJo's, he had to call it quits for the rest of the week. He has a deal, I understand, with the Really Useful Company, that he can only do the club so long as it doesn't affect his other show's work.

PR, with an uncharacteristic generosity and concern, offers to send Misha his own GP to check it out. It transpires that this was so he'd be able to shimmy in for Friday night's performance. Real concern about our futures is definitely not a hallmark of this organisation.

Needless to say, Misha was not going to appear on that stage without a wheelchair. And this is where things get really funny.

Now we have a drag show with no men. OK, we have the

barbettes, but in terms of star power it is all being generated by Becka and myself. If I thought it was ridiculous missing one person, two was even more hysterical.

I must confess I felt like we were robbing our rather packed straight weekend audience, to the extent that Becka and I dragged up early both nights to go out and 'do the floor', all the while calling each other John and Frank. Claire was loving every minute of it, coming into her own during a crisis. I think she enjoyed it infinitely more than the 'boring' normal nights.

Now George hates Carla even more than usual. That boy is going to have hell to pay.

Sunday, 22nd September

George welcomed the ailing Carla back on Monday with a bag of prawn spring rolls and she has not been let off the hook by anybody. We have teased, joked, and embarrassed her on stage, and I'll say one thing for her: she is the most consistent liar I have ever met. I almost had to admire her for not cracking.

Had a bit of a celebrity influx this week, starting with Stefanie Powers on Wednesday and followed by Major Ronald Ferguson. Got to drape myself around him and sing 'Barbette Express', all the while thinking what a field day the press would have if they could get a shot of this, although this is not the first member of the Ferguson clan to frequent JoJo's.

Fergie herself was apparently quite enamoured not only with her mother-in-law but queens in general it seems and, after seeing the old cast at the Hippodrome, promptly got mobbed trying to catch the show in Soho. Elaborate adventures ensued trying to get her in. I don't know why she didn't just dress up as a policeman again. God knows we get enough of them in. Be it as a party or even the mandatory 'raids', which always guarantee that someone will pipe up 'Grab a dyke and dance' in nostalgic recollection of gay club raids when homosexuality was strictly *verboten*.

Reminds me of some other stories of the rich and famous passed on to me by Ruby and cast. For example, the time Liza Minnelli was recording with the Pet Shop Boys and decided to put in an appearance. According to Ruby, George, who can normally be almost nauseating in his fawning adulation of the stars, doesn't even bother sending a drink over and they just get plonked at a table. Jason's ego went into overdrive when she informed him that she's 'been dying to come down', that is to say that she would want to see *him* perform.

Ruby has to go out and send a bottle of champagne over to her table, which she replaces the next day with an angry thud. George's only remark when they left at half-time was 'she said she loved it, but was recording early.' Apparently they would try to come down before she left London. The way I understand it, she left because they made an announcement drawing attention to her. Subtle as a bloody sledgehammer, boys.

Going from one strength to another, there was of course the Eartha Kitt visit, who apparently did not mind the spotlight flashed on her. According to them, she soared in with turban askew and loved the attention, until it was directed in a negative way. When Jay crooned out his 'If there's a right way' and replaced it with 'If there's a wrong note, she'll sing it', there was a *major* sense of humour failure. It was a stupid joke but she demanded more professionalism from that performer in a subsequent letter to the office the next day.

A bit out of character, according to Jason. He had worked with her in his early days in a drag club in Cannes, where amongst big hoopla it was announced that 'Miss Kitt will be choosing your songs, you must all be professional.' She apparently came down the next day, announcing a hellish hangover and asked which songs they enjoyed doing. Once these had been submitted she insisted upon champagne from the management, which of course they raced to supply, and proceeded to dispense this tonic among the cast. Needless to say, they loved her.

One thing I've noticed about a lot of the people who frequent the really late-night clubs around town – Trade, Fidenzi's, FF, even Heaven – is that they are generally quiet by day, wild contrast by night: a case of 'Essentially I'm a very shy person but for God's sake look at me'. Had the joy of going to 17's, a poxy little club on Old Compton Street, the other night – what a dump. One guy was dealing like he had a direct link to Noriega, orgasmic groans came from dinky loos and darkened hallway corners and there was an atmosphere that had long since made a rush for the emergency exits. Stained walls, crusty floors, peeling plaster and dangling red lightbulbs; a real dive, and peopled with characters who had the distorted, fish-eye faces you see through spy-holes fitted at front doors. Made the New York gay bath halls look like paeans to good taste.

Sunday, 29th September

I hate walking home alone at night.

Since my father's generous, if worried, offer of paying my taxis home (totally defeating the purpose and price of close proximity to the club), I have tended towards the lazy safe option of being chauffeured to my doorstep. Yet Friday and Saturday nights see me at a loss for transport. Everybody and his brother are looking for a cab, and still this familial closeness is not to be experienced en route to Drury Lane.

As a single woman, one is continuously exposed to the perils of late-night journeying, which I have mostly combatted by walking with Carla part of the way. What a joke, I'd probably have to defend *her* virtue if anything. As a made-up drag queen I appear appropriately whore-mongerish at night.

Having seen Jodie Foster in *The Accused*, not to mention the million-plus articles, programmes, etc. on the subject of female rape, the 'victims-are-guilty' mentality and prosecution is heavily impressed on most women's minds. Walking down the street in my 'face', I pile on self-abuse for my appearance with the attitude of '3am, you look like a tart, of course the unsolicited attention is to be expected.' Why don't I take it off? Curiously enough, it's one of the last acts of privacy at the end of the night, a chance to take off my 'persona' and go to bed as me.

This is not to say that I mind being seen 'au naturel'; I am forever arriving at the club looking like a washed-out Timotei advertisement gone horribly wrong. It is more the feeling of ritual, the cleansing pre-bedtime that I prefer to do at home; that, and the fact that it is a bloody messy business getting three inches of 4W, glitter and Rimmel off your face. *And* Carla hogs the sink.

Speaking of which, said party was plastered tonight. Always makes me laugh – she is really such a sympathetic, warm, giving person when drunk, not at all the self-righteous git she can be on sober occasions. Becka and I have decided she is definitely schizoid. She was even joking about Brie and weekends to Paris; she *must* be feeling secure.

I am still trying to figure Misha out. He is completely professional, more so in fact than anyone else in the cast, but never seems to let anyone glimpse the inside of the proverbial onion. I know he runs a trannie-dressing and kissogram service, I know he has an eight-year-old daughter with an estranged partner, I even know that we have jointly nicknamed his penis 'Penny'. But I don't really feel that I know *him*.

Then again I've never numbered transvestites amongst my pre-JoJo's friends and acquaintances which, after all, is a dominating part of his character. Actually, what am I saying? If a defining feature of male cross-dressing is secrecy, then who knows how many closet transvestites have cruised in and out of my life? One thing I've been learning from Misha is that you never can tell.

Previously my idea of trannies had been as portrayed in Woody Allen's *All You Ever Wanted to Know About Sex, But Were Afraid to Ask,* specifically the demented, if slightly sad, sketch about the middle-aged man at a dinner party furtively dressing upstairs in his hostess's clothes. A howl superficially, but the last line managed to capture the tragedy quite well: the newly enlightened, humiliated wife informing her relieved husband in bed that she understands, and immediately adding that 'It's OK, we'll never talk about it again' and suggesting therapy. She, like so many sheltered conformists, completely misunderstood.

Misha and Becka are off for a Sunday together, which initially made me jealous. Now these unadmirable emotions have been replaced by relative indifference. After all, I'm permanently matched up with Carla – what more could a girl ask for? *Brother.*

Good crowd last night, including an entire Irish rugby team from Dublin down for their first weekend in London. Talk about an initiation. Injecting 'I'll be your hooker any time' proved to be a bit of foreshadowing in light of my subsequent paranoias walking home later.

Speaking of outside, we were almost saved on the corner of the Piano Bar. Normally the types who loiter outside in the wee hours of the morning tend to fall into one of two categories: the 'Pssst, you wanna watch?' variety or those carrying on animated conversations with beings from another dimension. Yet in this particular instance, a lone missionary had stumbled across what obviously struck him as a meeting of Satan's henchmen and an evangelist fervour emanated from his insightful soul as he assured us sinners that we 'were not happy'. Sweetie, spare us, I could tell you that about 95 per cent of the population that walk through those portals, and this not even reflecting solely upon the welcoming door staff. Had dinner with an old male friend of mine, who took me out to a nearby vegetarian Korean restaurant and proceeded to bombard me about the possibilities of our impending nuptials. What? I would have hardly thought that my current career was indicative of a desire to settle down. I think I still have a lot of growing up to do.

Paid Dutch and felt terribly virtuous and emancipated.

Sunday, 13th October

Despite feeling shattered I must scribble down some sentiments. My current state owes a lot to the celebrations of our hundredth show of *All Aboard*, entitled 'Over the Top' according to Schnitzel's latest memo, demonstrating yet again how involved and on the pulse the office is, not to mention Schnitzel's true opinion of our 'art'.

What a night and what a fab audience. Went clubbing afterwards, which turned out to be a total drag and not in our usual sense of the word. A real letdown from the previous high.

Had a fascinating lift from some guy called Alan, whom we picked up en route at some club or other, and was initially concerned about possible kidnapping, rape, murder as I didn't even know the character. Halfway along, thinking that I really do have the most amazing luck, I started concentrating on the conversation. I can't for the life of me remember what he does now, but it transpires he was an ex-army guy, and had done stripping to make ends meet in a place packed with ex-MPs. Seemed about as unreal as a pimp I met tonight informing me I had 'class, girl'.

Anyway, chatting we discovered that JoJo's and his scene had more in common than I may care to admit. I gaze at people in a spotlight with half-lowered thick lashes, unseeing of the gaping faces, and consequently allow myself to be outrageous. He does the same thing, but for a hell of a lot more money. OK, so we're a smart cabaret but really it's all in the way you look at it.

Everyone in good spirits tonight. Mine to be precise, as I paid for our bathtub load of punch and never got my money back. Jamie is a lush. Oh, and our tabs have been called off which is a mixed blessing. It's a pain to carry money on the floor for courtesy drinks, but I'm fairly sure that whoever was totalling up our bills never passed maths O'level. We drink a lot but at this accounting rate we should have keeled over with cirrhosis at least two months ago.

Sunday, 20th October

The shit has hit the fan.

It's cast change time for the impending new show, set for the 27th November. I received a 'phone call from Schnitzel asking if

I would be interested – all I had to do was look at my mounting bills and the decision became quite a simple one. Misha and Carla had apparently also been requested, but our agreement hinged upon the fact that we would not breathe a word until the office's memo terminating the present show arrived yesterday. I couldn't help but feel that Schnitzel was enjoying the power play, like an elderly kitten toying with a ball of wool.

The new show, *Back to Havana*, is being orchestrated by someone called Pablo. He's been down a few times and has taken great offence to Becka and the boys, seeing one as too masculine and terrifying and the others as not enough.

Needless to say, all hell broke loose when the announcement arrived last night before the show. Great way to psych-up your cast. At this stage, Becka and Jamie were not talking to us and were alternating the grand mope approach with intermittent hurricanesque explosions. By the end of the night, and several tantrums later, our dressing-room was resembling a badly bombed make-up counter and everyone in the club was aware of the volatile scene being played out behind the stage door. Those of us who thought we had already heard our two formidable colleagues at full volume quickly discovered that they still had a few decibels in reserve and made a run for it.

Unpleasant.

Sunday, 3rd November

Things are calming down, although I would hesitate to assume that we have been forgiven. Let's just say that an uneasy truce has been met.

I hate being locked up together with these razor blade vibes being flung around the place. I almost find myself losing sympathy and wishing that they could take this development more gracefully, if not professionally. Then again, my contract hasn't just been terminated.

Two cast members who are overjoyed at the end of their performing era are Pepper and Tevita. They have become increasingly girly looking, which is in direct contrast with Pablo's aim to make the barbettes more drag and less feminine. I gather that he was one of the original directors at the club and favours a much harder, glitzier show over the musical-style fashion we have slipped into.

He and Ruby did not see eye to eye in terms of style and format, and it is his intention to recreate a glamorous Parisian nightclub with a fast and furious pace. Sounds different at least.

Therefore our two lovely transsexuals are now relegated to cock-tail waitressing the floor all night instead, which seems to suit them down to the ground. I think they have hit the stage where they want to be taken seriously as future women and no longer ogled as part of a freak show. They've even started talking about getting day-time jobs, which would be a real leap of faith.

Last night I had them showing me a book about 'le chop', and what they do to the candidates before, during and after. Incredible. I was aware of taking hormones, seeing the psychiatrists and going for speech therapy, but seeing actual pictures was enough to make even me cross my legs. I can imagine why guys wince at the thought.

They asked me to draw what a 'natural' woman's genitals look like and I have to admit I was really stuck. I mean it's not like you take a mirror and look at it every day. Of course I know basically, but would hardly class myself as a proper anatomist. I made an attempt and promised to do a self-portrait next time I took a bath.

Interview with Marcie & Misha
On Transsexuals and Hermaphrodites

Got talking to Marcie, who will continue doing the show as a barbette, and found out that she had contemplated transsexuality when she first started. As she explained, 'That was influenced by what was going on around me, especially Tevita and Pepper, and I thought well this is actually a channel for me to go in. I can see how I would go in that, if I copy them.'

How long did you take the hormones?

Two or three months. Until I scared myself.

Curious now as to the actual physical differences she felt, I pressed her further.

A lot of it I think was psychosomatic anyway. I mean the point of it physically was that my tits grew really quickly; within two weeks it was like buds. Not out to here, but really quick. And I was like really freaked out. And amazing, because it was just there. And I thought, this can't be possible, I'm just thinking it's there, but one day I was in the dressing room and Pepper came in, and she just looked at me, and she went oh yeah?

And I said what, and she was looking at my tits and there were tits there, although it was hardly anything. But my nipples came out – you know you can always feel a little lump, most boys have them and I always had large nipples, but these seemed to be right out, sort of swollen. And I looked like a little prepubescent girl.

Anything else?

The hair. If I creamed myself, the hair didn't come back like it would've done the month before. I do it now, I can shave my chest, and two days later I'm going to be very stubbly.

But then I could go two weeks, after two or three weeks of taking tablets. Hair stopped falling out. You know how you lose loads of hair? Around that time I was losing loads, and then it just suddenly stopped; when I actually stopped the hormones, it all came out again. That's one of the reasons I shaved it off.

That actually sounds glorious, and that scared you?

No the thing was emotional, but I think it could have been psychosomatic. All these hormones. It imbalances you, you know like when you were thirteen. Screwed up, crying all the time, really depressed. Whether that is actually a fact, I don't know, but that's what happened.

Having Caroline Cossey, a.k.a Tula of James Bond fame, come down to the club regularly is extremely encouraging for the 'Changes', but I could see how she would help confuse someone in-between like Marcie all the more. Tula has got to be one of the most beautiful women I have ever seen, to the extent that one cannot look at her and even imagine her ever having been male. Her personal tragedy incorporates a failed 'marriage', to an Arab who then whisked her off on a wildly romantic honeymoon. His mama was waiting at the end of the tarmac upon their return, opened the limo door for her son who promptly got in, never to be seen again and leaving Caroline standing alone on the runway.

Apparently she had discovered Caroline's past during the trip and although, according to Jay, her son already knew, Mama held the purse-strings and he heartlessly and unceremoniously dumped his new 'spouse'. It's all hearsay for me. Since the marriage was never legally recognised, I'd imagine Caroline had to pinch herself to establish whether any of it had really happened. Therein lies the paradox of transsexuality – once a man, always a man on paper. Should she commit a crime, she'd be chucked into a male prison even though she sexually qualifies and operates as a woman. The consequences of such a scenario are not a pretty thought.

Anyway, then Caroline's coming around being this gorgeous like woman, such a nice person, really sincere. She was ready to talk, I spoke to her a few times, and she said you know you are the classic transsexual, back from childhood, how you were brought up, your feelings . . . So I'm a classic, I should see someone.

At the time it was right, but I started going out with Brian, we were friends all the time, and I was really confused. Then I started thinking, my voice, it's a man's voice; I've got a feminine body, but it's very hairy. All these different things, and I started looking at the pros and the cons as to what I would do and I thought, for the time being, just get rid of the hormones to sort myself out and become a boy and then see how I feel about that.

So that's when I moved out, shaved my head, and changed. That's when I had my girly glam bob, and changed it all round – shaved my head bald, and started wearing loads of glitter, big make-up, painting spider-webs on my head. Went back to my Boy George look, because then it becomes androgynous, it doesn't become 'I want to be girly'.

I marvel at Marcie's adventurous spirit, especially as she doesn't strike any of us as future transsexual material. She is an effeminate man, but not necessarily a candidate for womanhood. Placed in her shoes I think I would have been absolutely terrified watching and feeling such changes occurring in my body, particularly a body that had never experienced anything of this nature before. For some reason visions of The Fly *keep springing to mind.*

One can argue that women on the Pill go through the same physical and emotional transformations, but we've usually had several years to get adjusted to cramps, swollen breasts and mood swings. It is, in fact, expected both of and by us. As a man, you must feel totally isolated; fellow transsexuals aside, no one can really imagine what you're going through.

I suppose that is why future transsexuals are put through such psychological grilling by appointed psychiatrists: to determine whether they can handle the changes and challenges. There must be so many mixed motivations, not least of all escapism, in what makes someone decide to drastically alter their entire identity. Furthermore, will they be able to handle the eventual 'neither fish nor fowl' status? Medically speaking, they are going to spend the rest of their lives popping pills. They develop breasts, have a constructed vagina and maybe, after enough electrolysis, won't even have to worry about facial and chest stubble. Yet that uncontrollable last chromosome remains a Y.

I sympathise with this testing predicament and applaud the guts of a man deciding to alter his entire history and future irrevocably, even at the risk of ostracisation by his nearest and dearest. Oddly enough, I can't quite grasp female transsexuality, and find it not only incomprehensible but quite off-putting. I suppose I am as narrow-minded in my own way as other men questioning why one of their own kind would possibly want to reject the ultra-symbolic,

53

virile penis.

Yet with the male transsexuals I cannot deny that, as a woman, I find it flattering. To have these individuals, still men, admiring your sex to this covetous degree is in screaming contrast with the distaste expressed by so many gay men for the female body. Admittedly there are enough married men who have the change, but my experience of this type is non-existent and totally confused. Often they remain with their wives, so do they become lesbians? Or were they gay men to begin with, and find themselves a 'husband'?

I find it much easier to grasp the idea of our gay transsexuals remaining true to their sexual taste but simply changing bodies, although what this says about their lovers is another story. There is the much discussed danger of attracting a trannie-fucker, who will dump the 'change' immediately after the operation; best hope really is to have someone fall in love with you, the person, as versus any particular genderised version of yourself. The best insight I have heard to date came from Tevita, who said that she had always seen herself as a woman and been sexually attracted to men accordingly. The only difference happened to be the appendage between her legs.

I find it a curious, but pleasant realisation that transsexuals should make me so aware and proud of my body. It's strange to think that a tiny stroke of luck in chromosome pairing should determine one's entire outlook and experience of life.

At this point Misha had walked in and started listening quietly, taking off his make-up. I have great trust in Misha's opinion on these matters, not least of all because he is locked in with Tevita and Pepper on a nightly basis and has occasionally found in their hormonal squabbles his own personal Carla equivalent. He started off by relating to Marcie's 'to be girly, or not to be girly' conflict, although not quite on a transsexual level.

I've gone through stages on that one, because when I was first here I purposely used to go out looking very 'geezer', or as geezer as I could do; to shock, in a way. And then as I was getting more girly looking, I rather enjoyed that. I love it if somebody thinks I'm a girly. I absolutely adore it. I think it makes you a hell of a big person to be able to accept it, Bea, as you do, and call yourself a drag queen which I think is wonderful. Because that then puts you in the category of being able to be even more female in many ways.

Because you're very aware of your femininity, and it's not a threat to your femininity, you know what you are. And that's as it should be. For me it's a bit more tricky, because I kind of know what I am but I think the rest of society doesn't want me to be it. I think maybe you choose whether to fight society, in your own little way, or you choose to go along with it. And live your life as best you can.

I'm really talking about transsexuality here. My view is that if you inhabit the body of a six-foot six truck, and you wish to be a woman, you will never be a woman. You will never be perceived by society to be a woman, even though in your mind you may be. And my heart goes out to somebody like that because it's the hardest thing in the world. Somebody who's small and petite and can make the change over to being a girly very easily . . . they've got a lot going for them.

Which brought us on to the topic of Pepper and Tevita, both of whom I think are enormously convincing. Misha agreed with their choice wholeheartedly.

I think it was very appropriate. Transsexuality goes down a pathway. If you start off as a guy, and you're saying you're a transsexual, people will look at you and say, well that's a guy. So you know they're going to be negative . . . this is not a good thing to do; don't do this, don't do that. And then, a year or so later, you have acquired a lot more female habits, traits, looks. People are now seeing it for themselves.

And in the case of Pepper and Tevita, with being very feminine in many ways anyway, it just seemed the most natural thing in the world. That people would say 'yes, this is the right thing'. And, in fact, in many ways, they could be pressurised into changing sex, which they shouldn't be.

The hardest thing is to make the decision yourself, because no matter who you talk to, they're coming from an angle. They're coming from a biased point of view. If it's the person you love, maybe they want to keep you as you are. If it's a transsexual who has a boyfriend, he may want her to have the change so he can have her as a woman, so *he's* coming from a biased point of view. Everyone comes from a biased point of view and, at the end of the day, it's only *you* who can answer to what you want.

To which I suggested that the difficulty lay in the fact that it was such a point of no return.

That makes it a lot more tricky. I recently went to a discussion where they were talking about the fact that this transsexual had an operation to remove a testicle, which was seen as a sort of halfway-house before the full op. I completely disagreed with that.

You can't put your testicles back once you've taken them away. So whether you're going to go through with the whole change or not . . . you know, you're stuck for the rest of your life without nuts. And that, to me, seems very stupid. It is a no return situation. I don't think that people talk a lot about the operation, and I don't think that that's the important part of it. It's about . . . being happy with your life.

And, presumably, being able to adjust?

Yes. I think it's very difficult for transsexuals to say after the operation, 'this was wrong, I should have stayed as I was.' Because that would be a complete admission to being in every way wrong. And there's no point to living.

So you very seldom – I've talked to a few and they've sort of admitted – hear that at the end of the day the grass is always greener. And that no it's not absolutely wonderful but it's better than it was.

At this stage we swung full-circle and started discussing hermaphrodites. I recalled Ferdie, a sweet pretty little Spanish hermaphrodite working upstairs in the Piano Bar. Operating as a boy, but looking like a girl, and I remember I was totally and utterly confused when I first met him. Very soft voice and skin, which in fact he usually complimented me on while gently stroking my cheek, but something a bit disturbing or rather disorientating about the feel of him.

Small wonder, really. Housing two sexes simultaneously in your body must be both intensely liberating and totally oppressive. Physical schizophrenia. I know that I have a masculine as well as a feminine side, but not to the extent that I am of undetermined gender or consequent identity.

It's exhausting: I never realised until I came here to what extent sexual pre-determination and inclination can screw up your life. Let me rephrase that: I never understood how many unnecessary hurdles are presented that we of the more common denominator never have to confront, much less deal with.

I think hermaphrodites must have a harder time of it than anybody. In order to stand up for their fairly unique needs, they first have to figure out what they are and where they're coming from. I mentioned this and asked them to expound upon this complete defiance of biological sexual determination.

MISHA: Hermaphrodites are people who are born both male and female. So they could have a womb and they could have a penis; often they may have a penis and not properly formed testicles. But they may have the whole bit: the men's genitals and the women's as well. Normally at birth, doctors 'sex' children if there's a problem and they'll leave the sex either male or female, whichever is more appropriate at the time. It's only in Third World countries that they tend to look upon it as a bit of a bonus and don't actually sex the child.

I don't always know why. Sometimes, well very few, but some of them go through the net, if you can put it like that. And in a funny sort of way, for a Third World country, somebody who's going to be in the pig slaughter-house for the rest of their life, if they're born as an hermaphrodite, they've got the chance of earning a lot of money. So I suppose it could bring riches. That might be it.

MARCIE: With Ferdie it has caused a lot of problems. She was eighteen when she came here, and at that point, Ferdie was feeling completely a woman. Completely. But with a boy's body. She went to see Russell Reed (the famed advisor and psychiatrist for transsexual cases) and she went to see everyone she could, and they said basically 'yes, go ahead and do it'. But the reason they couldn't do the operation was the pure fact that as she was sexed as a boy at birth, and then having done whatever they did to her vagina and having taken the womb out, her penis was actually too small to make a vagina.

Because most hermaphrodites aren't formed properly as a guy, the penis is too small to invert. So she could never have a full-sized vagina and if they had done it, it would probably do her a hell of a lot of damage if she tried to have sex. So they wouldn't do the operation and Ferdie had no choice but to live as a guy. As a child she was given male hormones so she could be a boy.

She still doesn't shave, she looks like a girl; I mean she can just put a bit of lipstick on, eye make-up, sit on the bus and no one would know any different. That's not just coincidence, that is the fact; the hormones are there as a woman. And so, she was. Even her voice is more or less the same; she doesn't have an Adam's Apple as such.

MISHA: There is an operation, and there must have been a reason why they didn't suggest it for Ferdie, because you can have your Sigmoid colon used. If somebody's having a sex change and say their penis is particularly small, having sex is always going to be a problem for them. So there is part of your Sigmoid colon that they can use, and this is more of a life-saving operation that they use if somebody has a prolapse.

So surgeons often don't want to do it, because if she's healthy before the operation, it's putting her life at risk. That can be a reason for not operating. But there may have been other reasons, I don't know.

So how does one determine the 'correct' sex?

MISHA: It's a tricky one, because there was another case recently where somebody was sexed as a male. He's got male on his birth certificate and had loads of problems until he was twenty-five. He had a relatively minor operation to become a woman, has got married and . . . had a baby. Which happens completely to contravene everything in English law because he's male on his birth certificate, you can't change that. You cannot marry because you're male, and as you're a man you can't have a child so . . . that's impossible. But this person has done it, and it just makes an ass of the law. But again, in this case he, or *she* it should have been, was wrongly sexed at birth. And it ruined a lot of her life, and probably is going to ruin most of Ferdie's life I would imagine . . . unless she sorts it out.

MARCIE: The thing is she's treated as a gay man and it's not the case really. Even to get a boyfriend, I've never known Ferdie to have a boyfriend. For the pure fact that a gay man wants a man. And Ferdie will never ever be that. It's like a little boy basically. They're very sad. If it wasn't for the pure fact that her parents wanted a boy . . . you know?

MISHA: And she doesn't have a choice, she was born that way. And society says she's a pervert, she's this, that and the other. But she's not a pervert. She didn't have any choice.

The interesting part on hermaphrodites is the theory in many ways on men being gay, men being transsexual, or transvestite. I think transvestite is slightly different, I think it's far more superficial than transsexualism. It's not so much – *I* don't think – a medical condition.

But the current theory, and this is just a theory, is that it comes from the women; that when the foetus is in the womb and receiving all the hormones it needs, if the woman is under a lot of stress at a particular time and a particular day, the hormones that the foetus should be receiving don't get through. And therefore there's an imbalance. Foetuses prior to birth can go either way. They can still be male or female. It's a fine balance, and nature isn't perfect; nature goes wrong.

That's probably saying it in the negative, because that's almost like saying that somebody is wrong. It's just saying that things can and do go wrong. A clearer case is a gay man. A gay man doesn't wake up one morning and say oh! I think I'll be gay. He just is. He doesn't know *why* – he just is. This is the most natural thing in the world to him. And the people who really want to try and understand that should look to the imbalances of a woman when she gives birth; it can't always be correct. That's a theory but it's the theory that I most like because it seems quite together to me.

It all seemed so terribly unfair. All this pain, this confusion, and to be treated like a freak on top of that. I realise now that what struck me as so unusual about Ferdie was not merely the obvious physical contradiction; it was something much deeper and more far-reaching than that, a weird blend of frailty and incredible toughness.

I recall her despondently telling me horror tales about some dodgy place she'd been living, with some less than palatable characters, I might add. Somehow her arm had been busted and she was looking for somewhere new to live, which ended up being New Cross. Not a terrible area, but hardly the place for a girlish creature to be skipping through at 4am. I expressed concern and Ferdie suddenly squared 'his' shoulders and announced 'I can handle it', in tough, butch mode. I still can't figure out if that was the boy in her speaking, or the woman.

By this point my head was whirling with all my new-found wisdom and I decided to go home, call my mother and thank her for saving me a lot of soul-searching confusion by eating the 'right' nutrients.

Sunday, 10th November

Re-reading my last entry, I've decided to start interviewing Misha properly at some stage. He is a never-ending fountain of information and insight, of the sort denied to me as 'merely' a female drag queen. OK, so I cross-dress as well, but somehow that seems more accepted by society. I've never felt oppressed or ashamed for wearing trousers.

This is, of course, assuming I ever get the time. Although we are seeing each other non-stop, this is thanks to our new rehearsals, which are due to continue for three weeks. Alternating this with temping in the mornings, racing to the club for afternoons and then doing the show every night is proving to be more than a little exhausting.

We started on Monday, with Signor Pablo as a new tyrant. And total misogynist, which is a joy. So we are getting the full Latin temperament and machismo in daily doses from a man about as pleasant as a full body wax. Oh rapture divine.

I can't quite suss him out. He has the most adorable boyfriend in the world who worships him, yet to my uneducated way of thinking has all the charm and charisma of a pet rock. Perhaps my insight is tainted by the fact that this opinion is probably mutual – I generally like people unless I feel disliked in return. Having said that, he has given me the majority of numbers and I get the closing curtain call. Carla, who if she crawled any further up his behind would soon emerge from his mouth, was bitching about the fact that he is building the entire show around a woman. Ha.

New cast members. Becka is being replaced by Teddi, a very handsome black guy who dances like a dervish and tops the scales on stage presence. Seems terribly nice and competent, if he doesn't drop dead from malnutrition first. He's totally broke which, with the £100 a week that he is being advanced – not paid, mind you – for rehearsals, looks unlikely to change in the near future. I was walking with him the other day, headed towards Marks & Spencer, and he revealed to me that he couldn't afford to buy food. This is crazy, I thought, and dragged him in and filled up a basket with all kinds of staples. I wouldn't have raced out to buy him luxuries, but something like this strikes me as desperate in today's times.

It's one thing to pass starving homeless in the street, but to be working with one is quite another. Carla bitched me out the next day, insisting that he was probably using the money for drugs and who knows what, but at least Teddi didn't look about to faint all the time, especially with his punishing 'Medusa' dance routine. All we have to do is follow a bit of foot, ball, step change or whatever the hell they call it, but his is serious dancing.

Which is more than can be said for our three new boys. Our token blond, Marcelle, was brought in to do a photo shoot with Misha, Carla and myself for the new poster, and is a complete bimbo. I posed à la Monroe for this shot, and Marcelle managed to make me look like a brain surgeon; vapid is not the word. As George put it, you could look into this guy's eyes and all you would see is a lone seagull flapping in the breeze.

Then there's Craig. Suffice it to say, nobody is going to be confusing him with Fred Astaire in the near future, maybe Mr Ed at a push. An ex-army boy, who seems very sweet, in fact scared of his own shadow and even more of the shadows of all the queens lurking behind him. I cannot for the life of me figure out what he is doing here. He has already expressed his undying love for Jane Seymour, the perfect woman. Somehow I cannot picture old Janey in this milieu, but I didn't have the heart to tell our soft-spoken new addition.

Finally there's Alexander. Dark, rather broody, I really can't draw any conclusions as I haven't spoken to him properly except to ascertain that he is not gay. They all say that. Asked why he had decided to join our little party he murmured something about a film project and paying off expenses. Could it be that we actually have someone with interests outside drag?

Night-times are punctuated with discomfort if and when we slip up and mention anything to do with rehearsals. If Pablo actually delivers tapes backstage it becomes a real torture; you could hurdle those hackles. Hope these rehearsals finish soon.

Sunday, 17th November

Not much to report. We had the show video-taped earlier this week, which consisted of Marcia's boyfriend spreading out the tripod and monopolising the Royal Box, to the extent that anybody wanting to get to or from the banquet would have to pole-vault over him. Being a typically lame Tuesday, this fortunately was not put to the test.

I gather we are merely following an age-old tradition of recording our drunken débâcles for posterity, but the cast performed as though we were up for a Spielberg screen test. Arguably, *Close Encounters of the Third Kind* works if you split mankind into male, female and in-between. We've all chipped in financially, so hopefully one day we'll actually be able to see ourselves in full technicolour glory.

Rehearsals are dragging on and we are discovering that not only can Craig not dance but appears to have swallowed lead weights that have deposited themselves somewhere in the vicinity of his feet. To call them both left would be kind.

At least he has a glimmer of brain activity, which is more than can be said of Marcelle. In the course of two weeks I have shifted from mild surprise and amusement to total irritation at this boy's complete denseness. The lights are on but not only is no one home, they appear to have moved out permanently.

Alexander, by contrast, is turning out to be a pleasant distraction. Went out for a drink together and discovered a highly intelligent, charming man who made me laugh uproariously. This was not hindered by the fact that we got completely sozzled at a two-for-one happy hour in The Boardwalk, but I feel like I've found something of a kindred spirit.

Ditto for our two new barbettes, who are turning out to be quite a surprise as well. Mitzi, a Teutonic goddess, has the frank outspokenness that I've come to expect and enjoy from our little circle and Sugar, equally stunning, oozes her namesake out of every pore. Quite a switch from the hormonal switchblading of our previous show's rehearsals.

About the only aspect that has remained intact from *All Aboard* is this curious lack of logical flow with regard to our show theme. Interestingly enough, this is the identical show that Pablo put on at JoJo's a few years back, and I attribute this repeat to sheer laziness. Makes me feel like we're really breaking new ground.

We start off with a stupendous opening of 'One of the Girls (Who's One of the Boys)' from *Woman of the Year*, an appropriate choice and set in New York City. The four barbettes set the raunchy tone, so favoured by our new director, by sliding up and down poles drilled into the stage and wearing less than you require to dress your average Barbie doll. They're followed by the three boys leaping on in a Village People ensemble, consisting of one football player, a cowboy and a construction worker. I defy anyone to scour the streets of Manhattan and come up with any of these professions being performed in a G-string.

Next, Teddi appears as a Josephine Baker-style showgirl, while

I get to be, revolutionary concept here, a man. Marlene Dietrich, eat your heart out. Well for half the number, at least. Then I rip off my gangster gear, in the form of velcroed d.j. trousers, to reveal stockings, suspenders and red basque. I've managed to insist upon hanging onto my jacket, although even my trilby goes.

I dislike the feeling of disinterest in the show that I'm getting from Pablo, even though I can happily live with his personal indifference. Professionally speaking, I have developed a pride for this club and my performance and would appreciate something more special than some half-assed imitation production. Admittedly the previous cast mimed rather than sang in his original show, and Pablo is a very competent director, but compared with Ruby's past commitment beyond the call of duty, Pablo's attitude seems a bit mercenary.

He directed Ruby in a past JoJo's show, and they apparently clashed in style and personality, which is perhaps why her approach was so diametrically opposed. We were her entire focus, whereas Pablo sees this as a second job.

Carla sashays on next as the glam movie queen, only to be upstaged by Misha's explosion onto the scene as the Statue of Liberty. I swear, if the real one had looked anything like this, excessive immigration at Ellis Island would never have been an issue.

We zoom to the beach to see Teddi emerge from a black oyster in his amazing Medusa routine, replete with snake headpiece and loads of attitude. Then Carla's 'Heatwave', and on to Cuba. Nothing strange about that considering the show title, but from there we whip through Casablanca, San Fransisco, the Clondike, the Amazon, Japanese and Italian divas, Betty Boop and a veritable smorgasbord of adventures. Keep it slick is the motto here, which at 1am becomes fairly crucial if you don't want your audience to pass out into inebriated slumber.

The costumes are marvellous and I am especially happy, despite the constant rebuffed attempts to remove 'significant items' from my person, such as my sequinned leotard bottom under-bustle of a beautiful, full-length Lillie Langtry dress. I soon discovered that its black twin is used in the Revue Bar show, 'derrière en flagrant' as it were. Hands down winners in this show, however, have got to be the wigs and headpieces: Rita Hayworth, Marilyn Monroe and Elvira on the quieter side, with three-foot diva beehives and boa-sprouting turbans on the more exotic. There are also ridiculous conical finale ones, for an effect that we have rechristened 'The Revenge of the

Killer Pencil-Heads'. This show could actually turn out to be quite a howl, if the minute-long proposed strobe lights during the finale don't inflict permanent brain damage first.

II

Back To Havana

Lordy, lordy, how do I even begin to cover the mayhem of our last week and new opening, let alone my personal developments? Well, ever onwards into the fray we go.

I feel like I've just survived an H-bomb. Preparations for the new show reached a frenzied pitch by the weekend, which coincided with our last night of *All Aboard*. Absolutely crazy, everyone swapping numbers with each other in the time-honoured last night tradition. I vaguely recall going out with a wig worn as a beard for Jamie's '16 Tons' number, while he and José dragged up to cover Misha and Carla in 'Speedy Gonzales'. In fact the schmucks managed to lose three pairs of my earrings in the process. One nice thing is I never have to sing 'Beat out that rhythm on a drum' in that absurd fluorescent leotard with the jump-rope headdress again, but afterwards the happy evening spiralled ever downwards.

Carla managed to get into a *huge* fight first with Robbie, our doorman, and consequently George. Ever seen two queens going at it, full hammers and tongs with no holds barred? It is not a pretty sight. There was emotional blood splattered all over the shop, and it has to be said in George's defence that it was in fact Carla's fault. And quite a surprise too – the first time that the bottle of booze has turned her into Godzilla rather than Little Bo Peep. She asked for it, and you don't mess around with George. Not if you want an ego intact afterwards.

He screamed that she was never coming back, to which she retorted that only Pablo had the right to decide that, so being the one man UN that he is, Mr Sensitive had to go to the office and straighten the whole thing out. As much as I felt fed up with her, we really did not need to lose Carla two days before our opening.

She came back for the Monday tech rehearsals, which were only marked with an icy visit by George. He stood at the back, arms folded and glaring at us all. Hey, wait a minute, what did we do? As far as he was concerned, we were all in it together. Carla of course managed to convince her mentor and defender that she was as pure as the driven snow. Slush, if you ask me. Nevertheless, Pablo continued to glove handle her and scream at the rest of us, especially me for supplying guacamole to the entire cast while wearing our new costumes. Actually, I think all the commotion was somewhat exaggerated considering that we were draped in lemon and lime satin sarongs for our Julio Iglesias backed 'Begin the Beguine' number; the dip would have blended in beautifully.

On a personal note, life has taken an incredible, if awkward turn. I slept with Alexander the night after our closing. I feel no remorse, only concern as I am not desperate for the entire club to be aware of this development. For starters, I am adamantly opposed to the idea of getting involved with a colleague, not least of all in these warped surroundings. I am convinced that he is 100 per cent straight, but everybody at the club is of the opinion that all men are gay until proven innocent. Or until coming out of the closet.

They almost had me convinced. I couldn't stop looking at all men as future homosexuals, no matter how macho and hetero they appeared. Alexander, thank God, has broken me out of that way of thinking. Now I only have to worry about hiding it, which considering that they were all certain that we've been going at it since the beginning is not going to be easy. Since when did I have to start hiding a straight relationship from gay men? This would be ludicrous if it wasn't so much a part of my reality.

Our opening night was an unqualified hit, despite the by now expected 'Darling I loved the old show so much, this is so different' spiels. You can never keep them happy until they get used to something, I guess. Then it changes, and you get the whole shebang all over again.

On this occasion it feels strange, but appropriate, to reflect upon how my attitude towards drag has been formed and altered since I first started working here. I recall my total sense of inadequacy in the field of camp as versus my relative confidence as musical/cabaret performer. In retrospect, I can't imagine why I was so petrified. Drag seems totally second nature now; lower the eyelashes and self-consciousness, then take control. Whereas at first I had viewed drag as a loss of control and self-exposure, I now recognise it as easy manipulation. Give the audience what they want, to be shocked, titillated and entertained, but all the while make sure you call the shots. We may be sex objects for them but ultimately the performer determines how far it's going to go – be it in raunch or coyness, aggressiveness or seduction – not the audience.

If anything, doing drag is in many ways easier than a regular musical revue in that the audience comes in *wanting* to be entertained, yearning for a bit of outrage. OK, you have to confront a lot of prejudice along the lines of 'Prove it, make me believe you', but this usually melts away into a willing suspension of disbelief. The bulk of people visiting us are not the most discerning types; they're straight and work in offices. In a word, they want excitement. About the only variety is what professional level they're on in terms of income and position, a direct contrast with the more critical and diverse gay crowds that we've been losing in direct proportion to our expanding heterosexual popularity.

I've been trying to figure out what contributed to this state of affairs, why the gay audiences started tapering off. Everybody here ascribes it to the club's increased publicity and corresponding influx of straight crowds, eager to sample 'the notorious Madame JoJo's'. Something to tell your mates about at work on Monday morning. While I can well understand that the ultra-modish gay clubbers might not favour rubbing elbows with 'boring' heterosexuals on their night out, I think a closer examination of the clubbing mentality provides a vital clue.

Gay 'recreation' involves a fickle club scene: vogue today, passé tomorrow. Hence the number of one-night gay venues around town. Even if JoJo's has a monopoly on drag, we certainly don't have enough of a changing atmosphere and our shows run for an average six months. Nor do we possess any reasonable sound system, up-to-date music or dance floor, especially compared to gay clubs/nighters like The Fridge, FFs, or Heaven.

Add to that the overstated, but nevertheless existent, promiscuity of 'the scene' and it becomes quite simple: odds are pretty minimal that a gay person is going to score sexually in a straight joint. 'Joint' being another factor: management is much stricter at JoJo's about client drug abuse in toilets and on the floor than a cavernous, dark airplane hanger of a club. George has thrown out and barred enough would-be dealers and users to filter out this knowledge. So combine all of this with inflated drinks prices and low shock value, and why are we surprised?

I do find one thing curious about straight audiences. So many of my colleagues are regarded by these people as freaks, and have been for generations. Suddenly a bit of decadence is back in vogue, voyeurism is again acceptable, and we're flavour of the month. It's all either very fickle, or people must be really desperate for escapism these days. A couple of drinks and these uptight city types are letting rip, enjoying themselves and are putty in our hands. Interesting when you consider that both the audience and the performers are seeking refuge and liberation in drag.

To round the evening off, Claire and Carla got into an almighty row, with both sides circling each other like spitting cats. Glorious way to start a new six months. Claire even had it flung at her that she stole Daisy's job, in which Carla was not far off the mark. Daisy had wanted to return and Claire managed to dig her heels in, by hook or by crook. That small grain of truth is what often makes Carla's verbal blows so lethal. Makes you anxiously re-run old confessions for future attack material.

Sunday, 8th December

New show moving along well. Ditto for my blossoming relationship.

Everyone has more or less cottoned on to the development and I now have seven older 'sisters' seriously analysing poor Alexander's 'intentions'. This is absolutely unreal.

At least their protectiveness takes on a semi-positive note in that it appears to be born of genuine concern. By contrast, my Irish friend John has been jealously glaring at my new paramour and hissing that he is certain that it won't last.

When this tact didn't work John moved into below-the-belt territory and began insisting that Alexander was gay. As John tends to visit the club on a regular basis this is turning into a painful non-stop barrage. I've almost stopped going out to see him because I know I'm going to get an emotional battering each time.

He bases his theory on the fact that he himself is gay, for starters, and that in running his very prestigious escort agency he has a lot of exposure to bisexual guys who will swap from one sex client to another. I have always had a great deal of faith in his outlook as he is an ex-Ulster constabulary veteran and has certainly lived. And died many times over, be it warming wounded colleagues' eyeballs in his hand or coming to grips with his subsequent nightmares in therapy.

What disturbs me is his motivation. There is a real lack of genuine concern in his eyes. He's supposed to be my friend, and yet he is hitting me in my most vulnerable, insecure spot. And he knows it.

He had me so paranoid that in the end I confronted Alex one night in Bar Italia. I told him flat out what John had been saying, explained my insecurities (developed over my time at the club), and asked him whether he was bisexual or had ever thought of coming out of the closet.

I am lucky to have found such an understanding guy. And, for that matter, such a sexually secure one. Rather than looking horrified or guilty he started laughing. We talked at great length, went home and he proceeded to make me forget all about it.

I've also been forgetting about Jay, whose evenings and earnings are now composed of three nights a week compering upstairs at the Piano Bar. Seems a step down from the club if we're looking at this as a critical career move, a sentiment his frequent appearances downstairs and backstage suggest he shares. We're moving apart and I feel powerless to change things, not because I can't but, even worse, because I don't want to. Harsh observers might argue that this is because I don't need him as much any more, be it emotionally or professionally, and they'd be right.

In a way, this growing discontentment feels closest to falling out of love. On an obvious level, developments with Alexander are partly to blame. For Jay and me, the honeymoon of our mutual fascination with one another is finished. Initially we clung to each other, and now I'm suffocating. All I see these days is a washed-out, nagging version of my beautiful original and believe me, this does not make me particularly proud of myself. I've never been a fair-weather friend before and am struggling against writing Jay off out of temporary boredom. It's just that our relationship was so overwhelming to begin with and I've realised that the reason we both succumbed to this intense closeness is the very same reason that it's now petering out. Neediness and the illusion of strength.

On a jollier note I have started doing drag gigs on my own, commencing this week with the Saatchi's Christmas Party bash for several hundred people. What a howl. And how nice finally to earn some serious cash. I can see how Ruby and all were able to survive on their meagre salaries – this is the only way to do it.

Misha saw the *All Aboard* video-tape a few weeks ago, and delivered the verdict: 'Hysterical'. Hysterical is what I *became*, watching the video last night in cringing embarrassment. If I'd had any idea that I looked so stupid . . .

One interesting switch in this show: Pablo has insisted on us pre-recording our vocals on most numbers and singing over them. This is fine in that people don't have to worry about battling the audio system, which is blaring enough to pulverise concrete and has ruined most of our voices by now, but a nightmare if someone should be off. I can just imagine trying to cover and blend with one of the guys' numbers; the audiences are going to think I'm the greatest ventriloquist alive.

This is also a real hoot when anyone is drunk, which is an increasing phenomenon. At least in the past you could sing what you liked; now you either have to mime or get caught out slurring some kind of mush over the mike. Unfortunately Carla, Misha, Teddi and I put down the lyrics on tape when we were not altogether comfortable in what we were singing, thanks to lack of practice. As we continue the show, we discover newer and better ways of attacking a number but are stuck echoing the same old schlock on the pre-recorded tape. No time (read money) for up-dating so far.

Fortunately I insisted on 'Put the Blame on Mame' not being done, so there is at least one number that is 'real' in the show. I think we are getting lazy and, worst of all, it is eliminating one of our greatest assets. Most drag shows internationally are mimed; we were the one exception, and now people can't tell that we are actually singing. I guess the one positive thing to emerge from all of this is that it means larger roles for the barbettes. For example Marcie has now been given a glorious diva number to mime to, in a three-foot high, ten pound Japanese headdress, and is hysterically funny being dragged to and fro by this monster wig from hell.

Teddi is finally coming up with some decent make-up, rather than his previous Diana Ross attempts which ended up looking like he'd had a dermatological incident with a brillo pad. He's discovered that shaving right before doing yourself up may not be the brightest idea in the world, and has improved the same way all of us except Carla did, who was already fantastic at painting on a mask. Now Teddi has visitors cooing 'Oooh, you look *just* like a young Eartha Kitt!' Unfortunately, only in appearance and not earning power; I think he's come to the sobering realisation that £200 a week is not as phenomenal as it sounds once you've hit Charles Fox for your monthly make-up supplies.

That boy had better be careful. I know this sounds very mother-hennish, but he is embracing this new life with an excessively self-damaging vigour and I can't help but feel that he is burning the wick at both ends. Then again, so did we.

Monday, 23rd December

Teddi is in my bad books. I had a pre-Christmas dinner for him,

Alex, Becka and Misha and he didn't bother showing up. Didn't even call, so I had to ring him to discover from his flatmate that he was passed out on a couch somewhere. Never again.

We had a wonderful night anyway and I'm off to visit relations in Germany for my three-day break. My first holiday since I started, and I am beginning to need it. Pakistan and my immediate family are too far away for such a brief stint, but Germany is beautiful at Christmas and is at least another country. Anything to get out of here.

Pablo echoed those sentiments by cruising off home this week. He's not due back until the middle of January and left us with the instructions to 'not do anyting wrong dat vould mean I cchaf to come back errlee.' Real commitment there, big guy.

I was supposed to be going to Belfast with John, but our relation-ship has taken a real downer since the entire Alex episode started. I feel terribly Tammy Wynette, but under the circumstances . . . I'm standing by my G-stringed man.

Initially I was worried about a male stripper becoming my sig-nificant other, even if I could elevate it by saying 'It's different, *he* only goes down to a G-string.' This sounds rich coming from a drag queen, but I identified the stripping 'career' with an IQ that hovered around gorilla level, with a body to match. As it is, *he* goads *me* into reading and questioning more. So far our only arguments have been political, usually degenerating into joking screams of 'communist' (me) and 'fascist' (him).

Somehow it makes it more tolerable watching women ogling him on stage, let alone gay men trying to pick him up. This has been one incredible lesson in jealousy control. Then again he claims the same applies to me, and he has a point. I may wear more, but many a character has seen the show and professed undying love afterwards. Makes our affair seem very 'deep' by comparison, and so far it hasn't been a problem. I'm having a great old time. We'll see.

Everyone seems set to see family during their break and I can't help but wonder what Christmas dinner is like discussing 'so what have you been up to' in their respective homes. Teddi is lucky in so far as both of his divorced parents have been down, and as an ex-child star probably see this as another stage of his development as a performer.

He has taken over Becka's spot in the dressing-room and his primary thought for the holiday season was just to get as far away from Carla as possible, a sentiment which most of us can relate to.

She has become devious enough to give even Joan Crawford a run for her money.

Merry Christmas, *dahhlings*.

Wednesday, 1st January 1992

Welcomed in the New Year in style. What a party!

People paid £25 to get into *the* scene for the evening, streamers and madness everywhere. We started early so that we could do half-time announcements for the usual birthday, hen nights, blah blah, accompanied by a midnight countdown. I was happily tossing back champagne all night, in between trying to protect my friend Frankie from John's amorous attempts to tongue wrestle him to the ground. An experience for all.

Friday, 3rd January

I don't know what to say or think anymore.

Teddi's been taken to an insane asylum, a 'psychiatric institution'. I can't believe it.

We discovered this turn of events yesterday upon our return to the club. Apparently he completely flipped out on New Year's Day and proceeded to tear apart his friend's entire flat. Then he became violent with everybody and ended up just standing there, screaming.

He wound up with a therapist somehow, whose final conclusion was that he needed a psychiatrist, and *pronto*. In return, the psychiatrist established that Teddi was suffering a nervous and mental breakdown and should be locked up for on-going tests and counselling. This just can't be happening. It almost sounds like some kind of 'Officer Krupke' scenario. Everybody passing him on like some wigged out vegetable which, according to reports, is exactly how he's behaving. Funny, energetic, talented Teddi?

Jay seems to think he's a classic case. I don't know, there were times when I thought Jay was pretty unbalanced but he just chowed down on Valium and got depressed. This sudden streak of anger and unprovoked aggression in Teddi has really got me re-evaluating my own judgmental capacities.

What a selfish thing to be thinking when this poor guy's life has suddenly fallen apart, but unfortunately we have to be self-centred now, as the show is a month old and none of us have a clue as to what to do with Teddi's numbers. Add to this that no one can get hold of Pablo and pandemonium has broken out at the club. The office is totally flummoxed; George is, for once, shocked but as usual already claiming to have foreseen the entire thing and using this and our beloved director's absence to slam Pablo to Schnitzel. Do the politics of this place never end?

The club has never seemed such a place of purgatory before. As the dictionary definition would have it: 'a place or condition of suffering or torment, especially one that is temporary.' I love it on one hand, but it seems to have taken on an almost evil or corrupt feel in light of Teddi's demise. I can't help but feel that we have all somehow contributed to Teddi's instability, even if by the simple virtue of performing drag.

I'm getting ridiculous. This club is nothing but a club, we are all entertainers and his was a problem waiting to be released. I just pray that we weren't the trigger.

Carla is showing her usually sympathetic side by putting on her mournful Basset Hound face and then announcing to all and sundry that she always knew he was a fruitcake. Misha seems saddened but continues to be practical, and the barbettes were all either dramatic or hushed. It's interesting to see what sides of people come out under the circumstances.

The only person who seemed to relate the same way I did was Claire. Maybe it's our maternal side, I don't know, but I felt downright grateful not to be burying Teddi right away, although I don't know how he could come back to the show, especially if they do find that this pushed him over the edge.

So now we are racing around trying to prepare for a few weeks off until we find a replacement or Pablo returns. He is going to be one displeased hot tamale.

Sunday, 12th January

The soul of sympathy is back. And fuming. You'd think Teddi had maliciously planned this to disrupt Pablo's frigging holiday.

We've come up with a replacement set-up incorporating the barbettes, and about the only amusing thing has been watching Mitzi tackle the Medusa dance. God, she's brave. And completely mad. She returned from her self-imposed exile to the club and has brought with her a taste of the club's old zaniness. Totally crude, lewd, and not afraid to shock. She thrives on it.

Sugar is happily thrusting herself forward in as many scenes as she can. This one is superb in terms of self-promotion, and I can still recall her trying on my dresses during the last show and constantly volunteering to cover me should I ever be ill. I know she's desperate to take over as a principal, an ambition which she only slightly glosses over, whether she's wearing stilettos during a tropical ballet number, or blocking whoever's number it is. From the bitching I would say she is well on her way to becoming the Carla of the back room.

No one has actually been able to see Teddi, not that I think there would be many volunteers. I guess it's one thing to go out and party with someone but another to deal with them when they're down and out. Kind of like a smoker visiting the lung cancer ward.

Speaking of ailments, I have an uneasy feeling about Jay. We were chatting last night in the Piano Bar before his act and he was again complaining of fatigue. This has been going on for nearly a month, and while he's never been a ball of effervescent activity, I've become aware of his increasing listlessness. There's no sparkle, which I initially attributed to unhappiness but am starting to regard as medical. I remember going through an unenergetic, mildly depressed period, which an iridologist diagnosed as a lack of vitamin B. This did the trick and I've been chugging Berocca ever since. Bought Jay some – hope it works.

Otherwise the show seems OK, to the extent that my permission to go to a wedding in New York next Saturday night has not been reneged upon. I cannot wait.

Monday, 20th January

Wonderful, wacky, wild weekend with exciting people in a fantastically vibrant city. God, I need more adjectives.

As with my life in general it was raced, this time in my capacity as bridesmaid to my old St Andrews friend, Vivian, singing with an amazing blues band and yet again blabbing about the club. Shame I was only there twenty-four hours, but was nevertheless exposed to the film *Paris is Burning* by some acquaintances, with the explanation that this was an insight into the New York drag world. Having seen it I would say it was more on a par with one of our many Kinky Gerlinky evenings.

The idea of 'balls' and 'vogueing' would appear to me to be more of a statement of fashion and style aspiration than a question of drag. There were some similarities to our set up, for instance the idea of 'mothers' for the various houses. Ruby was our mother, although I would hesitate to equate her with the (House Mother) Peppa LaBeigas of this world. As for the thought of her vogueing like Willi Ninja . . . well, summon up the vision of a water buffalo breakdancing and you kind of get the picture. Ruby's routines tend to have more in common with the Anchor cows.

As I saw it, the movie was about the ball circuit and who was involved and how they wound up there. Describing it as 'Wonderland', a feeling of belonging somewhere 100 per cent in a world in which you don't always feel accepted, rings a familiar chord. The most common sentiment expressed was that 'a ball is to us as close to reality as we are going to get to all of that fame and fortune and stardom and spotlights.' That is what Kinky, with its mix of hairdressers and accountants, is all about.

I think Peppa LaBeiga summarised it quite well when she said that 'a ball is – the very word – whatever you want to be, you be. So at a ball, you have a chance to display your arrogance, your seductiveness, your beauty, your wit, your charm, your knowledge. You can become anything and do anything, right here, right now, and won't be questioned. I came, I saw, I conquered.'

I've seen that desperate need in so many of the quiet, staid gays that go to Kinky's or even come down to see us. The exposure to glamour and excitement, the chance to be a part of something that sets you apart. Unfortunately, being gay often means having to suppress that side of yourself, as established queen on the scene, Dorian Corey, explained in *Burning*: 'If you're a man or a woman, you can do *anything*. You can almost have sex on the streets if you want to. The most anybody will say is, hey you got a hump for me, you know? But when you're gay, you monitor everything you do. You monitor how you look, dress, how you talk, how you act, do they see me, what do they think of me?'

The difference for us in the professional drag community, I would suspect, is the fact that it's very blatant and it's all encompassing. Admittedly, you don't walk around in your gear twenty-four hours a day but doing it as a job means that people have to accept that part of your character. It is, in many ways, a complete act of defiance and rejection. Which, I know, is the general feeling of the queens in the club.

In some ways the film left me feeling quite saddened. Because really, it wasn't so much about drag or balls as simply the desire to be a bit different, to shine for a few moments, that transcends gay or straight, any kind of sexual boundaries that we place on ourselves.

As the ageing Dorian Corey concluded at the end of the film, 'I always had hopes of being a big star. Then I look – as you get older, you aim a little lower, and I just say well yeah, you still might make an impression. Everybody wants to leave something behind them – some impression, some mark upon the world. And then you think, you left a mark on the world if you just get through it. And a few people remember your name. Then you left a mark. You don't have to bend the whole world. I think it's better to just enjoy it. Pay your dues, and enjoy it. If you shoot an arrow and it goes real high, hurray for you.'

Friday, 24th January

Went to see Teddi yesterday.

A shock. A completely horrible shock. Fortunately Alex came along because I needed someone else to see what I did.

Teddi was in a room with handles on the outside. A dingy, yellowish room with crusted bloodstains on the walls and bed frame. Somewhere in one of the remote wards in Finchley. Talk about feeling cut off.

The oddest part was how totally normal he seemed. And subdued. I don't think it was the drugs because he made way too much sense. Call it the curse of being intelligent, but Teddi seemed as knowledgeable about the diagnosis as his rather confused-sounding psychiatrist was.

Obviously, it was depressing. But curiously enough, also encouraging. I had come expecting to find a basket case and found someone not terribly far removed from the person I'd come to care for. While some might argue that this should be even more frightening, it made me realise that sometimes a breakdown is neither permanent nor irreversible.

Discussing it further, they seem to have concluded that this was all based on Teddi's rather insecure upbringing. As a child adopted by two white parents who subsequently divorced and used him and his adopted brother as weapons against one another, his experiences in the fast-paced gay world and attendant sub-cultures would appear to have promoted his instability. As did his past as a child performer in rep and constant swinging from stage school to 'proper' education. We gathered that JoJo's was just the final straw in his fairly turbulent existence, and that he has hopes of returning, depending upon his final condition.

This, I must say, did not thrill me as much. I can't imagine that going right back into that world can do him any good and, egotistically speaking, do not revel in the idea of his spontaneously combusting in our dressing-room in the middle of a show. This is a very dicey business.

As was Carla's birthday, I understand. Having been in New York I fortunately missed this blessed event and simply gave her chocolates beforehand, cherry- versus cyanide-filled. This was as good as it was going to get, and she is now still holding a grudge that no one gave her anything or made an announcement. Sorry babe, reap what you sow.

Sunday, 16th February

Teddi is back, which is about the only pleasant situation in the club so that is saying something.

Hurricane Carla has been unleashed. Or make that blizzard Carla. Misha's birthday this week was fêted by all, rather cruelly I must admit, since this incorporated George's deluge of attention and gifts: champagne and a birthday cake on stage with a happy birthday sing-a-long. Not that George has developed a sudden weakspot for our favourite trannie. This was a calculated stab at his personal nemesis – he was going to sock it to Carla whatever the cost, and if he could have showered Misha in jewels as well he would have, screw the cost.

Carla has taken understandable offence, but to such an extreme that she became totally irrational and lost what little remaining sense of humour she possessed. She has now complained to Daddy Pablo, who is coming down on us like a ton of bricks. She's off and screaming about quitting and everybody's crossing their fingers. Except Pablo, who is trying to soothe her ruffled feathers and convince her that we would be sunk without her limited talent. *Puh-lease.*

So we are left in a Siberian dressing-room, and it has hit the point where Claire, Teddi and I carry on conversations while trying to ignore the Ice Queen in the corner. God, she drives me nuts.

Sunday, 1st March

I can't stand much more of this.

Pablo keeps coming back and preaching about the difficulties of living in a submarine. What do *you* know? She's sweetness and light to you, we're the ones stuck in your proverbial submarine with a shark.

The worst of it is that it has started interfering with the show. It is difficult, if not impossible, to perform with someone who is not only sending you bad vibes on and off stage but deliberately ignoring you in joint numbers.

Teddi and I are talking about going to the office. Personally, I think we are the worst hit, being stuck with that witch two-and-a-half hours a night in a confined tin can. Let Schnitzel deal with some of our real problems for a change.

George is gloating and in the meantime even he is bugging the hell out of me. It's not enough to have this guy sympathising with us. In this case, bark is less preferable than bite, and infinitely more tiresome. Why doesn't he do something? He talks a lot when the day is long about all his power and of getting rid of her, so damn well do it then. If she doesn't go, I happily will.

My God, I'm becoming a queen.

Sunday, 15th March

An uneasy truce has been met.

This was entirely thanks to negotiations from above, which were only triggered by Teddi's and my arrival at Schnitzel's office to pull out ultimata, although we tried to be more gentle and understanding at first and deferentially explained the situation.

I actually felt sorry for the guy for the first time. He'd had his ear chewed off by George, then Pablo, then Carla, and now us. He listened attentively and made clucking noises, all the while fixing us with a stare that said 'God, why do I have to deal with these hormonally imbalanced people?' Then called up Pablo to come around to the office.

So there we are, a cosy little foursome. I felt as if we were on trial with Pablo as prosecutor, until we swung the tables and started telling him some home truths. Which of course he pretended to acknowledge, while not believing a word. Carla must be convincing; I should take a course from her in the innocent victim routine.

We finally concluded that we would all try harder. Can you believe it? Like we really felt that remorseful. The only advantage was that Pablo would use his considerable clout with his golden child to get her to snap out of it which, in a half-assed way, she has.

So we're all civilised to each other now, sort of like locking Yasser Arafat in a room full of Jews. Why am I here?

All I can say is Carla better be on stellar form when my parents fly in from Pakistan next weekend or they are going to find her wearing cement eyelash curlers at the bottom of the Thames.

Monday, 23rd March

Mom and Dad came, saw, and were less than impressed.

What a way to meet your girlfriend's parents. Poor Alex was looking good and green before and throughout our performance, trying desperately to ignore Mama and Papa up in the Royal Box. We'd had a perfect foursome dinner beforehand and I know that both Alex and I would have been happy for the evening to end there.

Unfortunately it didn't, and Alex-babes had to perform in the knowledge that the people he had so tried to win over as prospective son-in-law material were sitting there watching him parade about in a G-stringed pouch. From a blackly humorous perspective, it was comical in its sheer awfulness. At the time, we both just died.

For the first time I felt like I was involved in some amateur production and I can't place my finger on why, as the show was actually very good that night. My father especially managed to cope quite elegantly and, according to Alex, simply said afterwards 'Well, at least you've got a good ass.' Alex was mortified.

Mama merely remarked that she thought, in contrast to Ruby's show, that I was being used and abused. Basically that while I may be the star, it was in a less flattering, too sexual light and that the entire show lacked the charm and stylishness of *All Aboard*. I could have told you that.

Wednesday, 25th March

A crisis is born. Again.

I knew things were getting too normal. It just had to happen. This show has been fraught with tension from the start.

An explosion of testosterone occurred last night, this time between our two entrancing, G-stringed wonders, Craig and Marcelle. Now, while Craig has occasionally had us raising our eyebrows with comments like 'I'd like to take a Kalishnikov to this audience', none of us were prepared for the violence of last night. Nor do we really understand it.

Previously the only sentiments he had laid out were an oedipal-like mother worship and a very black and white approach to women in general. All madonnas or whores. Fortunately I did not appear to fall into the latter category, although God knows I would hardly qualify for the former.

While we have all been irritated by Marcelle's complete inability to grasp stage directions, none of us was about to beat him up for it, as Craig proceeded to do during the intermission. I gather that he had made a comment to Marcelle about some move or other, to which el bimbo had only semi-responded. The next thing we know there's the sound of cracking cartilage and Marcelle's nose is being prised away from Craig's fist by Pablo and Alex.

We managed to separate them into the two dressing-rooms, with Craig in the back repeating 'he had it coming' and Marcelle vowing to avenge his honour. Carla and I just looked at him with amazement as we were attempting to mop up the copious blood splattered all over his face. Even the concept was ludicrous, like pitting a dormouse against a gorilla.

We calmed Craig down, or so we thought, only to have the two meet up on the backstairs and to have the whole rigmarole start all over again. Alex was most shocked by the whole thing I think, being the one in between them yet again. As he described it to me afterwards, the terrifying part was Craig's face. He was in complete killer mode. Alex was convinced that if he hadn't stopped Craig, Marcelle would have been history.

This event sent understandable unease throughout the cast and we are all now looking around warily for the next person to flip out. There is a very tangible feeling of danger, although with Marcelle sent away for the second half Craig behaved like a complete lamb.

Now Marcelle is in negotiations with the office and they are debating whether to sack him or Craig. I should have thought the choice would be fairly obvious.

Saturday, 28th March

Apparently it wasn't, not until last night at least.

Craig had continued doing the show and was talking to the very sympathetic Carla, who has now managed to convince him that we are all evil and that she is the only decent, hard-workin', law-abidin', kinda gal in the club.

In this frame of mind he and Teddi started 'chatting' last night. The next thing we know, he's got Teddi by the throat against the wall and is threatening to kill him. What is happening in this place?

I've only discovered now that part of it was because Teddi is aware of Craig's fledgling ventures into the gay scene. What exactly this entailed is still slightly vague, but it must have compounded Craig's aggressiveness somehow.

Considering Craig's macho background, this must make him feel terribly vulnerable. Despite all the talk of secret homosexuality in the military, I doubt that Craig has had much sexual experience with anyone, much less a man. Making up for lost time, Craig apparently also had a fling with one of Teddi's best friends and manhandled this guy in the nastiest way.

God, are we all blind? You work with these people six days a week and they still have the capacity to swing round and scare the shit out of you. Craig was going out with Alex and me after the show for coffee counselling sessions with Teddi just three weeks ago, and now he's turning homicidal on him. It's reached a stage where Teddi is even scared to go outside the club, frightened that one night he'll find himself on the edge of a knife, as Craig has now been sacked and threatened to get revenge.

This feels more and more like Cosa Nostra territory every day.

Wednesday, 1st April

I feel appropriately foolish today for thinking that I could go to a little party at the Revue Bar last night and sit through the entire show without feeling nauseous.

Not that the girls were bad, mind you. They were perfectly competent, even if they did rip everything off within the first two seconds. I think I fall into the *Dance of the Seven Veils* approach to erotica – I would find it infinitely more arousing to have a gradual exposure of flesh rather than legs akimbo in my face immediately. Having said that, I start at a disadvantage anyway, not being a heterosexual male.

It was quite an interesting situation. Sitting there with my straight boyfriend, who was looking even more turned off than I, and our slightly queasy, if unmoved, gay colleagues, between the Japanese businessmen and stag night parties. There were even some women there. I excused myself, citing a previous engagement, during inter-mission and left poor Alex, whom I had forced to come along, stuck with the queens watching replays of the same tired thing. Definitely not my scene.

Alex ended up having quite an unusual conversation with Tevita last night, who suggested that once a sex change has taken place it was difficult for a partner who didn't know to find out. Alex snorted at this thought, claiming that he would know and anyway how could you disguise not having periods. To which she responded that women often go without periods. Sound familiar? This actually had Alex thinking. I think the whole evening did his head in.

As for me, I'm finding a need for an intellectual outlet that drag really has not provided. Something beyond my regular temping stints, which really have got to be the most soul-destroying tortures ever devised. I'm the only one at the club, besides Alex, with a university degree. Consequently I've been treated by my colleagues as some kind of super-achiever. So what could combine my love of performing with a chance to use my academic background, or at least my brain?

Interview with Misha
On Transvestism

We started off discussing his background and La Cage Aux Folles.

I'm a trained classical dancer, and I went into West End shows, musicals, and survived on my ability to do classical dance. But I've always loved dressing up, and I always wanted to dress up, so when *La Cage* came along, it seemed it was my little dream. It actually was a springboard in many ways to me taking my dressing further and saying I don't know why I should be embarrassed by it. This is me.

It broke up my relationship, which verged on marriage. It meant, really, that I didn't see my daughter again. It meant that I re-evaluated who I was, if you can do that. It's very difficult to do that. Transvestism, and this whole dressing up, this gender thing, is very difficult to work out.

If you have enough people saying to you you're a male, you'll be convinced that you're male, whereas what is happening in your head may be slightly different. But you'll ignore it, because everybody else is saying 'you're wrong'.

So when did it first hit you?

I suppose when I started to grow up, when I was about thirteen. I think men grow up a little later, generally. I started to say to myself, this isn't going to go away, you're always going to dress up. But I didn't particularly want somebody tapping me on the shoulder saying 'I saw you in a frock'. I wanted to be able to wear a frock, and I wanted to be able to do as I wanted. But the way I got round that was to start legitimising my dressing up. And the way you do that is by working in drag.

I started off by doing kissograms, and things like that. So if anybody said well you know, it's bloody odd wearing a frock, I suppose my answer could have been well yes, but I get paid for it. And so it legitimises it. And then as I gained in confidence in that, I moved on from that area. And if somebody would say 'Why are you wearing a frock?' I'd say, 'Because I like to'. And that's quite a different step. That was the way I stepped in to it. And then JoJo's came along, which was fabulous. It's a bit like going back to *La Cage* but in a nicer sense in that you were being a principal, so you could . . .

Create your own persona?

Yes, exactly. In an artistic sense, I've spent all my years dancing. Dancers really don't have a character, they are dancers. If you're a principal dancer, you do a principal dance, but you're not a character, not a person. And all of a sudden, having danced for so long and not had a character, I was thrown into having a character and being able to express myself, and also was not pigeon-holed as a certain type, i.e. young man. I could now be an old woman, glamorous queen, you know.

People often get confused at the difference between a drag queen and a transvestite. If anyone can explain it, you can.

A transvestite is a man who wears women's clothes, or is a woman who wears men's clothes, female transvestites.

A drag queen is somebody who dresses normally very glamorously, and enjoys performing. And the actual dressing is not a sexual turn-on, it's a professional thing. The two things do not normally mix at all. I don't know anyone else, besides myself, who is in the same category. That's not to say that a gay man does not enjoy putting on a frock, and does not enjoy putting on a frock outside of work. I think they find that they can be a different persona, and do do that. But I don't think that makes them into being a transvestite.

So is there a common denominator for transvestism candidates?

There is no common denominator. I think I would say every man has the ability to be a transvestite. It depends on his upbringing. In many ways transvestism can be about getting in touch with your female side. In England, we live in very much a macho society that encourages, in every way, men to be macho, and be the provider, and not to be emotional, or not to be too emotional, and be strong. And transvestism can often be a cry in the dark because, hang on, I can be gentle and feminine too.

I found that with my dancing, it was always a confusion to me that if I was gentle and graceful it was considered a female trait.

I don't understand this, I don't know why women should have the monopoly on this, it's not a female trait. It's just you being you. I think men generally are more aggressive, and I don't like aggression, I never have. So I think it leans me towards a female disposition.

Now you run your own trannie service. What kind of people enlist your services for their hour of fantasy?

Well, I run a transvestite dressing service and it goes across the board. I see any and every person, there are no barriers between class or age. There is race. There are very few black transvestites. You get black transsexuals; I've yet to meet a black transvestite. So there's something there, in their upbringing, a real sort of macho thing. They'd shoot themselves before they put a frock on.

But besides that there seems to be no boundaries on that one. I think with most transvestites it's very much a sexual thing. In the majority of cases it's men looking – I would say coming to a mid-life crisis – and looking for alternatives, because they think that life is passing them by rather quickly and they want to experience everything. And they can be very misguided on that. They forget the loyalty of their wife, and for a brief moment – if they had the opportunity – would like to have a fling with me, but I don't give them that opportunity.

Tell me about some of the characters that come to see you at home and the types of fantasies they live out.

Well, the maid one. A lot of men, for some reason, want to dress up as maids. There seems to be a time warp, that they want to dress up as Victorian maids and be chastised. If they pay the mortgage, they pay the bills, they're in charge; if they're then taken out of being in charge and put in a subservient role, it's somehow very appealing.

The particular one I'm thinking of came along dressed quite normally, and then it came out that he in fact wanted to wear a French maid's outfit. And I think this is very cool, this is fine. I'm sad that he can't do it at home, and I think his wife is cutting off her nose to spite her face – she could have her house cleaned quite happily, as long as Auntie Ethel doesn't come around! But in fact, he came round and cleaned my house up very nicely and then paid me for it. Which is quite fabulous, and I don't have a problem with that at all!

It's the people who don't come round that really piss me off. People

85

who are time-wasters. Again it's very difficult, because somebody who has lived with this secret for so many years and wants to dress up but is really scared, doesn't know what they're coming to.

The most positive thing I enjoy about the dressing thing is when I talk to women. To wives and girlfriends. And because I've faced it in my own life with my relationships, if in some way I can give them the education that I know to be correct, I can help put their mind at rest and we can analyse what he wants to do, and what he is.

I've always been curious as to how women react to discovering that their partner is a transvestite. By now I probably would not be shocked but that is a conditioning acquired over the course of a year. Do you think that increased exposure to the idea might have changed the stigma in any way?

No, no, that's not changed at all. It's changed in the respect that it would be slightly more acceptable, right up until the point that, possibly, women now are a little bit more informed, that they sort of say well I realise that 98 per cent of transvestites are not gay, therefore I'm not going to lose my man to another man. But then, if they think on on that, you're man is wearing a frock. He's wearing a dress. Therefore, if he goes out he wants to be attracted by a man. Or, if he stays indoors, he wants you to be the man. This is very confusing. And no way can a woman accept that.

Because it puts traditional roles on their head?

It does, yes. And traditionally women. We like to think of ourselves as very equally minded in this society but, when the chips are down, men still are seen as the stronger ones. You know, everything's gone wrong honey, help me. And that's going to take a long time to change.

It's very important that you can distinguish between being a transvestite, a transsexual, a gay man, exactly what you are. And when you get those distinctions then it's not as scary a thing because, as an example, if at the end of the accounting session, you can quite clearly see that he is a gay guy, then in many respects the relationship with the woman is going to stop at some point. But at least that's clear. You know, why carry on lying?

It's not always easy to analyse it and define it, because we like to put people in boxes. You're gay, you're straight, you like to wear frocks. The unfortunate thing is you get gay men who like to wear frocks, or straight guys who like to wear rubber; you know, you can't put anyone in a box. They're all different.

So it's a tricky one. But it's nice to be able to put women's minds at rest, because I think – particularly if a woman's been in a marriage for fifteen, twenty years – suddenly her world's blown apart. It doesn't have to be quite as bad as she thinks. That's the best part.

So how do you think transvestism is viewed by society?

The general view of transvestites in society is hairy truck drivers in dresses, and that's not *entirely* true. People of every different sort of job, different size and shape, can be transvestites. They don't tend to look very good because a man doesn't know how to dress and he'll tend to go to an extreme. So he'll be either very much like a tart, or just dressing in such a way that a woman wouldn't dress.

Therefore the truck driver idea isn't entirely untrue either, that's often what they do look like. I think transvestites who go out often do dress a lot better because they realise that they have to cope with society. But for the transvestites who stay at home, it's more of a fantasy thing. And I think if they stay at home, I don't see what harm they're doing.

What really does annoy me is the gay population. On the most part they're very accepting of dressing up and love drag queens, but they're not very accepting of transvestites. Ten years ago, gay men were in the closets. And now, at this point, transvestites are in the closets.

Where do you think transvestism or drag queen ends, and transsexual begins?

The two don't really cross.

Could one be a route to somewhere else?

Well you'll always get transsexuals and transvestites involved in the drag world, because they see very glamorous people, how they'd like to be. But most transvestites have no wish whatsoever to be drag queens, and transsexuals even more so. Most transsexuals just want to live a normal life and be women, and just be left to be women as a normal life. That's why there's a lot more transsexuals who are very successful and you don't know about them, because they don't want you to know about them.

They *want* to be the woman next door. If they have a history, then they can't ever be the woman next door. There's quite a few more transsexuals around than people think.

So what do you think of the transvestites that come around here?

I think they can be very sad individuals. Which is partially a reflection on them, but mainly a reflection on society, which says that transvestism is wrong. That this is almost like a perversion or something. That's a great shame. I think women have come of an age that they can wear a pair of jeans. A hundred years ago if a woman wore a pair of trousers, people would say, what you gonna do? And I suppose the answer would be 'Well I'm going to walk away'. You have to think in a different way. It would just be so out of order.

And women have come of an age that they can actually wear anything, and do, and that's right, that's as it should be. Whereas men have just stayed in their particular little closets, in their suits, and the only inspirational thing that's come in the last hundred years is turn ups, baggy trousers, and we've got to the stage of wearing a very colourful tie. Well whoopsy-do! You know, we're really getting somewhere here boys. I don't understand it. If a Scotsman wears a kilt, this is very acceptable and he can be seen as being very smart. A kilt is a skirt. That's what it is. We're very puritan in our outlook, and what we consider as normal, if the truth be known and if we went into every household in England, you would find that most people are not 'normal'. They have many, many quirks.

And this is a fairly harmless one?

Yes, a very, very harmless one. I've yet to meet any violent transvestites. Most of them, they're showing their gentler side. The other thing, that people say that transvestites are more interesting people, I think is rubbish. I think transvestites can be very boring, just like anyone. Just because you're a transvestite doesn't make you a special person. By any means. It makes you more aware of women, and many transvestites make slightly better lovers because they're more caring with their women, but that's a generalisation. There are some very selfish transvestites around as well.

Any other commonly held misconceptions?

Everything else, like in the past these blokes were being brought up in girly clothing, so that's why they turned out gay or transvestite, things like that. Well that's a load of rubbish. And there's a lot of men being brought up as girls because their mother wanted a girl, and it has not affected them in any way. So I think *that* one can be knocked on the head relatively easy. Also, the thing about transvestites is they often start dressing up when they're forty or fifty. They've never dressed up before.

I think with the forty to fifty category it's more a fact of a change in life, rather like women. They're thinking life is passing them by and they should try every avenue, so in that respect I don't think it's so biological, I think it's far more superficial.

At this stage we shifted to philosophy, and Misha expounded his developing theory on the animal kingdom, the natural order of things.

It's just a little theory that I think goes back to the Puritans. They started it off and got it wrong, I think. In the animal kingdom, the best example is a peacock. The peacock, or the cock bird, is the most colourful thing in the world. Gorgeous. Whereas the pea hen is quite dowdy and brown; she's going to sit on her eggs and she doesn't really want anyone to eat her.

And that's true of most of the animal kingdom. You will find the male of the species is the bright one, and he's going to do the little dance, and he's going to be really flashy. It's not entirely true of every species, but the majority, and I think it should be true of humans as well. I wouldn't want women to have their bright feathers taken away from them in any way, but I'd just like to see the men with a few bright feathers as well.

It doesn't have to confuse the sexual stereotype. Over three hundred years ago, for Elizabethan men and Elizabethan women, people knew what a man was and what a woman was, but an Elizabethan man going into battle would wear make-up, earrings, pearls, and in many ways peacock feathers. Women would be in the very restrictive dresses. But the main thing about it was that they were both peacocks, in their own way.

In many ways the men were more peacocks than the women. But at least they were both powdering their faces and displaying.

Being close to my parents and having their support is something that makes me reflect upon the difficulties confronting my colleagues. How did your parents come to grips with JoJo's, having already had a near heart attack when you unveiled your idea of becoming a dancer?

I'm a bit unsure about this. When I was a ballet dancer, and when

I told my mum, she said I was gay and didn't talk to me for two weeks. My father took it very well and said you must do what you want to do, and was, in fact, very supportive in many ways. It was only years later that I finally got my mother along to a ballet that I was in and she was like a kid at the candy shop. It totally changed her outlook on it, and she was as proud as punch.

I don't think they're so proud of me now. My mum's been down here to JoJo's to see me perform, and that was very nice and I think she enjoyed it. She knows for me it's more than just performing – it's a way of life, and that's a confusion to her. My father's never been down and I find that slightly hurtful. A recent comment that he made was that probably the reason I got so depressed was because of the people I work with. And my answer to that was I *am* those people. And everybody gets depressed.

So that's slightly hurtful, but only because I think he doesn't understand. But they're very, very supportive, and their answer is 'We love you, we want you to be happy'. I can't really criticise that in any way, because you know that's what most children want from their parents. You can't ask for more. It's a very, very dicey situation: how can you be proud of your son to all your neighbours, and your aunties and uncles, when he wears a frock?

I personally think whatever you are, if you're a good person that should be enough. If I want to have my hair long and go around with nail varnish on and make-up, that is my own affair. And if people can see past that and see that I'm a good person, or I'm not a good person, or I'm a selfish person or whatever, surely that's the way it should be. We all, in this society, look at people very much on the surface, as if good people are pretty people. And that's often not true.

I always think of JoJo's as a world which accepts people as they are. Accepts the peacocks again. I think it's a lovely place to work, mainly because you're accepted for what you are, as opposed to having to fight all the time. And people are coming into this world, and they accept you for what you are. And if they don't, they get out. And that's . . . fabulous.

I suppose what it boils down to is being able to work in a frock. I don't see why I shouldn't be able to work in a frock, and here I can work in a frock and it's accepted. I don't want to have to fight society all my life. And maybe working down here is a bit of a respite. Besides the dressing, it's lovely to work and to know people, and it's lovely to go to work, although it can be very boring.

If you don't have work, then life falls apart very fast. And I do think that if I didn't have JoJo's, I would be in a lot of trouble.

But you know, particularly in my case now and for the people who work here, there's not really another JoJo's around. So you have to go into normal society again. And that's what I think people don't really want to do, because this is . . . fantasy time. You can be somebody else. I think everyone likes to do that, but it can be dangerous. But it can be a lot of fun. It's nice being somebody that you're not, I suppose.

You know, when you put so much glitter on and stuff like that, it's easy to have and be what you want to be.

Well, amen to that.

I marvel at how similar our outlooks on drag and the club are. Madame JoJo's and the attendant genre promised us both a freedom that extended far beyond financial compensation. I was permitted a raunchy outrageousness that was totally out of my public persona, while Misha was allowed to adopt any variety of female guises under the more accepted face of male cross-dressing. Even though they are different by nature, drag and transvestism are related; I would be inclined to classify drag as the older, tougher sister.

Transvestism may have been around just as long but it is by no means as aggressive or defiant, whereas drag has asserted itself as a legitimate, if 'risqué' profession. In my experience, drag earns more grudging respect than the secretiveness of transvestism, which to society as a whole suggests some deep, debauched and twisted character flaw. According to Misha, he's heard women who discover their husband's transvestism tearfully question their partner's 'moral strength'. 'Is he a paedophile?' for some bizarre reason crops up more frequently than 'Is he gay?'

Unfair, yes, but who is going to be the transvestite to come out of the closet to dispel the fears and stand up for the cowering majority? So far Misha is about the only one. He has even been on a chat show in Birmingham as the token trannie, and generally done enormous amounts on behalf of the cause. He is still not content, however, and now that Aspects is closing will have the time and energy to combine his entrepreneurial skills with his beloved one-man crusade.

He's talking of opening a 'proper' trannie clothes shop, complete with changing salons for the 'ladies' to have consultations, take their tea and find an oasis. He's thinking of staffing it with a few barbettes, who can pass on their undeniable make-up skills. This is probably as close to going public as any of these men are going to get, which seems sad in light of its apparent harmlessness. Misha, by comparison, is one brave soul. I am so proud of him.

On a less promising note, we're both growing concerned with our increasing reliance on the club as sole artistic and financial provider. The fact that we enjoy our jobs, by and large, puts us in a precarious position with regards to the office. It is never good to be too needy with them, or allow them any kind of advantage. In the past we've all been told that we 'are easily replaced'. While experience at the club auditions belies this tough stance, you never want the Paul Raymond Organisation to have power over you.

Sunday, 12th April

Have been giving a lot of thought to transvestism, especially in light of one of our visitors last night, Dane. Dane is probably the notable exception to the 'trannie-in-hiding' rule. Perhaps it's because he's an avant garde fashion designer, who has used the barbettes in a number of his catwalk shows, that he can get away with it. Whatever the reason, he merrily trots down in female gear, arm-in-arm with his stunning girlfriend, Charlotte. She is totally unruffled and accepting, which I admire immensely. Meanwhile, they have become two of our most beloved regulars.

Not all women would be able to deal with this kind of situation, and not all do. I recall the experience of two dear friends of mine who are, surprisingly, still in a relationship. I express surprise simply because of the nature of their experience, which was as follows.

Let's call our two lovebirds Amanda and Andrew. Both had been down to the club several times before this fateful night, when Amanda intended to celebrate someone's birthday, JoJo's style, with a group of girlfriends. Now, injecting some background information about Andrew, he had always loved dressing up as *Rocky Horror*'s Frank-n'-Furter for cabarets at university. Not that he was necessarily a habitual cross-dresser, but he was an actor; Amanda knew of this, but had never witnessed renditions of 'Sweet Transvestite' as produced by her suave, handsome boyfriend.

In a fit of inspiration, Andrew decided to come down and surprise Amanda at the club that night, with one slight variation: he wanted Misha to do him up as a barbette. We all thought this would be a howl, and proceeded as planned; Amanda, unfortunately, did not. When I introduced him to her, or should I say 'her' to 'her', Amanda smiled unrecognisingly at what she presumed was a new barbette. All of her friends, by this point, had already sussed it out, so perhaps it was a case of subconscious denial on her part.

When Amanda finally twigged, she blushed to the roots of her hair, and gave an embarrassed laugh. They watched the show together as a group, but not 'together' as a couple. I could see the gap widening from the stage and pondered this development.

It takes a very strong, secure woman to cope with seeing her man in a dress. I know that as much as I see men running around in frocks, jewellery and make-up, I would not take to my man imitating this behaviour and asking to borrow my perfume. I think I can honestly say that I look beyond the dress with all of my colleagues, but it helps that I don't plan on sleeping with them.

Amanda confirmed the next day that not only had she been totally taken aback, she had been repulsed. 'I've been down countless times,' she said, 'and I happily accept the guys at the club in drag. But it's an entirely different thing when it's *your* boyfriend . . .' She admitted that the thought of sleeping with him, the memory still being so clear in her mind, was enough to make her feel queasy.

It all boils down to what turns you on. And what doesn't.

Sunday, 19th April

Surprise, surprise, surprise. Ruby's back!

She and Jason have finally knocked together some kind of arrangement and, after dramatic stances on both sides, the office and old cast have decided to bury the hatchet. And not in each other's backs for a change. At least not for now.

Suddenly they are welcomed back with the red carpet treatment after being banned for a year, and George is falling over himself in ingratiating mode. These people display more sides to their faces than a Rubik's cube.

George is not my favourite person at present, having gone on a ranting rage at me for nothing. I was teasing Tevita during my 'Whatever Lola Wants' number, where she and Pepper had come to the front and started yelling 'string!' to get me paranoid about tampon visibility.

We all laughed, and the next thing I know George hurtles in after the show, turning purple and screaming at the top of his lungs. I had joked to the girls during the number that I was going to deck them, to which they had cackled 'You and what army?', and now I had a demented George on my hands demanding how I could have been so insensitive in light of the Marcelle and Craig saga. Not only am I the biggest pacifist in the club, but this happened a month ago. I was livid in response and stormed out. Not least of all for being placed in the same position as Carla.

George was a complete darling to me the next day, acted as though nothing had ever happened. I seriously had to start questioning his sanity. Especially when I later saw him kissing Ruby and telling her how much he'd missed her. The guy is bonkers.

Got a new guy in, Zach, to replace Craig. Happens to be the son of one of Schnitzel's very good friends, and has consequently been teased incessantly about 'Uncle Carl'. I bet this is the first time nepotism has landed someone in a G-string. Zach intends to become a stuntman. Watching him dance and act, this is probably a very good aspiration.

Pablo video-taped the show last night for the *third* time. What is he planning to do, market it? He says he wants to mix and match, to ensure that he gets a uniformly excellent recording. While I am all in favour of this, especially having been sloshed on recording number two, I'm rather sceptical of his intentions. He has already informed us that he has exclusive rights to this tape, as he did a few months ago with our 'publicity' photo-shoot spreads, and it makes me uncomfortable to know that he has us on film, to do with as he pleases. He claims he 'may' let us have a copy, but knowing him, it'll be a cold day on stage before that materialises.

I marvel that Alex is not more concerned, especially about the painting that Pablo did of him, Craig and Marcelle, from one of the G-stringed show photos. Supposedly Pablo only wants it for 'personal' purposes, you can just *imagine*, but how do we know this painting won't make its way out of Pablo's living room and into some publication? For someone as nervous as Alex is about his family and school friends finding out that he works in a G-string at a gay club, he is taking a very relaxed stance on this one.

Sunday, 26th April

Misha and I have been asked to rejoin Ruby and Jason as the four principals for the new show, *Forty Years a Queen*, a reflection no doubt on the length of time Ruby's been involved and a nodding acknowledgment towards the country's sovereign.

I am seriously tossing the idea around. Part of me is so fed up with this place that I'd like nothing better than to get out now. I've been here for a year now, six months longer than I anticipated staying. Friends and family have started nagging me about planned departure, new options, and the all-time favourite: 'long-term career goals and prospects'.

The worst thing is that I agree with it all. I've tried a few tired auditions but haven't made great headway into any decent alterna-tives. Part of it is that although I've now got a more respectable agent, he still puts me up for few worthwhile jobs. When I leave JoJo's, I want something decent to give up my security for.

I suppose that's really what it boils down to: security. For the first time I have a regular job as a performer, and am loath to sacrifice that comfort. It's a very seductive existence and, if I'm honest, a very lazy one. I know too many 'resting' actors for my liking, ones that would happily leap in to fill the gap of my departure. I'm also nervous about giving up my role as decadent wild-child, the infamous 'Queen Bea'. My life sounds such a thrill that sometimes I almost believe it.

I am currently in the process of expanding my career field. After substantial internal analysis and agonising, I think I've finally come up with the career that incorporates both my performing and intellectual sides. Broadcasting. It spells out a world of challenge and excitement to me, important prerequisites for a long-term commitment in my book.

At present, I'm awaiting a *Buddy* recall, so maybe I'll agree for now and see what develops. Also, I've gone for a temporary broadcasting job touring the country. Let fate decide.

One point in favour of returning is that Carla is out. O-U-T. Teddi has sadly been 'released' as well, ditto Alex, a development I welcome with some relief. It will be interesting to see what tone our relationship takes against a 'normal' backdrop. At least now we may have something resembling stability return to the backstage. Also, it would actually be quite interesting to learn from one of the first ladies of drag. And no doubt phenomenally different to perform with her.

Carla has been kissing ass to Ruby and Jason in a major way, who fortunately cannot stand her anymore either. There is a God.

Sunday, 3rd May

One more week to closing night and I've decided to stay. No word on the broadcasting front and *Buddy* was a farce. All those recalls to discover that most of the cast is not even thinking of leaving, so we all get to pad out a few more files.

Have decided to visit my parents in Pakistan for two weeks' break between shows, followed by two weeks' rehearsal. Apparently Terri LaTour is in during the interim doing her one-woman show. As long as we get out of here for a while, I really could not care less if it were the flying Wodenzi Brothers. Even if it does mean two weeks of parental angst regarding my future; at least they care.

Had a woman come up to me last night and start telling me how lucky 'we' all were not to have to worry about female things like cellulite. I clucked sympathetically and she started on her list of female woes and how we men had no idea how difficult it was. Tell me about it, sweetheart.

Sunday, 10th May

The show is over. Hallellujah! Good final night, and now I am off faster than a bride's nightgown.

Strange week, as the spectre of AIDS seems to be moving in ever closer. Brian, our HIV barman, was terribly upset with Irish John for jealously – or perhaps rightly – informing the guy that Brian was flirting with that he was positive. Then my gay ex-flatmate rings me up out of the blue to announce that he's been feeling tired and has gone for a test, and could I come with him to find out the result.

Not a task to be undertaken lightly and I felt sick the entire time, especially sitting in the waiting-room, twiddling my thumbs and feeling totally ineffectual. Fortunately he was negative, but it really made me think – what would I have said or done if he hadn't been? What can you? To comfort someone with a still terminal illness, no matter what the future prospects of a cure are, is a difficult thing. If not impossible.

I've recently learned that a frighteningly large number of our club employees are HIV positive and the deceptiveness of the disease is reinforced to me by the apparent healthiness of those afflicted. Sufferers handle it in their own fashion: some openly acknowledge their status, while others follow the favoured trend of secrecy. In a high profile, gay club that attracts a mostly straight clientele, with their possible attendant prejudices and fears, the latter option is not entirely inadvisable.

While on the whole I am assured that consideration for others is paramount and safe sex a priority, I've never heard much talk about condoms or restraint when the day-after reports of clubbing and orgies are related. It concerns me, although I would be a hypocrite if I claimed to always be 100 per cent certain of a sexual partner's 'safeness' myself, especially in the flings department. Having said that, my sex life has been downright nun-like compared to my col-leagues'. Not that this is any guarantee, but it certainly reduces the odds.

I have no understanding, however, of and for HIV positives

knowingly infecting another person through negligent sexual prac-
tices. Reminds me of the case of the HIV positive prostitute, aware of
her condition, and hauled up on charges of wilfully selling her infected
body without warning her customers. She effectively signed the death
warrant of not only hundreds of men, but simultaneously sentenced
their wives and possibly children. I see very little difference between
that and premeditated homicide.

So after these harsh, condemning words, how squeaky clean am
I? I've never even had an AIDS test. I'm hardly one to preach when
the only thing shielding my conscience from potentially murderous
actions is ignorance. A pretty lousy excuse.

Question is, what do you do if you are positive? Most people
expect to be negative, but options are rather limited when that's not
the result. There's always suicide, like Brian's lover, but generally
you have to come to terms with it. To live with it rather than use
it maliciously as a tool to drag others down with you.

The primary reason this topic weighs so heavily on my mind
right now is Jay. We've found out that all of his fatigue was in fact the
early stages of AIDS, something I think all of us dreaded but secretly
feared might be true. He's pulled away and now gone into virtual
recluse-mode which, as much as I find it harsh on friends and loved
ones who want to be supportive, is fully understandable. He has so
much pride and does not want to be seen wasting away bit by bit.
I don't know which would be worse, to decay slowly and then die,
like Jay probably will, or Auntie Bob's route of seeming healthiness,
sudden transformation and then tortuous hanging on interminally in
this half-state afterwards.

I feel very guilty for all my negative thoughts towards Jay, and
sad that it is now too late to rectify the situation. I used to shake
my head in disbelief at all the fervent believers, spouting that AIDS
was God's revenge on the gay population; now I feel active anger and
defensiveness on their, and Jay's, behalf.

Maybe I should go for a test. We tend to be lackadaisical as
women, but totally unjustifiably so. It's all around us.

III

40 Years A Queen

Karachi was hardly a vacation, but at least it was a break. In between constant power failures and drought rationings, I somehow managed to give my body its long overdue rest. I made the discovery that homosexuality is probably more widespread in Pakistan than on Old Compton Street. There again, prostitutes are not as easily available so I guess a large chunk fall into the homosexual category by default. The paradoxical liberality of Pakistani society is that practising gay men can at least walk arm-in-arm down the street, whereas Western convention dictates this as serious stigma territory. Bizarre.

Now back from Pakistan and into our first week of rehearsals. I'm living at Alexander's place in Hampstead, although we are talking of moving to West Hampstead and sharing a flat together. '*Aaaagh*, commitment!' was my first thought, but the knowledge that we will no longer be seeing each other every day at work has allowed eagerness to replace my initial hesitation. Have just entered telethon negotiations with Schnitzel, who has only now informed us that he has no intention of paying anybody for rehearsals. Are you serious?

It wasn't so bad last time round as we were working and earning at night, but this is absurd. Schnitzel keeps skirting the issue, claiming that the club hasn't been making enough money. This is also his excuse for getting out of any wage increase. We had agreed upon our initially paltry sum with the pact that we would earn more eventually, according to audience numbers. The gist was, as I understood it, that the office was nervous about the effect that Ruby's departure would have on punter influx, and would therefore ensure that we were getting in crowds before making the commitment of upping our salaries. The club seems to be pulling a profit, so Schnitzel's stance seems a little weasel-like.

I had almost forgotten what working with Jason and Ruby can be like. That is to say a totally absent Miss Venezuela, madly running around organising costumes and sets, who may or may not make an appearance by dress rehearsal. Jason ordering everybody around, although for a change not bossing Misha and myself. Could it be that we will actually be treated as equals? He is currently releasing all his venom on the boys – Steve, of old show fame, Zach, and a returned (*All Aboard*) Marcia.

Jason and Steve's vicious verbal interplay is underscored by a long and deep friendship, but it does illustrate one very fundamental aspect of gay culture. The art of character decimation, or even assassination, with one word. Queens especially have mastered the technique, and seem to know instinctively how to spear a person's vulnerable spot. Heaven help you should you try and defeat them at their own game. They'll massacre you.

For example, do not even contemplate calling someone a 'fag' if you are outside their circle, not even in jest. Then it is considered absolutely non-PC and highly insulting, whereas if you are within the 'family' it is often warm and affectionate. I've heard it described as linguistic judo, the ability to disarm insulting outsiders while simultaneously demonstrating that one is in-the-know.

This is best illustrated in this year's Gay Pride T-shirt logo: 'We're here, We're queer, Get used to it.' A means of confronting heterosexist attitudes, a sort of 'New Queer Politics', it is not derogatory in context primarily because it was scripted and worn by gays. Other interesting words I have since added to my vocabulary include 'Rice queen' (that is to say those attracted to Oriental men), 'Snow queen' (figure it out, but the clue is fairly black and white), and 'checkerboard' (happy with both).

I had always been aware of 'fag hag' and 'fruit fly', falling into this category as I do, but going into poultry territory was a new one for me. There's 'chicken', young male homo, who may hang out with his peers in a 'chicken coop', being preyed upon by 'chicken hawks' and old leches, who, when in Scotland, are prone to 'bin-raking' after a night's 'cruising', although it has to be said that I know plenty of heterosexual people who dive into their last-minute desperate quest to attract anything that breathes or has a pulse.

Speaking of which, Zach's pick-up attempts are starting to bore me. I just wish he didn't feel he had to prove something to me. Living with Alex, I feel quite the domesticated housewife.

Sunday, 7th June

Never in a million years would I have guessed just how domesti-- cated my future is to be. On an immediate level, Alex and I are playing happy families in our new place: painting, decorating, and christening every room in a very personal, hedonistic fashion. On the career score, I've landed the temporary broadcasting job as – wait for it – 'The Radio Chef'. BBC and independent culinary adviser to eleven million people throughout the country on all things healthy and economical, and styled 'The Green Queen of Cuisine'. Little do they know how revealing that title really is.

The only down side to this double career deal is going to be finding enough hours in the day (and night) to squeeze everything in. While I couldn't pull both jobs off without their opposite time requirements, it's going to be pretty tight. A round-the-clock schedule, interrupted only by a quick wink of sleep. Thank God the tours so far are only one week long, every six weeks, so I'll just store energy in advance. After all, I managed temping simultaneously, I'm young and healthy, I can do anything. Right?

I'll judge early July, when my first tour is launched. For now, all I have to do is get trained in time. An exciting prospect as I know practically nothing about broadcasting, except that it seems the right direction. Time to take that leap of faith again.

This blast of fresh air into my increasingly stagnant career has helped me immeasurably in negotiations with Schnitzel. Misha and I went in, and I think I managed to impress both of these inflexible businessmen with my negotiating. And surprised myself more than anyone. Previously, my idea of bartering was 'Twice the hours you initially suggested for half the salary? Great, I'll take it. Thank you so much.' Then again, maybe some of the hardness of this place is rubbing off, and I've just grown accustomed to playing dirty pool with suggestions that I can't rehearse if I'm stuck temping all day for income. Either way, we ended up £100 a week wealthier during our prep period, although we were warned not to spread news of these joyous developments about. At this point I was so relieved and exhausted that I was ready to have our hard-won prize attached to my body by steel cables if need be, not to recklessly endanger it by blabbing. We were to discover the office's unexpected generous side later, however, when the three boys also received a payment. Whether this was an advance remains unclear, but everybody is now receiving some wage or other, which is going far in improving company morale.

We've lost Sugar to Mykonos and a hormonally-inspiring job as weight-room cleaner/attendant. So now we have Barbie, Marcie, Mitzi and a reluctant Tevita, who looks set to be replaced by someone called Mo. Need we say more. With a name like that, she was

101

probably a short order cook in some northern greasy spoon.

Tuesday, 9th June

Had our by now typically manic, panic preparation weekend, everybody sitting around sewing sequins onto costumes and no proper dress rehearsal. Ruby stood in for a few light cues and otherwise got shorthand directions before each number of where to stand (centre stage), and whom to avoid (everybody).

The show did go brilliantly, however. After a frenetic opening which consisted of a Ruby whirlwind running amok and causing global mayhem, we all raced from 'Campalot' through Scotland via Las Vegas, and ended up somewhere in Wonderland with a bunch of nuns. Don't ask.

As usual, mother's muse had visited her in the guise of one Venus ManTrap, alias Jason, and several gallons of alcohol imbibed before, during and after their traditional brainstorming dinner. Not surprisingly we have the stampede through places, times and styles, that has more in common with a particularly violent acid trip than any subliminal artistic design or vision.

Our costumes reflect the Ruby-n'-Jason show style; a blend of high camp, outrageousness and tongue-in-cheek. Pablo's shows were slick, sexy and predominantly tacky. Ruby's involve a sense of humour and pantomime-meets-music-hall approach, while Jason manages to keep a foothold in contemporary tastes by injecting a few up-dated songs and dance moves.

This show sees Mother emerging 'through' the stage as the legendary Arthurian Lady of the Lake. We, of course, have no mechanical stage opening, so this consists of Ruby lying on the floor and gradually dragging herself up Steve's leg to standing position, all the while swinging a potentially lethal wooden sword in the vicinity of Steve's genitals, torso and head. Considering the number of times she starts the show sozzled, our major (justified) concern is that she'll simply fall asleep. Especially with the weight of her Valkyrie opera wig and four diaphonously-clothed barbettes wafting around the stage with flowing chiffon cone hats in UV lighting. Much more effective than counting sheep.

Jason bounds on after her, dressed in the most ridiculous outfit I have ever seen, which with fourteen months spent in this place has got to be saying something. Truly, it makes my fluorescent 'Beat Out that Rhythm' gear from *All Aboard* look trendy. Enter the Venus ManTrap in a striped fluorescent body suit, with long dragging strips, and a bright pink fluorescent hoola-hoop with more strips of material extending down the sides and up towards the top of his headdress. This is the *pièce de résistance*: a fluorescent pink ball, with green plastic circling it, one of those children's toys used to bounce on that resembles a psychedelic Saturn. Said *objet d'art* has been attached to a spandex bathing cap, with various floral arrangements scattered randomly over his person.

The effect is hysterical, sort of like Mike Tyson in a baby doll outfit. To add insult to injury, our own little heralder of spring has to shriek out 'It's May', surrounded by tambourine-rattling barbettes and boys. Julie Andrews didn't know how lucky she was in her version of *Camelot*. His warm-up offstage consists of the gurgling shriek usually associated with strangulation victims, followed by a satisfied 'Ha! Now I'm ready.'

I follow in dominatrix thigh-high boots to attack 'I Wonder What the King (re-titled Queen) is Doing Tonight', which at Ruby (read: warp) speed has become my own personal version of 'The Modern Major General'. I've managed to alter some of the lyrics to a more accurate description, along the line of 'Oh, the final hour, As she takes her Golden Shower, Being regally, illegally prepared.' Whether anyone will be able to understand it at this pace is another story.

Sadly, the rest of the outfit consists of a huge, nightmare cape, that constantly trips me up when reversing, and royal purple page-boy gear, all offset by what has now been laughingly rechristened my 'King Rolo Crown'; this constantly threatens to fall off my head as those demented barbettes cruise-missile their way around me.

Misha brings up the rear in 'The Simple Joys of Maidenhood', a topic which he knows oh-so-much about. He is, of course, in seventh heaven in his long, permed blond wig, flowing cape and leotard, and chastity belt. A chain with a Master Lock on it that you could pick with a hairpin, which somehow seems rather appropriate. The boys proceed to start stripping him down to his leotard, all accompanied by trannie shrieks of '*noooo*, don't, stop it, get off, oh all right.'

There are fun and frolics with Ruby's 'Masochism Tango', and a highlight is sure to be the 'He Had It Coming' number. This involves the four principals and Marcie and Mitzi, dressed as the six wives of Steve's Henry VIII. Huge, stupendous period costumes designed by Ruby from cheap but stunning cloth purchased in some Indian bazaar in Brixton: gold and coloured threads, tight waists and bodices, and gigantic hoola-hooped skirts. Manoeuvering on and off in these contraptions is going to be the acrobatic feat of the decade.

Misha is on first as Catherine of Aragon, equipped with a Spanish accent that she obviously picked up on holiday in Israel. I'm Ann Boleyn, although I've already declined Jason's offer to 'authentically' carry my head on stage with me. Marcie gets to be wet and pathetic as Jane Seymour, and shows her true dramatic potential in a teary-eyed 'I gave him Edward, Then I kicked the bucket.' Mitzi stomps on in her Visigoth rendition of Anne of Cleves, followed by Jason's sluttish Catherine Howard – no typecasting, please. Finally, Ruby bundles on as a gigantic Catherine Parr – if the real one looked anything like this it's small wonder she survived. She probably ate Henry VIII for breakfast.

If the stage doesn't eventually collapse from the assorted weight, we move through Ruby's 'Dancing Queen' into a Vegas finale, then quantum leap into a second act of highland dancing in the Heather and Glen of Bonnie Scotland.

Somehow I don't think we're going to get a commission from the Scottish Tourist Authority. Sporrans have never been so strategically placed as on the boys, who then go through the further indignity of becoming de-frocked monks and wailing an ear-shattering 'Bells of St JoJo's'.

Misha and I attack 'Ring Them Bells' as Liza Minnelli would have sung it; playing Sally Bowles, that is. Jason and I hot-trot it on as Christopher Robin and Alice in Wonderland for 'They're Changing Guards at Buckingham Palace', which gives wonderful scope for alternative lyrics and promises to emulate childlike behaviour all too realistically: kicked shins, yanked hair, sibling rivalry and professionalism at its best.

Finally we end up in a weird medley of traditional, patriotic numbers that have the misfortune of being massacred at our hands and springing from the song that nobody ever really needed to hear again, 'The Land of Make-Believe'. Appropriate title, crap number, and the only amusement value is seeing a silver sequinned Venus-Unicorn and gold encrusted Misha-Lion attempting to yowl their way through the number while performing an overly ambitious dance duet. I say overly simply because they are weighed down in what they already refer to as the 'Bacofoil outfits'; it's also near the end of the show, and we all know that Jason is usually plastered by that point. I join them in some absurd red sequinned soldier-type thing, and Ruby comes on as Britannia. Long live the Queen.

Everybody was happy, including PR and Schnitzel who seemed to herald this one as a return to the golden days of yore. I'm sure they are hoping this is the case in terms of coinage as much as sentiment. The club is, as is to be expected with a darkening theatreland, feeling the recession, even if we are still cashing in.

Sunday, 28th June

What a relief to be back in a semi-normal working environment again. Sharing a dressing-room with Ruby means a lot of laughs, a lot of booze and three square inches to get dressed in.

Jason and I have settled into a sibling setup, that is to say lovingly abusing each other and being totally rude. His motto for life: 'Bea, everything has a HOME', usually in reference to any of my possessions infringing his space. This could not be further removed from the last two shows and I sometimes find myself pessimistically waiting for the dam to break.

The only leak in our dike now is Claire. I guess no situation can be completely perfect, but I do know that she makes Ruby uneasy, partly because she's a female dresser but also because she has started whining about too much work and Ruby ends up having to do half the costume reparations. Jason and Claire inhabit the same room but different planets, so there's not too much loving interaction there.

I actually like her a lot, but must confess that the result of her divorce insecurities seems now to border on egomania. You can talk to Claire about Claire and you're fine. When it's anything outside of that spectre, say one of your own problems, she will empathise, promptly fail to deal with it and then quickly move on.

I recently did an interview for *The Word* radio programme with Kim who used to work here, which threw me as I thought it only existed in televised form. This foray into the unknown was prompted by a photo exhibition done by an acquaintance of ours, entitled 'Men At Work' and consisting entirely of shots of everybody at the club in various stages of preparation. Some were absolutely hysterical, such as Marcie with wig, make-up and hairy legs doing her sex goddess routine in a bathtub, and some were quite thought-provoking. There is always an interest in this world and it is a shame that our exposure is so monitored by the office, if not restricted. With more public relations work I'm sure we could have the people swarming in.

Sunday, 12th July

Did a mad Soho Festival performance on behalf of the club today, followed by a laid on dinner at Kettners for the entire cast. Drank way too much and now have to deal with the panic of doing my first radio tour as of tomorrow. Help.

Met the most incredible 'woman' trannie-Annie as she is known. She helped dress us during the festival, as a favour and, husky voice aside – which I would classify as very sexy, very cigarettes and whisky – there is nothing that gives you a clue that she is man. Even her hands are petite, which my photographer friends assure me are usually a dead giveaway. We chewed the proverbial cud for hours at dinner and discussed trannie prostitution and shoplifting, two subjects on which she speaks with great authority. Wonderful creature.

Sunday, 19th July

Have finished an exhausting week's broadcasting tour. This involved getting up at 6am to prepare food, which, for radio, initially seemed absurd. Now I've discovered the reason – sound effects and happy, well-fed presenters, which entails a whole lot of cooking when doing three shows per day at various radio stations and driving hundreds of miles with my tour manager. Monday saw us in Leicester and Blackburn, Tuesday in Kent, Cambridge and Bristol, a pace which we were to maintain for the rest of the week.

Basically, I prepare an international menu and do a cross between an interview with the presenters and my own tips/consumer advice, all the while cooking on air. For someone with limited culinary expertise this is trial by fire, especially as I try to concentrate while desperately warding off personal questions. The company that employs me has stuck to facts with regards to my life and family history, which BBC and commercial radio presenters seem to find particularly fascinating. If only they knew that the best, the real 'juice' of the story lies just below the surface and comes out to play at night.

Afterwards we race back to London, and I get delivered straight to the club for about 11pm, do the show, and crawl back into bed at 3am to start the whole shebang all over again. Alex is a great help, going through my 'image' packaging with me and calming me to sleep when I get wound up at 3am, knowing that I only have three hours to go.

Thank God it's only once every six weeks and at least the club is not as emotionally draining as it used to be. If there are any demands it is for me to bring food in. In your face, kids.

The hardest part is continually switching modes. My day-time persona comes complete with Alabaman accent which, while it may have been my birthplace, is not my instinctive speech pattern nor, for that matter, is what comes out of my mouth. I feel a bit of a jerk, not to mention imposter, with these very receptive presenters, and try to rationalise my guilt with the knowledge that we are producing high-standard radio material. Nonetheless, I feel for the first time as though I have something to hide and realise that while London may be very open-minded to our brand of bohemia, the rest of the country is probably not.

Interview With Steve and Jason On Northern and International Drag

Drag is an international art, subject to varied interpretations. Britain seems to have cornered the market in pantomime and it is this speciality that is still most associated with English drag. Yet drag varies drastically throughout the country itself, although I base this statement on hearsay rather than personal experience. From Ruby's proclamations, I gather that Manchester is as close in style and acceptance as we 'London Queens' can hope for outside of our little southern niche. Following this line of thought I asked Jason and Steve about their recent experiences up north.

Was northern drag any different?

JASON: Oooooh, very different. Much coarser, much more vulgar.

STEVE: Traditional sixties drag really. There's like twenty years difference between there and here, and we said that when we went up there. We tried very hard to adjust and get in.

JASON: You get a lot of third-rate London acts that move up north and get to be big northern stars. They get themselves trapped in their own little world.

So we are talking second-rate in a way then?

JASON: Not even second-rate, because there are some good northern acts as well, don't get me wrong. But it's like they sneer and feel vulnerable when somebody comes and takes over their territory. At the same time, you go there and you'll see certain acts up there that have been to London and seen some other show and ripped it off. Like Terri Fox kept ripping off Lily Savage for ages up north.

But we get people down here from places like Munich, who come down and watch our show and then rip it off over there.

STEVE: While we were up there, it was quite strange, because we were involved with this show which, of course, never really happened.

108

But La Cage, which was the next club down from where we were 'appearing' but never *did* appear, had this one act on one night which you [Jason] and I went down to, and it was a new male group that is now the number one group in Britain, Take That. We went down to their opening night in Manchester, and both Jason and I said 'Wow this is the most amazing thing' that we'd ever seen. And they were all non-plussed by the whole thing, weren't they? They had no idea what was there. What I think is they want the same level, they're not into seeing anything new or different. They want the traditional.

JASON: It's not that I consider myself as that alternative, or that different, or more special than anybody else. I'm only doing what I know I can do and hopefully I'm doing it well. That's all that I'm saying. But the northern circuit especially will look at you like who the fuck does he think he *is*? I don't think I'm anyone special, I don't think I look down on people like that. I know when I see something, and I will say whether it's good or bad. I mean hopefully what I do is better, but I don't sneer at them and go, oh my God, what a pile of crap, thank God I'm something special and wonderful.

STEVE: I will never forget as long as I live the day that that queen said to me, 'Who does that trumped up little drag queen think she is, coming up from London and telling us what to do?' That is the one thing I'll never forget.

I have always thought that our show would easily make it in New York – because it's different and because it's good. Then again, my experiences of the Big Apple's drag scene are far from multifold. Again, Jason and Steve were to enlighten me.

STEVE: It's rougher. It's newer, if you like.

I think the drag that we do here is very drag, and this is from an outsider's point of view and having seen both. I think drag here is very traditionally British, in as much as it is a very pantomime sort of drag, in which the men are very obviously men, dressed up as women, doing the traditional British pantomime thing. Whereas New York drag has always been very much more alternative, very much more.

JASON: Well it's either alternative, or it's transsexual. There is a lot more silicone over there.

So what do we attribute that to?

JASON: Because that's New York for you. If you're a feminine drag over there, you've had your silicones done. If you're outrageous drag over there, you're completely wacky. But, at the same time, there's a much more positive view of drag over there than there is over here. Drag over here is, in some respects, sneered at by some parts of the community, whereas other parts love it. New York, I think, has got that early eighties feel we had here; you did it for fun, whereas now you do it for competition. A lot of these queens, they have to be the best. They can't go up to someone and say 'God, you look fabulous'.

You go up to someone at Kinky and say that you like the way they look, and they're like 'What's fallen off, what's gone wrong, you're taking the piss out of me.' Whereas in New York they are all so friendly. They're not worried about competition, they don't look on it from a competitive angle. Whereas unfortunately in London, they do. Of course everyone wants to be the best, everyone strives for the best they can do, but that's New York in general. They're more positive. If you want to do something in England, and tell someone, they will give you the downer, or the bad way, or what will go wrong. You say it in America, and they'll look on the bright side. You can go here, you can go there, you can do this, you can do that. That is Americans in general. Therefore, it also rubs off on the drag community as well.

And they do have more fun. As an outsider, again when we were in New York, you go to a club and OK, it was new for me, it was exciting, I was somewhere new in the middle of New York in this fabulous club. But at the same time you look across the bar, and you see these boys; *that* is their local and they're behaving in a way I would behave here on a fabulous one-nighter, not in my local pub. Do you know what I mean? That's them in their club which they go to every week.

So do you think what we do here could be transferred over there?

JASON: I think it could be. I think it would work very well over there, because it's something they haven't got. It's like Steve said, there is definitely that 'panto' feel with what we do. It's more of a theatrical show than even a drag show or a transsexual show. I mean, you go to Malaysia, see these amazing Malaysian drag queens, and it might as well be a stage full of women.

STEVE: What I feel, and what I see, is if you transported this show to New York today, put it on in a huge venue, it would just completely knock the socks off them. And it would run, it would go on Broadway. Because they don't have it over there. All their drag is lip-synch or miming, and they're all looking so perfect, and they're doing Diana Ross, they're doing Madonna.

JASON: Even American tourists who come here are like 'I can't believe this show is entirely live, just to have a completely live show.'

I marvelled that this should be so unheard of.

JASON: They're more like hostesses, that will get up and do a couple of numbers. They will host a club. It'll be *Lady Bunny Presents*, and the club will be full of outrageous people and she'll get up on stage and say welcome to everyone, she'll sing eight songs and she'll go off, then later on she'll sing another eight songs.

STEVE: It's fabulous what they do, don't get me wrong, but it's different. What makes this so unique is that there's nothing in the world like this. Anywhere in the world.

JASON: We get public appearances over here, where, for example, a pop group will come on and they'll sing their hit single and two other tracks. *That* is what a New York show is.

But we've been allowed to evolve here. When this place first opened the shows were ridiculous. You know what I mean? Ask Ruby. Very small murky affairs, all the drag artists provided their own costumes . . . Eventually, over the years, we started getting a budget for shows, the shows started getting longer, and we started doing a full spectacular. And like with Manchester, yes they loved it when they came down here; we went up there and they didn't realise how much money was involved.

You go to a backer or you get backers coming to you sort of saying, yes we'd love to see you do a venue, but they don't realise that it costs them an arm and a leg to open and refurbish a venue anyway, and they could open that club on that level. And then you ask them for the same money again to put a show in, which is an 'unnecessary' expense as far as opening a club goes.

I mean, when you get a backer coming to you saying they want you to come and work for them, you say how much does it cost to run a club. Right, well double that and you've just about got us there. They see what this club is doing now and think they can do it instantly in their venue. But they can't. They forget how long it took this club to build up, and how it got more and more expensive, and how more and more people get involved.

I guess we do have something to be grateful to PR for.

Whatever grievances we may have against the office, at least they know what it costs to put on a decent show. I wish that our show turnover was less than six months, as by then not only are our 'regular' audience members bored to tears but so are we; then again, I don't view things from any financial side other than my own.

I occasionally fantasise what it could be like taking the show to New York, and agree with Steve's belief that we would cause a sensation. Admittedly I have not had opportunity to sample the drag scene there myself, but coupling what they've just told me with the countless over-awed New Yorkers who have come down leads me to a confident assessment.

British drag has obviously stuck with a very popular formula, the pantomime or music hall style, but I sometimes wonder why it is so acceptable as part of the nation's cultural heritage? Is it because the ugly stepsister drag performance is self-mocking, and therefore non-threatening? One thing is for certain: I have never seen a race of men so willing to throw on a frock when drunk, all in the name of 'humour'.

I guess every country has its unique peculiarities. For example, one thing I can't work out is why the drags in New York go for silicone breasts. Perhaps it makes them more 'realistic', but to me the whole genre is based upon pretence and suggestion; ergo, plastic surgery should be off-limits. It's almost like cheating, although then again some people could probably argue the same about my situation. Certainly we were informed that transsexuals could only stay up to a point at JoJo's, and then only on the understanding that they would be preparing to leave sooner rather than later. Anyone else popping the pills better watch their bust measurement, or the office 'reserves the right' to dismiss them immediately.

Wednesday, 26th August

I owe Ann Smith. This is, or was, the first woman to do a show at JoJo's, and it was thanks to her stellar performing that PR decided to employ one woman on a regular basis. She only stayed for six months, I believe, before being snapped up by *Chess* and *Evita*. A comforting thought when I hear voices of doom grimly announce that no one has ever left JoJo's and become anything. In this case I wouldn't mind a bit of a gender distinction.

Saw Ann last night, recreating her role in *Good Rockin'* at the Prince Edward Theatre and she was fantastic. We had a brief chat in the pub afterwards, and both commiserated Jay's fate along with the lack of knowledge about his current state. Jay had always thought of Ann as a goddess, especially once she made the leap to the West End 'proper'.

Ann was followed at JoJo's by my immediate forerunner, Izzy, who by all accounts seems to be using her contacts well, appearing in every *Hello* edition until she drops dead from flash-bulb over-exposure and gets buried in one. Also performing at quite a few venues, so maybe my two predecessors' fortunes bode well for mine.

Although it didn't seem like it for a few terrifying minutes during Misha's and my 'Ring Them Bells' duet, the other night. I thought we'd never make it out of the club alive, populated as it was by about thirty Italians over for a madcap weekend. The blasphemy of the two of us running around in nuns' outfits with thigh-high slits, revealing fishnet stockings and stilettos was enough to have them crossing themselves and doing at least ten Hail Marys. We didn't know whether to run for it or just sit down and recite the Lord's Prayer. Then again, having the boys on before us as monks, stripping during 'The Bells of St JoJo's' and not being crucified proved mildly encouraging.

Sunday, 30th August

A calm show run does have its disadvantages – no juicy gossip to report, no wild dramas or tantrums being flung.

Even my home life is the picture of tranquility, although Alex is finding the job hunting especially frustrating in these recessionary times, which often leaves me carrying a heavier financial burden than I would like.

Friends raise their eyebrows in silence, but I love him. I know he would do the same for me and furthermore think of all the times others have cared for me, both emotionally and financially. Philosophically, it seems a case of what goes around, comes around. You may not be able to repay the person who has helped you, but one day you are allowed to help someone else in return. Call the Samaritans, I'm ready to join. Coupled with my radio tours, all this doesn't really leave me the time to get involved in our never-ending power politics within the club.

One thing I am sticking with is my ambition to interview various club members with a unique outlook or experience of a certain aspect of the gay scene somehow denied to me. Teddi invited me over to his new flat for dinner the other night. This translated into too much red wine and a take-away pizza. He really seems to have pulled his life back together in the most amazing way. I'm not overjoyed about the fact that he was acting as a 'guard' or bouncer for a rent friend of his, but he assured me that it was easy money and all he had to do was sit tight and watch TV. Whatever. It's his life, I guess.

He's also now hostessing upstairs in the Piano Bar and making the most amazing progress. When he started he knew all of three songs, and those not even in their entirety. Now he whizzes through several sets a night, and is negotiating appearances on the James Whale show. I decided to go from a chronological approach initially. Take it away, Teddi.

Interview With Teddi
On Homosexuality, Drag and Rent

We started off discussing homosexuality generally.

Early stages, being gay is a big argument I think. Some people believe that you become gay when you're a certain age, sort of a social conditioning, which every gay man knows is not true.

So do you think it's more genetic?

Genetic in the sense that it's there from birth, from the early stages; even if you don't have any sexual experience, you know there's something different. When you look back, when you establish yourself as a gay person, you are then able to look back on your life from a very early age and think, 'My God, when I was three I fiddled with so and so instead of Missy-something', and it makes sense then. All the time it's actually a very natural way of life in your head, I mean it really is just a part of you, as is sexuality full stop. If you are heterosexual, you don't really think about it being social conditioning.

So for me, I was very sexually active from a very young age. I mean at the age of four or five, I would find I'd want to play with girls, I found girls more contrasting, more appealing, more sensitive, but . . . as playmates. But with men, I don't know, I got a different sort of high from being with boys. This was like when I was at school.

Parentwise, I've grown up in a completely liberal, middle-class, white family. I should really have come out when I realised it myself; deep down, when I was thirteen, when I started being bullied at school being accused of being gay. I mean, children are very astute and they pick up on things, and kids at school know, they can spot the queen though they don't know it themselves.

But they obviously spotted that something was different . . .

Exactly. Hanging around the girls, being effeminate, not liking football . . . all the things the boys did. It's a really odd irony actually, because you fancy men, you want to be with men, you

115

want to settle down when you're older with a man, yet when you're at school, most gay men do not like to be with men. They do not like to be with boys, because boys are threatening. So you want to be with women, and that's where I think a lot of gay men get their femininity from: from the women they spent time with when they were growing up.

And whom they developed with . . .

Exactly. I think there is something in the argument that gay men have more female hormones because, like women, most gay men have developed sexually and mentally quicker than heterosexual boys did. I mean, I look back now and I think I was sexually aware, despite lack of experience because I hadn't slept with men. I'd slept with boys, but then it was more groping, it was more fondling, as do heterosexuals. So lack of experience stopped me from understanding it fully, but I was very, very aware at the age of thirteen or fourteen, as were the girls of that age. But the heterosexual boys, they were still playing football, they were still smashing windows until they were sixteen. Then they suddenly discovered women.

So your sexual experiences, your initiation shall we say, was much earlier?

Much, much earlier. And I also found it an irony that people would mock, that all these boys at school who would laugh at me were unaware, and I thought 'I know more than you.'

I asked him to tell me about his family. I was especially intrigued in light of their partial responsibility for Teddi's breakdown, and was curious to fit together the pieces of the puzzle.

Very middle-class, very turbulent in the sense that my adopted parents divorced, and then my mother once tried to, with the little homophobia that she does have, say that maybe my sexuality was . . . My mother always tries to question, she doesn't want to appear to be offensive in anything because she's so 'right on' . . . so she'll question me, do you think that maybe my and dad's divorce made you . . .

Was she trying to push the blame on your father, or was she perhaps trying maybe to accept a sense of guilt about the situation?

Everything – both, I mean. It's funny, I think no parent, no matter how liberal or left-wing, can really come to terms with gay sexuality; because society hasn't, and no matter how 'right on' and strong they are, they do have elements of embarrassment.

I imagine that parents often feel it reflects upon them. That if it's a genetic situation then it's their 'faulty' hormones and if it's social conditioning then it's the way they've raised their child. Either way, they feel a sense of blame.

Exactly, and they do look. Now, I remember my mother battling very hard because she didn't dare think she was homophobic in any way, and that actually made it harder for me to tell her that I was gay, because I thought . . . she's so full of herself, she likes to think that she's so 'right on', but she's not. And my telling her that I'm gay is going to challenge her and send her into oblivion. I mean, if you know you have a parent who's anti-gay, you just don't tell them because you know what their reaction will be if you tell them. It's going to be a slap around the face, blech . . .

It took me a long time. My father, who is one of the most laid back men in the world, said that he's glad I was, glad that I *am* gay, sort of knew all along and glad I was gay. He thought that if I were a heterosexual male, I'd probably be a nasty person . . . because of the kind of person that I am.

I had to explain to him that I am the person that I am *because* I am gay; I am flamboyant, I am sensitive, I have an understanding of women that a straight son would not have had because I am gay. And I am the sort of person that he quite likes because I'm gay. And he said that's really interesting, and he was very cool and quite proud.

So what about siblings?

A brother who is more heterosexual than most heterosexuals.

Is this as a means of compensation or a natural situation?

Natural. He really is. I mean he's one of the boys who's got a trail of broken-hearted young women and abortions and children lying all over the place. He's younger and he surprised me, because I thought that he was the person who would react badly, and he reacted . . . wonderfully. Jumping ahead, he was the first person that I told in my family. And then subsequently went and told my father, who subsequently told my mother. He was fantastic – intrigued by the whole thing, that he had a queer brother. But, when it comes to drag, he can't cope with it. It's not a problem for him, he's not like 'ugh, disgusting', but he's never come to see me. He constantly tells me to be careful, because he thinks I may get beaten up. Being gay he can understand for some reason.

Because you're still being a man?

Yes, exactly. It's a lot easier for him to cope with that, but as soon as you bring in the female imagery, not real female but the whole drag imagery, it's something people can't quite grasp. Because what is it? I don't even now like to say that I am emulating women, because I'd hate to be any woman who acts like I do when I'm in drag.

The thing about drag is that it does challenge everything. It throws everything out of the water, because when women, gay women especially, say 'Oh, it's offensive to women', then I say, 'Well then you must have a very low opinion of women to think that a) women behave like I do when I'm in drag, and b) basically all drag is, is a man.' I am a man, people know I'm a man, I never try and disguise that fact, although I have long hair, with a wig, I have make-up, and I have clothes that women in society have worn.

How do straight people who come to the club react to you?

I think it really does vary, because I like to think that I look good, it's taken a long time to look good in drag, and it's a job for me. And my job is being an actor, a performer . . . I can act, I can dance, I can sing; I could – if I wanted to – go into any one of those three categories. I don't wish to just be in one of those pigeonholes, so I've tried to combine the three to propel myself. And as any performer who wants to be a star, I found myself as a man not getting as far as I wanted to as a man performer; I found drag a way of becoming that star. I've been able to propel myself, in a year-and-a-half of drag, faster than the first eleven-and-a-half years.

As a child performer you developed a stage personality from a very early age. Do you think that influenced you?

I think so, I do. The funny thing is, as a child, when I used to dance around my living-room, I used to dance to all the girl parts because the girls had better parts. Then, going into another even smaller piece of irony, women suffer in theatre and in performance as they are always pushed down, but women are allowed to be superstars.

There are so many female superstar performers, like Shirley Maclaine, Barbra Streisand, Diana Ross, all these people who can do everything, and not so many men like that at all. So my desires, the kind of performance I wanted to do, was to be that kind of superstar, the person who did everything.

So presumably there are no role models or heroes in drag considering that it is such a limited field and there are few, if any, superstars that fall into that category?

No, there aren't. The only superstar drag queen, as in all singing, all dancing, all acting, is Danny La Rue. I find he's from the old school, he's from twenty years ago.

How would you classify his style versus yours?

Danny La Rue cannot dance. If I was required to, I could. I mean the ideas I have for my own work are that I could buy a pair of pointe shoes and I could dance *Swan Lake* properly, and beautifully, and on a big stage. I could look like a woman, and it would probably be the only time I would actually emulate a woman and actually do everything that a woman would do without offending women. I'd be a man, dressed as a woman, doing the woman's steps as best as I could. I also have images of contemporary dance in drag, and why not?

I find myself gearing it towards a more modern audience, but bringing in the old theatre. People like Barbra Streisand, Diana Ross and Shirley Maclaine, people who are icons to a lot of people in the superstar genre, are not modern performers. They can do modern numbers, they can be in modern films, but there is an element of the classic about them.

It makes them completely adaptable, because I think you have to be able, going back to influences, to look back in order to go forward, and you have to be able to do everything. Everything, all music today, all performance today, has influences from ten, twenty, thirty, forty, fifty, sixty and seventy years ago, all in it, rolled up. It's moved on from there, it's all a steady progression, so people like that, what they've done is remain classic. They've been able to evolve into the modern. So someone like Bette Midler, although she's a modern

119

actress, in whatever she does, singing, acting, whatever, there is something very 1930s, 1940s, possibly 1950s about her. The same with Barbra Streisand, even in film . . .

I would be the last to swarm about Madonna, but I acknowledged that she tried to recreate that era in some fashion as well . . .

She has but she's done that in a look, as opposed to a sound and style, and that's not enough, you have to really combine the whole lot. At the end of the day, Madonna started off as a modern pop star with something completely new. When she started, there was no one like her at all, and what she's actually done is gone backwards as other people have done, recreate other people; like she does the Marlene, she does the 1930s chorus girl look . . .

So what is the fascination of the gay community with her style and persona?

She's dangerous, she challenges. Again, going back to the school thing, I've always found girls to be the challenge at school. Boys I found boring, because they just did everything they were expected to do. Boys were expected to break windows, girls threw temper tantrums; girls were always doing things that weren't expected of them and I always found that challenging.

I think a lot of gay men, as with any minority or any group of people which is put down by another group of people, by a mass group of people, have to fight back. Gay men fight back. Ethnic minorities fight back. And the only way, especially as children, to fight back, is to do something dangerous, to do something which challenges society. Madonna's done that. As a woman. And, like most gay men, I find that intriguing, because it laughs in the face, the boring face, of your average convention. Convention is one of the saddest words in history.

What in a woman do you find attractive that you would want to reproduce in drag? We've said it's a caricature, so on one hand we're getting away from the idea that it is a woman. Is there any element of being a woman in drag that does influence you?

I think we all crave, deep down – and anybody straight, gay, male or female who says otherwise I think is a liar – we all crave to be in a sexual element, in an erotic element; to be adored by people, in a pseudo-erotic way. That is one thing that women can do which men cannot do. I mean a man can try to look good, a man can dress up, look a million dollars, walk out, and he gets attention because people say 'Oh that's a good-looking guy', but it's always such a surface bravado. A woman can dress up, look a million dollars, walk down the street and heads will turn and people will stop.

Trying not to get into the sexism element of that, a woman can, like Madonna, have so much power by looking beautiful, by looking sexy, by using sex, and I think everybody wants that. But men can't have that. Straight men can't have that. A lot of gay men cannot have that, and don't desire that as a man. I love to go out and have people say he's a good-looking boy, but I don't want excess attention, I don't want it like that. I don't have that kind of vanity.

So by doing drag I'm able to lift out that little bit of 'power' that we all have. I'm able to put on the outfit, put on this image, caricature or whatever it is, and have that minute of absolute sexual glory. And the thing is, I can get away with it because I am a man, again another irony. I am not a woman; I know that, people know that, it builds another surface.

I don't want to offend women. I don't want to offend anybody. Women specifically because, as I said as a child, women were my saviours, and a lot of gay men will say that. Women helped me through the really bad times, and even now, if worst comes to the worst, it will be a woman who comforts me, be it my mother or my friend Carol. I can only get my complete and utter self-esteem back with the help of a woman, because they are the only people that have that ultimate sensitivity. Not all women, but I think most women.

Now this came as a pleasant change of tune from the old 'fish' song. I suggested to Teddi that he might be a bit of a rarity on this score, unless the usual insults were just an act of bravado.

Bravado and insecurity. I don't have a problem with being gay. I don't like to *think* I have a problem. Obviously, there are times when I think I am challenged with that, but you'll usually find, although they'll never tell you, that the drag queens and the gay men who mock women have a problem with their own sexuality. It's so much easier to mock other people; it's a classic syndrome.

It's almost a horrible form of sexism. They think because they're gay, they have a right to be angry. Gay people *do* have a right to be angry. Most gay people have suffered in some way, but what they've done is they've been weak by taking it out on what they think is the weakest type of person to take it out on. It's so much easier. They're not going to go up to a straight man with his pint of beer in the local pub and call him an asshole. It's so much easier for them to call a woman a fish, and say 'Get that fish away from me'.

So let's examine gay women. I know from experience that straight women who come down really don't react that badly against drag, if anything they revel in it. The gay ones tend to either try and pick me up or save me, so I was curious about Teddi's experiences.

Lesbians who come down to Madame JoJo's tend to know what the club is about. A lot of gay women enjoy the glamour, which is why a lot of gay women enjoy Madonna.

You'll find that very few gay women are the stereotype. Homophobic straight people will have labelled gay men as effeminate queens who swing handbags and gay women as butch bulldykes who hate men, and cannot stand anything that's offensive to women. That's actually not true. I mean there are gay women like that and there are gay men like that, of course there are, but that is not the general rule.

The thing is, some drag queens are offensive to women. I'm not going to be there to hoist the flag for women's lib obviously, but yes there are drag queens who are offensive, who sit there with their microphones and slag off women. But as I said before, those are drag queens who are uncomfortable with their sexuality and who can't think of anything funnier to say.

That's why, for me personally, I'm trying to change the face of drag. At the end of the day, I'm a performer, I need to pay my rent. I have a talent, and I'm marketing it. And if I'm offending people, then I'm sorry. I'm not intentionally offending people, and at the end of the day my little self and all the billions of the people in the world . . . I'm sorry. I've got to look out for number one. If I thought at any moment I was offending anyone, I would try and veer away from that because I do have a conscience.

What would you say your life is like outside of drag? Would you as a person go out in drag for kicks?

No. At one point, before I started doing drag, I was an average gay man who enjoyed being a man. Had a little bit of butch about him, a little bit of femininity, as all gay men have; enjoyed the attention of men that were men and repelled the attentions of drag queens sexually. *Then* I thought I could never be a drag queen. Never thought about it. It happened through whatever circumstances, fate or luck or whatever, I don't know, and you, as you yourself know, get propelled into a world which is so unreal, so different from anything, that it challenges everything.

The club itself challenges everything. It's men looking like women, it's a gay club but it's a straight club, and there are more straight people than gay people; people are trannie-fuckers down there, it's everything we don't understand basically. It blows everything out of the water. And I found myself wrapped up in that. As a gay man, most gay men's ideal man is a straight man. Growing up as a child, your only images of gay men are of effeminate men. I can say 'gay children' because there is such a thing. They may not know they're gay yet but they're going to be gay. Gay children's images of gay men are based on what society gives them: effeminate queens, and that's quite repelling to a lot of people, to most people. A real screaming queen is repelling to anybody, even to most gay men. There are very few screaming queens.

And what you find is that as you evolve you have fantasies of the opposite of that, you want someone hard and strong and protective. The only images of this that you have as a child are of straight men. Your fathers, your brothers, your schoolfriends, your rough and tumble around on the rugby field, your schoolteachers, everybody who is 'butch' and forceful.

And it's a shame because by the time you reach the gay scene, you realise that 85 per cent of the gay scene is actually made up of very, very butch men, lots of bodies, lots of good looks, lots of beautiful hair, lots of muscle, lots of jockstraps and G-strings and whips and chains and boots and Levis – and it's too late. Your fantasies have already evolved inside your mind. And I'm obviously not speaking for all gay men, but for me . . . my ultimate fantasy was of a straight-acting man, a protective man who didn't embarrass me in the street, didn't scream around.

So what kind of lovers has this translated into? I can't imagine that your ideal would react happily to a drag queen boyfriend.

At the end of the day, most of the people I've slept with, last year especially with the transition from JoJo's to the Piano Bar, have been with men who have been interested somehow with the fact that I do drag. For instance my last boyfriend was a trannie-fucker.

I used to always believe that as a sound gay man I had a knowledge of sexuality, whether gay or straight. There are always people who are very dubious about bisexuality, but I do believe now that there is bisexuality, I do know people now who are genuinely attracted to men and women equally. It's very bizarre, very strange, but there is another sexuality.

There are what some people would call perverts, others would call fantasists, but there are a lot of people out there who couldn't sleep with a man as a man. They just couldn't do it. It would be like you being a heterosexual woman not being able to sleep with a woman, it doesn't do anything for you, it's not there for you. You don't have any problem with it, but it doesn't turn you on, so why do something that doesn't turn you on for the sake of being politically correct?

And these men, they couldn't sleep with a man because they don't fancy men. They want what I would call a trans-bisexuality, which is some sort of femininity: the women's make-up, the women's clothes, the sensuality of a woman but with the tool, for want of a graphic word, of a man. Because women's sexual order is internal, it makes them more passive. Things have to come into them, as in heterosexual, man-and-woman sex. Even if the woman's on top, they're still being penetrated. These men want the knowledge that you are a man so you will have that power. A lot of these men do want to be penetrated. I find that a lot of these men that I've been with immediately want me to lie on top of them. Upwards they hold me as a woman, but they spread their legs around me wanting that domination down there.

So even if it is obviously a physical desire, we're talking about an attendant mental need to be dominated as well?

I think a lot of men who want to be dominated can get that from certain women, but then how far can a woman dominate you, I mean really dominate you physically, without using something? Like a chain, or a whip, or that whole dominatrix imagery. How much can a woman really truly dominate a man with her physical size being so much slighter than his? And that's what these men want. Then you've got the ones who are gay but cannot come to terms with it.

So, going back to our initial definition of the ultimate attraction . . .

At the time, but not so much now, as a gay man I used to crave a straight man. The thought of a man with a wedding ring on, who I knew was going back to his . . . that's my perversion, that's my kink. So I was able to get that. And underneath the make-up and the wig and whatever, I am a man, and I was a gay man enjoying my final fantasy with a straight man. He was enjoying his fantasy, I was enjoying mine.

But presumably with a gay lover . . .

As a gay man, they want me as a gay man, and I completely understand that. And that's why my life has changed again. Because after a while I found myself losing, from two years ago being able to go into a club, whenever I wanted to, my short back and sides, and looking fit and picking up men as do all gay men, and feeling good about myself sexually as a man – I lost that, because the gay scene in London is very small and people know you're a drag queen. Especially if you're in the paper, or if you're on television; it turns gay men off.

So you get labelled?

Yes. And they presume that's what you're like all the time and it does turn them off. It turns me off. I had a snogging session with a certain drag queen at work who recently started, but before he started work at JoJo's. Attractive man, I found him attractive and he's really nice and then a few weeks later he gets a job at JoJo's. I knew he'd been a drag queen before, but I'd never seen him in drag, never thought of him in drag because he was such a big butch man.

And then he starts drag, and I think 'ugh', and it's an instant turn-off. I don't find it sexually attractive at all. Now he personally accosted me when I was in drag, in a late-night drinking bar a couple of weeks ago, and told me he's in love with me and wants a relationship with me. I could not, could not for the life of me, conceive of sleeping with him, or having anything sexual. As a friend, fine, but not sexual, because he's a drag queen. And that's what made me think, 'Now I understand what other gay men are like with me', and that upset me; I had to look at myself and think, right, I've got to change. I am a man, whatever man, a girly one when I'm a girly for want of a better word, but I'm tired of drag destroying my happiness as a gay man.

And therein lies a sub-title for Torch Song Trilogy, *the eternal dilemma confronting a gay male drag queen wanting a 'normal' relationship with an accepting homosexual partner. One of our most common heartbreaks at JoJo's. Even as a straight woman I am encountering Alexander's aversion to my drag face.*

That also shows you how fickle and how shallow the gay scene is. In a year and a half, I have only met two men who have been willing to accept me, to see the man in me, to enjoy me sexually as a man, and to put the drag aside.

But then I say to myself, if they've got the strength mentally to see through the drag bullshit and accept me as a man, then they've got the strength to handle the kind of stigma attached to it. And, as a relatively sensitive person and a person with a brain, I hope, I want someone who's going to stimulate me not just sexually but mentally as well. I need someone who's going to be strong for me, who can say 'I don't give a shit what you say about him, I like him or I love him, I don't care what you say'.

At this point I wanted to get some kind of perspective on the murky world of rent. Tentatively, I asked Teddi what it was like.

It's a very, very sad world. Prostitution full stop is a sad world, because it's not marketed well. Prostitution has got a stigma to it, and it's sad in a way because some people actually enjoy it. As far as male prostitution is concerned, the only reason it's sad is because it's boys. All of a sudden, everyone gets moral when it comes to male prostitution.

I know it sounds awful, but my argument to it in a nutshell is – at the end of the day, someone's got to do it.

In the whole of the natural world, there's a market. It's that list of sexual kinks again; punters who pay for sex come in categories. For example, they come into a category of actually sexually enjoying paying for sex because either they are married, or they have commitments to other people and they don't want any strings attached, so they pay for their sexual kick. It's like going out and buying a dress – you have to pay for it. If you don't have the means or whereabouts to make it, then you have to buy it. In the way of the world, someone's got to do it to fill that need. There are no rights and wrongs about this, I don't think.

I get very saddened when I see fourteen-, thirteen-, twelve- and eleven-year-old rent boys on the scene. I think that's wrong, but then I say to myself that's society for you; society kicks some children in the teeth, leaves them to their own devices and they immediately scrabble to their feet to do the best that they can. Most rent boys, 80 per cent of the rent boys if not 90 – 95 per cent, are gay. Five or 10 per cent are bisexual.

Are they predominantly picked up by gay men? Or women?

Gay men. Women don't buy boys. It's very rare and there is a very small percentage of that kind of prostitution. Five per cent are heterosexual; heterosexual in as much as they can be heterosexual. They have some sort of sexual release. Some men are so wound up in their own machoism, so aggressive and so violent, that they need to release it sexually.

Now, if they were to release it on a fourteen- or fifteen-year-old girl, they'd kill her. It's so much easier to release it on a boy. If you have a fifteen-year-old girl, if you're going to fuck her senseless and beat the shit out of her, she's probably going to be dead; and that's why a lot of girl prostitutes die. From punters like that. Then you find these fifteen-year-old girls dead, in gutters and rivers. Boys, on the other hand, are stronger; they'll be bruised and scarred, but they'll still be alive at the end of it. That's your heterosexual five per cent.

I personally don't ever frown on male prostitution at all – if you're going to do it, do it. Whatever you're going to do, do it well. I get very upset with some of the boys around the Piano Bar, because they're not doing it well. They're making money, they're making something like £250 a week, and it's not a lot but they're earning more money than, for example, someone down at JoJo's.

So what is the background of most of these guys?

They leave home, and a lot of them have left home because they're gay. They've been kicked out because they're gay. So they've used the only other thing that they have. They don't have a knowledge . . . for example, if you are from Manchester and you are fourteen or fifteen, and get kicked out of home because your parents find your gay porno magazines under your bed, all you know is those gay porno mags. All you know is sex. You don't know anyone, you don't know that there are gay men who sit around and hold each other, you don't know that there are gay men who care. You know the violence and the sex side of it.

Don't they at least eventually mingle with the gay world once they arrive in London?

No, they don't tend to. Again, gay men tend to sneer at prostitutes. If you're a known hooker on the scene then you are as much of a pariah as you would be in the heterosexual community.

So how long do they work for?

It depends when they get the knowledge. And again, it depends on your education . . . your street knowledge of life. You've got a boy, about fifteen years old who comes from the north: he's not very bright, he hasn't done any O-levels, he hasn't got a clue. Now, he will come to London, and he will use prostitution as a way to make money to pay for a place to stay. And because he's not bright, he doesn't move on, he doesn't get himself into the gay scene. And then, in five years' time, you find that gay boy working in a bar in Soho or running a business, or whatever.

You'll find a lot of gay men have done some form of prostitution when they were younger. And those are the ones who've moved on. I think a good 80 per cent of gay men have at some time in their lives had sex for money, but then they got the credibility, they suddenly, somehow clued into the gay scene and that there was a very strong supportive, so therefore they grew up in that because they had a brain. But it's the boys who don't understand who end up being rent boys until they're . . . until they don't look like boys anymore. And then they disappear into oblivion, and you never see them again.

It depends on what the prostitute looks like. Again, it's looks. On the gay scene, it's looks. The Look. It depends if you've got a good body, a good face, or something that's appealing to a certain man – it's luck. It's all about money. And if you are lucky enough to be gorgeous, and on the game, you're going to get snapped by everybody. You're going to make a lot of money. If you're not so gorgeous, or you become not so gorgeous, then you're going to fall.

Leaving this interview on a positive note, I asked Teddi how JoJo's had affected him personally.

If I was to stop drag now, I could turn around and say it gave me a hell of a lot. It made me move on, it let me into a world which I never knew anything about and if I hadn't discovered it, I would have passed on oblivious. This whole transsexual, transvestism, prostitution, drugs underworld scene, which I had always been wanting to be part of but never knew existed, never knew how to get into it. Through working at JoJo's I've learned a lot about things that I would never have learned about before.

And I thank it for that, because it has made me stronger as a person. I can sit here now and have a conversation with you on tape, because I know what I'm talking about. Whereas before, I could never have done this. I could never have told you about prostitution like this, I could never have told you about transvestism.

The breakdown knocked me for six. Completely knocked me sideways. I mean, it was other things, a million other things. JoJo's was like a miniature, miniscule atom in the things that caused me to break down, but it was one of the final pushing-over-the-edges because it was so intense. I couldn't cope with it all. All the new emotions and the new experiences. It pushed my already slightly unstable brain over the edge.

But I fell off the edge and landed back on it, and came up with the knowledge, and much stronger. I look back now and I remember smashing up the dressing-room, and I could never conceive that in me now – I would never lose my temper like that now, I would never feel so insecure, so hurt and so weak again. I have hit rock bottom. It took me many months, from being in the hospital, months of therapy. It's only recently that I have realised it, when situations happen like you have an argument with someone where you think, my God a year ago I would have burst into tears, but I'm not crying. A year ago I would have been pulling my hair out and screaming, and I'm not now.

I think a lot of it had to do with drugs, a lot. That again was the other atom that pushed the balance over.

So do you think that's a very predominant feature of this particular world?

Yes. On the gay scene on the whole it is. Because it's fantasyland.

Prior to JoJo's, 'fantasy' had always held positive connotations for me. Fantasy versus nightmare was my simplified black-and-white outlook. To fantasise was to take a trip through the realm of possibilities; to daydream, to succumb to imagination and create your own ideal world. I suppose nightmares could be similarly construed, except for one vital difference: nightmares are uncontrollable and usually far from ideal. Perhaps therein lies the abyss Teddi talks of, the point where fantasy careers out of control.

I support Teddi's analysis of the gay scene, although in fairness I think we are all equally prone to fantasising. It's simple escapism. Having established the 'rules', however, our heterosexual realm of reality is that much broader, that much freer. Not for the first time am I confronted by the pain and restrictiveness of homosexuality, that sense of having to develop your own boundaries. As heterosexuals, we seem to ape society; be it by mimicking our parents, our teachers, 'our' history. It seems perverse to think that homosexuality, which has been around nearly as long, should in many ways be so undefined, so tentatively building an identity, so young an 'open' movement. Oscar Wilde aside, and bearing in mind his ostracisation, how many strong role models were there before a few decades ago?

One thing I am slowly learning is to recognise tones of grey, to drop the moral high ground. Whereas prostitution may be the oldest profession, female prostitution to me was a sign of male oppression and abuse. Male prostitution was practically unheard of for me before the club, and my attitude initially was 'A man being forced to have sex for money? Yeah, right.' I had no idea, no concept of the sad world that lies behind the tough picture. Only now have I come to appreciate the tragedy of these boys, and recognise the potential strength and power of many of these women. My heart goes out to them, even the empowered ones, because I still cannot believe that the majority actively want to become prostitutes if offered better alternatives. And yet they manage to cope, and Teddi's tale probably illustrates one of the truest examples of Darwinian theory around today: only the strongest survive.

Sunday, 6th September

Talking to Jason and Marcie last night about trannie-fuckers evoked an entirely different response from Teddi's. Jason told me of one the night before who liked the idea of Jason stomping up and down on him in thigh-length boots and then tying him up with silk stockings. And who said the age of romance is dead?

Apparently there is a type of unspoken interaction that is to be expected in these cases, although Marcie helped by explaining that TFs do tend to fall into two categories and how you handle them varies accordingly.

'If we're talking big TF, what I would call a big TF, he is like a dirty old bastard who comes down and checks your ass going round and is turned on by it. I hate them, I really hate them. Then you have the ones who are slightly younger, who are actually quite charming; the ones about fifty are the ones who chase you around. The ones about thirty are much more charming. Buy you a drink, chat you up a bit; maybe they leave you and come back later, or they try and get hold of you in bed that night. And it's amazing that they all have the same lines. "The fact is I've never done it," and then you get into bed and they give you the most incredible blow-job you've ever had in your life. And they know exactly where to touch, where to feel, and what to do.'

Marcie ended up agreeing with Teddi's analysis of motivation though, saying that 'we have younger ones who are just dabbling, or having fun, or that's what they like, but they're still trying to believe that you are a woman because then it doesn't make them gay. You know? All of them do it, the trannie-fuckers, all of them do it. The fact is you have women's clothes on, you have make-up and a wig, or make-up and you're own hair if you have long hair, then you are a woman. I don't look at them in disgust, but I look at them quite sadly because they are obviously the men who are having trouble with the fact that they are homosexual. Or bisexual. Normally bisexual. They need something else, they need something sexual, and they can't come to terms with it basically.

'The other two types are the ones that are bisexual and the ones that do find it attractive that I don't look like a man; but then the other ones just can't come to terms with the fact that they are gay. I'm not confusing bisexuality as being people who can't come to terms with being gay – they are two completely different things.'

I think the whole territory is very confusing, especially at first exposure. I vaguely recall a guy nicknamed 'Tiger' who used to come to the Piano Bar during *All Aboard*. A gorgeous man who saw me in drag and asked me whether I was a man or a woman. When I responded the latter, he proceeded to really charm the socks off of me. Whether he would ever have got to the tights is another story, but I soon found out from Jacquie, our barbette toilet attendant, that he was a renowned TF and had had affairs with various barbettes already. Blew my mind, and unlike with my colleagues, that's all he blew.

Sunday, 13th September

Jay is dead.

I came in on Monday night from my tour to discover Ruby giving an interview to a *Guardian* reporter in our dressing-room, and Jason just blurted out something about were we all going to go to the funeral together? Not realising that I hadn't been home all day to field my calls, I had no idea that Jay had even died. It was like a bucket of cold water from nowhere, and worst was having it all played out in front of this complete stranger.

I couldn't go to the funeral with everybody else because of my conflicting broadcast so I went to the cemetery an hour after the service and tried to figure out where exactly he had been buried. The duality of our lives really hit me when, asking the groundkeeper for the site, I realised I didn't even know Jay's real name. We had to go through a list of three names and concluded that the 27-year-old male must have been Jay.

I found the grave, filled with flowers and notes and lay mine among the pile. In a way I was happier to say my farewell in private.

It was somehow ironic to see the large wreath 'To our son' lying there for him, having heard him say how separate his and his parents' worlds were and knowing how they really didn't ever want to acknowledge his gayness or profession. In the end they showed great generosity and acceptance by asking Ruby to ride in the funeral cortege with them. I guess what it boils down to is that death is a great leveller and, sadly, it often takes that to make people overlook their superficial differences. Always too late.

The HIV positives at the club seemed saddened, but don't let it affect them too much. Seeing how often people refer to it as a psychological struggle or fight, I guess this is their way of holding on. One good thing – barman Brian has found a wonderful lover who has whisked him off to Cornwall to love and cherish him while he still can.

I wish Jay had had that.

Sunday, 27th September

What a bizarre week. We are now making our mark on the popular music front, normally a contradiction in terms when discussing any musical output at JoJo's.

Thanks to an aerobics acquaintance of mine who handles a major band's albums, they decided to celebrate their newest release with a party at the club. We opened at 6.00pm for them and did a special show, all the while being video-taped on and off stage by some dodgy character from the record company. He assured us that this was only for private company purposes, although I can't really imagine the execs sitting around watching our backstage changes in a yearly review session. I for one was careful not to be caught in any state of undress as I had already had that experience with some newspaper photographer during *All Aboard*, and had to move mountains to get my full frontal snapshot back.

While the new album sounded dreadful, not assisted by our eardrum shattering sound system, the show was a hit. I say this in unqualified terms because it makes the subsequent article in the *Daily Mirror* all the more inexplicable. We left the club afterwards to go for drinks at the Café Royal and then do the nightly show, bidding our guests, most of whom were still downstairs drinking, farewell.

Two days later we get a newspaper clipping from a rather perplexed office, in which it's claimed that Ruby sat on someone's face during the performance and that we whirled amok throughout the club before running screeching into the night, across the road and into one of the sex shows. About the only thing they left out is that we burned effigies of the Pope and tortured small animals in a live devil worship rite.

For starters, if Ruby had sat on someone's face we would have had to scrape their flattened head off the floor afterwards. Furthermore, what on earth would a bunch of gay drag queens be doing running into a live girly sex show? I mean, while we want publicity for the club, and this certainly does wonders for our wild and crazy image, this was about as realistic as announcing that JoJo's would soon be re-opening as a convent school. I don't think so, guys.

The office is happy though, in that JoJo's is once again being used for various outside groups and pulling extra income and kudos. The Revue Bar has already been put back into use, apparently for one of Kylie Minogue's latest videos. (As Jason joked the other day, 'What's the difference between Kylie Minogue and a Skoda? You feel a tit in a Skoda.' Then again, with my flat chest I should probably keep my mouth firmly shut.) Anyway, since Euronox closed and the Limelight has been overused, there appears to be no decent alternative venue, so JoJo's is coming into its own.

Sunday, 11th October

Jason just had a phone call from a friend of his in the Canary Islands, who excitedly announced that he had just seen us all on MTV. Put two and two together and you get no money and a video for one major band's newest single. If this is true, then I am furious.

I don't think anybody minds the worldwide exposure so much, but the fact is that we didn't sign any releases and for that matter weren't even consulted as to the final destination of their sneaky video-taping. Jason and I were screaming lawsuits and revenge (read money), the office is giving us the raised eyebrow treatment and Ruby is sitting there like a beneficient Queen Victoria. Schnitzel, grandmaster of the big Sue, is doing sweet FA. Maybe they consider it too small time, or just aren't interested, but this is very out of character. What is going on?

We're off to a Sunday 'family' dinner at Mother Ruby's and I'm in charge of the Bloody Marys. Maybe if I put in enough tabasco it will light a fire under her bum and she will turn into the shot-gun waving Granny Clampett that we need to make headway with this potential injustice.

Sunday, 25th October

Well, we can kiss that lawsuit goodbye. How infuriating.

If anybody would have been hot on the trail I would have thought it would be Misha, but he seems preoccupied with suing another party who have used one of his audition tapes for their own purposes. That and dealing with obnoxious trannies, like the one he was bitching about last night who insisted, against Misha's advice, on shaving before being made over and then started whinging about stockings when he wanted to wear tights. The final straw came when he complained to Misha that the outfit supplied 'breaks me up', to which Misha snapped 'Well, you're six foot two and you're fat', then stomped off to make a forty-five minute phone call which he only interrupted to get his payment. There is no such thing as easy money.

Speaking of la trannie, Misha is making us all roll our eyes with his constant habit of shrieking and ad-libbing his way through numbers, rendering them completely unrecognisable. Jason has decided that Misha is getting a Stephen Sondheim number in the next show, announcing triumphantly 'Let's see him put extra words into songs that already have too many words for the music.' I had to squash this prospect of victory by reminding him that Misha would probably just bellow his normal welcome, 'Hello, chicken, I'm a lesbian too' to some poor unfortunate and scratch the song altogether.

Another current trannie focus is imperative weight loss. Misha was horrified to find himself bulging over the sides of his corset the other night and I think our constant ribbing about his developing chubbiness is finally getting to him. The fish and chip inhaler is now talking about 'Flab Attack', which must make a first; as a dancer, he has never had to worry before. I reckon this transformation is due as much to the absence of *Aspects* exercise as to the hormone pills he's been popping with alarming single-mindedness. He'd better be a little more cautious with all of this, or the office will sack him. Ruby and Jason are already concerned as Misha's tits are seriously protruding and the alteration is becoming physically apparent, even from a distance. This does not suit the type of drag image JoJo's attempts to project.

Ruby, Jason and I are equally confused about Misha's motivation. He claims to be a heterosexual transvestite, he has a girlfriend he adores, so what does he want to keep developing breasts for?

When I put this question to him, I got a vague, confused response that implied experimentation. Call me a hypochondriac, but I don't think chowing female hormones, as a man, is the healthiest form of testing. It's not just the physical impact on your body, but emotional as well; after years on the Pill, I should know. Misha is now far moodier and more highly strung than I've ever seen him and I can't imagine that his girlfriend's understandable confusion is helping clear his perspective any. It just makes no sense.

Friday, 6th November

Sometimes, sadly, the learning procedure can prove fatal.

The club is in uproar at the untimely, shocking death of one Debbie Raymond. I mean, what was she, thirty-eight, maybe? Everybody is reeling, not least of all Ruby, who was thicker than glue with the late deceased and is absolutely crushed. George is running around like a headless chicken, professing a sibling-like closeness which I gather from my two teary-eyed 'dressing-room-mates' never existed.

If JoJo's has been numbed by this sudden tragedy, then this is more than can be said for the press. We have been inundated, often surreptitiously, and have been consequently 'warned' by the office to not speak to anybody *under any circumstances.*

I'm hardly surprised – the death of the beloved child of one of London's greatest magnates, add to that editor of his eight-odd magazines, from a suspected heroin overdose is not the kind of story that falls into your lap all the time. Quite a coup.

Rumours are already flying about as to her induction into the drug world and reports are stating that she was an habitual cocaine user. Supposedly it was the fact that she tried the unaccustomed heroin that, in Eliza Doolittle's immortal words, 'done her in'.

Our profile as scandal pit is soaring sky high, and it is tragic that it had to be at this poor woman's expense. Even if it was self-inflicted, she has left behind two young daughters aged six years and six months, and I can't help but wonder what kind of legacy they are being left courtesy of every broadsheet and tabloid.

PR is reported to be devastated. And completely uncontactable, even to the office at present.

Sunday, 8th November

Well, our keeping shtum is of little consequence in light of Debbie's divorced mother's damning newspaper indictments. She did a whole spread for the *News of the World* today, slamming PR and his exclusion of her positive maternal influences on her 'baby'.

Word is that PR has aged at least twenty years through this nightmare and it is Ruby's one hope that Debbie's kids will force him to be strong. Everybody is already asking who will take over the business. Probably PR's nephew, although judging from the family head's absolute indifference to anything at the moment that is the last thing on his mind.

On a far more trivial note, Bea Arthur came down to the club, doyenne and role model to half the guys here. I've held her in high esteem since I was still padding around in fluffy 'footsie' pyjamas, and listening to her Matchmaker in the Broadway/Zero Mostel version of *Fiddler on the Roof*. For someone of such tremendous stature, I was surprised to find that she was much smaller than I expected; especially when you see her towering over the other three *Golden Girls*. OK, I was wearing five-inch heels, but I was already so much taller that I could have checked her roots for regrowth.

In spite of my respect for her, I couldn't bring myself to join in the grovelling and prostration; actually, maybe it is because of that respect, although I can't stand behaving like a fan to most people. Probably just a huge ego complex on my part. Anyway, she looked like she could use some peace and quiet.

Oh, and Steve has a new admirer. A 'straight' one, no less.

Some very good-looking guy has been coming down to the club fairly regularly and fallen in love, or lust, with our forty-year-old sex bomb. Jason was laughing, knowing what a tart Stevie-boy can be, but Steve was definitely lapping it all up. Hell, if *I'd* been sent a vintage bottle of Perrier Jouet backstage I'd be engaged by now.

Ask him about prospects though, and he seems to back off from any kind of serious involvement. He's still smarting from this summer's split with a long-term lover, with whom a lot of water and mutual open affairs had flowed under the bridge. We got to talking about the lead up to this demise and he suddenly revealed that he had forayed into the US rent scene for several months at his boyfriend's instigation. Now there's love for you.

Then again, that's Steve for you as well. His entire history is an exploration in sexual freedom, and I decided to interview him on both the contrast in American versus British rent as well as the generational gap growing up as an older gay man. Despite the mature impression Ruby gives off, she's only thirty-eight; Steve is older, and yet acts the proverbial spring chicken. We're meeting tomorrow.

Interview With Steve
On Sixties Homosexuality in Australia and the Navy, and the US Rent Scene

We started at the very beginning.

Well, I had a very traumatic adolescence really, beginning with a stepmother and a father, who I thought – and all children do at that age, I think – didn't understand and all that sort of thing. I thought that I had an ogre of a stepmother and a father that didn't love me. It really was just adolescence rearing its ugly head. The fact was that I was very, very headstrong, very typically Sagittarian. Independent, didn't like to be tied down, didn't like to be told what to do and never did it anyway if I was told. If I was told to do anything I would *immediately* say 'Right, I'm doing the opposite', as you do when you're developing into an adult.

So at fifteen they said you've got to knuckle down and go to school and do all your examinations and all that, and I said 'Fuck this darling, your mother is going off and doing whatever she wants to do!' So I rebelled at school and it all came to head in an English class.

I was getting very bored with this Shakespeare shit they were shoving down my neck. Drama was my main subject at school, but to be lectured on the pros and cons of the *Baaard's* wonderful language . . . And I was playing at the back of the class, as you do at fifteen. Probably with the boy next door to me. I can't remember exactly what I did, but all I can remember is calling our English teacher a 'ridiculous woman'. So she sent me to the headmaster, but he was never told why. You had to tell him why you'd been sent to him but I said 'I have absolutely no *idea*. As far as I'm concerned, I was just being perfectly truthful and honest.'

The next day my parents were called, summoned to the headmaster's office, and he said 'Well, we've tried very hard but there is nothing that we can really do for Steven any longer, so we would really appreciate it if you would take him out of school.'

In other words, it was a nice way of expelling me, so at fifteen I was expelled from school. Which was of course in those days, we're talking early sixties now, quite scandalous. To be *expelled*! So, off I went into my hairdressing career, into Raymond's. I obviously wanted to go to the best hairdressers that there were, and that happened to be Cheezy-Weezies, as it was known, and Raymond. I hated it because it was even *more* disciplined, you know, being a French sir. I did that for a while then thought I can't bear this any longer. I was hating living at home so I said I wanted to leave.

I ended up, aged sixteen, boarding an aeroplane at Heathrow bound for Australia on the 'Big Brother' movement, which was an emigration scheme they had for young boys aged between fifteen and eighteen. They paid for everything: going out there, training you in a skill, and placing you in a job. So it was all very exciting and off I went to Sydney; it was a bit of a wrench, I must admit, because I suddenly felt that I'd been sort of torn away from this family environment that I'd always had all my life, into a void, the unknown. At the same time, it was extremely, wonderfully exciting because I hated family existence.

So there I was, sixteen years old, 12,000 miles away, in this very hot climate, which I loved. And the first thing they did when we arrived in the airport was put us all on a coach and drive us out to this training ranch. You had dormitories and a big house with the farm men and instructors. All I can remember is that they had five ranch hands that worked for them. And I wasn't sure, I was almost positive that I was gay but I didn't understand what gay was in those days. All I can remember are these five Australian late teens and early twenties gorgeous men, who used to ride around on horseback all day and I was totally smitten by every single one of them. Instantly. On arrival.

These *gorgeous* men. And that kept me occupied for the six weeks, otherwise I wouldn't have stayed more than a day because I hated the place. It was pissing down and you had to get up at five o'clock in the morning and go and milk the cows, then you had to go and do the chores . . . And so I thought, OK this is new, brought from an industrial Midlands town going into *daaairy* farming, it's interesting enough. So I did that, finished my course there. And then they sent us off into placements, so-called jobs. I was sent out to this dairy farm in the middle of nowhere; it was practically in the bush. Having got up at five o'clock in the training camps, they said 'Oh no, we get up at three o'clock because we have a larger herd and we have to milk our cows earlier.' So I thought 'OK, I can cope with that', so for two days I did. And on the *third* day I thought 'I've had enough of this', so I ran away to Sydney. I had nowhere to live, I had no money, I had no clothes apart from the clothes on my back and I didn't know what to do.

So, how it happened I can't quite remember exactly, but I ended up living with a transvestite sex-change. But I don't think she was a real sex-change then, although she told me she was. It was too early, it was 1965 or '66, and there weren't many sex-changes around in those days. This was the King's Cross area of Sydney, the red light district, darling! And of course she was a prostitute but she took me under her wing. So there I was, living with this transsexual prostitute, and she used to bring home all these straight men that obviously thought she was a woman, or they were too drunk to know whether she was a woman, but there were never any problems.

I used to sleep in the next room, go out, and was gradually introduced to this very underground, because it was illegal in Australia to be gay or under sexual age, *very* underground existence. And I sort of gravitated towards *the* drag club of the sixties in Australia, which was very similar, in every possible way, to JoJo's, called Les Girls. It's an icon of history really, it was one of the most famous drag clubs in the world. They got to know me after a while and I used to get to know the drag stars because I lived with this transsexual – as you know, they get intermixed. I used to sit there every night, getting in free, watching all this drag. It was all mime, there was no live acting then, but I used to think they were the most incredibly glamorous, wonderful creatures. I did that for about six months. I was this little boy that used to watch this and of course know everyone's part by heart, thinking 'I want to do this, I want to do this'. But I didn't, because the next thing that happened was that she got busted by the police and I had to get out quickly.

So I phoned my mother, who was living in Australia at the time, in Perth, on the other side of the country. I had never really had anything to do with her but she said 'Come and stay with us'. So I did. That lasted for two weeks, because we couldn't stand each other. We clashed terribly; too much alike. But during that two weeks she had this barbeque and invited all her friends and relatives and friends of relatives.

This young, gorgeous dark-haired god was there with his girlfriend, with whom I fell – this is the first and only time it has ever happened to me – *instantly* in love. Just totally, on the spot, there it was. All these feelings I'd never had before for anyone I knew. And there was something about him, because he was obviously intrigued by me and

Queen Bea

Ruby Venezuela

Misha

Teddi

Venus ManTrap

Jay

Mitzi

Barbie and Marcie

Becka

Becka, Ruby and Bea

three weeks later we were living together. He'd left his girlfriend. He was a few years older than me, but I thought of him as this *terribly* older man that I was living with, as you do at that age anyway.

It was like setting up home. Going into a relationship without any previous experience, but going to live with this man and sort of setting up home, you take up a 'role', if you like. I took up obviously from where his girlfriend had left off. There we go . . . And I was totally and utterly in love with this man. Six months later I found out that he'd been seeing other people, and there were girls *and* boys.

So, being me, I threw this *huge* drama, this *monstrous* wobbler, walked out thinking that he was going to come after me – but he didn't. So there I was, I'd left my parents, I'd left this guy, and I was, for the very first time in my life, totally alone, totally depressed, suicidal and thinking my life was over. So I did a *huge* suicide attempt, took a monstrous number of sleeping tablets and I can't remember exactly how and why I was found, but I ended up in hospital, stomach pumped up. Everyone found out, the Big Brother movement found out it was me, and everybody found out where I was.

I'd sort of surfaced from this underworld existence. And I didn't really know what to do, I had no idea of where I should go at this point, so I had about a couple of months thinking, oh I don't like this, but then I don't *like* being a suicide case. I didn't *like* being depressed, I didn't enjoy the fact that I had to go around with a long face all the time. That's not like me . . . you know, I'm a happy person basically. So, I decided I had to do something.

I was walking through Perth, and the next job that I had was as a porter in a hotel, the Palace Hotel, which was *outrageously* camp, full of queens. Which I really enjoyed. I had a good time in my little bellboy's uniform, operating the lifts and taking people's bags to their rooms. You know, I was a pretty naive little thing really in those days.

Then, as my personality was and still is, I get bored very quickly, within a few days in most things. I wanted to do something new, something different, something more exciting. So I was walking past the navy recruitment offices, and standing in the doorway was this *stunning* sailor (just shows you how influenced I am by men, and have been in my life) and immediately I presume this is a fabulous glamorous life full of gorgeous men. I was soon to realise they weren't all like *that*! I went in, signed the papers and two days later I was in the Royal Australian Navy! Fortunately for me, because I found out a week later that my mother had papers saying I'd been called up for the Australian Army, as you did for National Service, for the Vietnam War. So I wasn't going to be going to the Vietnam War as a soldier, where I very easily could have been shot and killed in battle, but I was going to go in the slightly less risky Navy. Or I *thought* it was slightly less risky. I soon learned the Australian Navy was more risky than anything else you could possibly imagine in the end!

They had this terrible habit of carving ships in half with each other, when they went on exercises; aircraft carriers kept slicing through destroyers, two destroyers had actually sunk by hitting them. Anyway, I went and worked in Melbourne to do my recruitment training, and they said what do you want to do, what sort of career do you want in the Navy? And I thought, what's the most *glamorous*? What's the thing that's going to get me the most flirting potential? Of course, it had to be an operating theatre technician. We were at war, and there were these huge dramatic scenes played out in the operating theatre, so I trained to become an operating theatre technician.

I did my basic sea training, which was six weeks on a ship, sailing around, scrubbing decks and being very butch. I had some *very* interesting sexual experiences at sea, I can tell you. With numerous other young boys of a similar age, that were in a similar situation; you know, hormones flying around the room like *crazy*, testosterone for days, darling. We slept in messes that held about eighty or ninety men, you know, so you can *imagine* the pheremones. Pheremones for days. That was when I had my first drug experience. We had to do night duties in the sick-bay, and the drugs cupboard was locked but I knew where the key was. So I was learning about all these drugs and what they did, and there were sweetie-jars – I'm not joking, these big medicine jars full of Dexedrine. Six thousand Dexedrine tablets, which is like pure amphetamine. So I thought I'll try one because I'm very tired tonight and that was my first introduction to speed.

For the next six weeks, I was a speed queen. I lost all my weight, I would go out every night: I never slept for six weeks, I didn't eat for six weeks. It wasn't until they did their inspection, their stock control takes if you like, that they came around and found this full jar of Dexedrine was now half full; and wanted to know what had happened to them and who'd been stealing them. So this full investigation got underway. I suddenly realised I might be in very serious trouble soon if they sussed out who was the one that was looking like the shaking drug freak in there, which I *obviously* was. I didn't realise at the time. So I stopped taking them, and at that point, I met up again with the transvestite because I was based in Garden Island. He'd just come out of prison, and in one night, I disappeared.

It was basically sexual harassment I suppose. I had this petty officer that was harassing me for sexual favours, and I wasn't really into it. I did it a few times with him, but I thought 'Oh God I don't really like him'. But he was really insistent, he was very rough about it, very cruel. So I avoided him by going AWOL, by deserting the Navy at war, which is a capital offence.

I lived with this drag queen, and got very heavily involved in the whole rent scene there. I didn't do any myself then, because I was too inexperienced really and too frightened to do anything about it. So I avoided all that issue. But they were catching up with me, the MPs (Military Police) were very close at hand. So this drag queen and I had to think of the best way of getting out of this. We staged, and it was staged, this very dramatic suicide attempt again. We had Nembutal, the barbiturate, and I only took a very small amount. She was going to come home, such a dramatic scene, and find me dying, come with me to the hospital and, while I was being pumped out, which I realised I had to go through, do this 'Oh my God what's happened?' This whole thing to convince people that I was suicidal so that when the MPs caught up with me, well it would be NPs, Naval Police, as they were called, I wouldn't get thrown in prison.

As it was, I was thrown into a psychiatric ward of the Naval Hospital where I was supposed to work during the day, but would be enclosed in this locked ward during the night. I wasn't allowed to go out, I had to stay on the base, and I had to do this, that and the other, because I was still under age, I was still under eighteen. Which of course was the worst thing that had ever happened to me in my entire life. I was in prison as far as I was concerned. During the day I would go and work in the theatre; quite interesting work actually as it was the main plastic surgeon and he'd done many, many GIs.

They had had enough of me by then because I was starting to become difficult, and starting to show what I thought were classic signs of all that I'd read about: paranoia, schizophrenia, manic depression. It was completely freaking them out. The doctors were saying 'oh my God' under their breath, and the one doctor who had to do it said 'That's enough I can't cope with him anymore.' So he went to the Surgeon Captain who was in charge of the whole hospital base, and said either he goes or I resign. The Captain phoned my parents and said you've got to bring him back to England. Things were arranged and when they came to collect me – 2 NPs – I was escorted to the plane because they knew I would try to escape. They took me by Naval Police Car to the airport and the Captain's leaving words were 'Goodbye, you're going home now', then he turned to the two NPs and said, 'If either of you come back and that man is not on the plane, you will be out of the service, it will be more than your life is worth.' So I was kept under the strictest supervision, practically handcuffed, and escorted onto the plane. I flew home to England, oh God, and had years and years of indecision.

Which led you down many paths and eventually allowed you to foray into the world of rent yourself?

I felt that I wasn't getting anywhere, and I wanted to do something different. My last, but one, boyfriend, Peter, with whom I had a very open relationship suggested that one way of earning some money would be – OK, let's not beat around the bush with this, I was skint, I needed to get money, and the best way you can do this is go and be an escort.

I met two American guys in Heaven, and one of them was over here with someone famous who shall remain nameless, and travelling with him. We met him and had a wonderful night, really lovely personality, wonderful. They didn't have anywhere to stay in London, so I gave them my flat in Earl's Court to live in for the week. They were great, they came out with us and we had a wonderful time, and they said 'Why don't you come over and go do what he does?' He was an actual escort. He was also an interior designer and very good, very well known, but this was extra cash. Which is the normal thing for American gay boys to do. They all do now, they work as escorts. If they're good-looking, they're going to make money where they can. And it's a service that's provided, it's a service that is needed, so it keeps people; it's wonderful, it's such a relaxed attitude that American people have. He said 'Come over and work for X who runs the agency in Philadelphia and he'll get work for you. A good-looking boy like you.'

So it was all arranged, and Pete said 'Go, it's the only way you're going to earn money.' So I went over for ten days as a 'guest' escort from London. It was a bit difficult at first, but I soon realised it wasn't a sexual thing with these men. All they wanted was company, they wanted to feel wanted: someone to talk to, someone to relate to. Because it was difficult for them. The ones where sex was involved were no-hassle sex; it was sex that they didn't have to go out to bars for and work for. It was someone they could just relieve themselves with. They had the lifestyle and the money, they could afford to do that; they could just do it and it would be all over.

What I found from the very beginning, which is really interesting about it, was that you could talk to these men. They needed to feel wanted, which is exactly what I needed, anyway, at the same time. I was used to that, and I was able to do that. *Very* comfortable and very easy, so I liked this. I was getting paid a lot of money. I did that for ten days, had a very successful time and made quite a few thousand dollars, and came back. Peter, my boyfriend who I was living with at the time, said 'Well this seems to be what you should be doing, and I think you should go out. You know, I'm not going to be able to keep you because you're not working, I think you should go and do this.'

So there I was. I'd just come back and Peter and I were not really hitting it off, I suppose. I didn't realise at the time, because I was madly in love with the guy and he said 'you should go'. For *him*. Mostly. So I planned a six-month tour of America, as an international travelling escort from England. It turned out to be the most interesting five-and-a-half months of my life. I started off in New York, and worked for one of the big agencies where it's *really* hard and really competitive, and the guys, really edgy guys, very streetwise, look after themselves. They don't take any shit from anybody, they know exactly what they're asking, and everything is very upfront. Then on to Chicago, where everything's changing, everything becomes subversive. It's mostly straight men that you're working with, that are married with families, that have lived very closet lifestyles. Their only way of getting into the gay world is to have an escort.

The guy that ran the agency ran it on a freephone, toll-free number. This guy was the biggest crook that ever walked on God's earth. He operated from LA, which no one knew; no one ever met him. He used one of these escorts that had been working for him for a long time to interview all the new escorts. He had over a hundred guys working for him every day, who were doing at least five or six jobs a day for him. He was making *at least* twenty-five to thirty thousand dollars a day from his operation and he was ripping them off. He'd make sure that guys that he knew were leaving or going to try and find someone else, did as many jobs to be paid for as possible. He'd get someone to collect their money, which sometimes was over a thousand dollars and he'd take the thousand dollars away. They'd then get their cut out of it and the guys would just run off and disappear. And that was the end. That was the sort of merchant he was.

So I flew to Hawaii and landed in Honolulu. Phoned up some agency there, although the detectives were really trying to close them down. So I booked into a hotel right on Wakiki Beach and thought I'll just enjoy my holiday here. I had a fabulous time, met a few film producers there and worked a few jobs for the agency, but not much work really. So I thought, time to get out, I think California is now the place to go. Off to California, where I worked in Out of Hollywood and obviously you can imagine the people and the names that crop up there. Because of my accent and the way I looked (which is very un-American but in a way very compatible with American looks), but especially the way I spoke, got on *really* well. Made a little bit of money, but made a lot of friends.

That's when Pete came out, for his ten-day holiday, supposedly with me, and spent the whole ten days totally ignoring me. I then realised that something was up with us. Obviously this wasn't quite what I was expecting from him and I thought 'What am I doing this for? Please, why, why am I doing this?' I then went back up to San Francisco, where things were rather unfortunate for me; it was a rather harrowing time I spent there.

At the time I was in San Francisco, I found the whole community had grouped together as one big family and become very insular, very protective of their own little circle; almost like being in a kibbutz, if you like. It was like a totally enclosed gay community, totally self-supporting. They have one of the largest percentages, or did, of death from AIDS, but are also one of the largest self-supporting groups of people anywhere in the world, and they had become very suspicious of outsiders. Straight people especially, but even those not straight. I found it very sad because I think they missed out on an awful lot of what was happening worldwide, as far as acceptance of gay people. Because it's gradually becoming more and more acceptable everywhere; in some places it's not unfortunately, but in their case they really separated themselves. They've got a very powerful lobby on a lot of councils, and the mayor is gay, and all that. But I found them very old-fashioned in their approach; I find gay men in

San Francisco very seventies in their attitude, that attitude of we are being aggressive. Everywhere else there's a mingling of gay people with straight people. You can feel it everywhere now, this acceptance, and gay people are spreading out, in a way cross-matching everywhere. There, they're still 'We are gay and we're staying here and we can't let anyone in.'

So I was very uncomfortable there, and left and went back to LA for a few days. And I partied, partied, partied, with all the stars in West Hollywood, and I was there for the demonstrations before the Oscars against the Sharon Stone movie, *Basic Instinct*. All the gay activists were saying that it was anti-gay and that it was portraying lesbians in a very bad light. So I was THERE, I was actually part of all of those demonstrations, obviously blowing whistles and all that sort of thing, which was faaabulous, being in Hollywood, while all this is happening, two days before the Oscars. The actual Oscar day I really desperately would have loved to have gone to, just to see all the stars and everything, but my flight was the last day I could go, and I had to go to Miami, so I flew out. *Rushed* and booked into the South Beach in Miami, and watched the Oscars on TV.

Then there it was, the Gay Mecca: Miami, South Beach. It was as though the whole world, the most beautiful men on the planet, had all congregated into one small area. They were from every country in the world. It wasn't like LA, which is very California; they all come from California – well New York and California. It was Europeans, Asians, Australians, Canadians, all the people from LA there. Madonna's got a house right on the beach there and Versace has this beautiful old colonial-style villa, so it's become THE stretch. It's about 800 metres of frontage all in art deco buildings.

I didn't have an agent in Miami because I hadn't seen any previous advertising, so I looked up this guy in their local phone book and he said 'Oh yeah, come around for your interview.' Of course he was immediately fascinated by the accent, and said 'I want you for porno movies, we want you to do this,' because he was the agent for Falcon Movies. So they took all these photographs and sent them away to head office.

In the meantime, he'd taken a very unhealthy interest in me; he was a very gorgeous man, an ex-escort himself. Stunning looking. I'd really fallen for him. So I ended up, instead of just working for him, *living* with him the whole time I was in Miami. Sleeping with this man and working for him in the day-time. All these escorts kept phoning up saying 'Why aren't we getting any fabulous jobs any more, why aren't we doing this and that?' But I'd been flown down to Key West, flown down to here and there. I had more flights from Miami to all these fabulous overnight resorts, then I did the whole time I was in the States. Most of the air miles that I did came from Miami. And it was fascinating, because he picked out all these really nice people. I met some *wonderful* people, and I had the best time of the whole time I was in the States, working out in Miami. I earned a lot of money there as well.

Then up to Atlanta for a couple of days: I didn't like Atlanta. I felt as though I was in the deep South, plus a hundred; it was a really heavy atmosphere, very homophobic, very racist. It was just their whole attitude, even in a big city.

Then back to Philadelphia, my alma mater of the States. Funnily enough, for an English person in Philadelphia, although it's a sixty per cent black population and really not the historical place that it was, it still holds this immense European culture. A wonderful orchestra, wonderful artistic culture and everything else. I had the best time there and met some wonderful people and stayed there for another month and a half.

I finished off in New York, where I had the most drugged weekend of my life. I ended up arriving in New York, stayed with my friend Kurt, one of the two boys I'd originally met in London, who had an apartment in New York. We went out for a weekender, which started on a Friday night with a big party. Then it was the White Party the next day, which is like a *huuuge* gay party that they have, with everybody dressed in white obviously, and there were lots of drugs flying around, off your face. Then to the Sound Shop at South Battery, for their birthday party, so it was an all-nighter and an all-dayer. It went on from 3 o'clock in the morning, all day and all night, until about 9 o'clock the following evening. And I met the guy that invented Special K, which was the big drug in New York then. He also produced a new drug called Product 19, which is the powdered form of Special K; cocaine, speed, a tiny bit of E in it as well. Phew! This amazing drug. And also this LSD drug called Green Pyramid, which are tiny little green crystals of LSD, which is *the* most powerful drug that I've ever had. I was *completely* on another planet for three days. Completely gone. I came out of this, and thought get me out of here!

I decided I'd better come back to London, so I caught a flight back and Peter met me at the airport. I had this fabulous job offered to me before I left in New York, hairdressing in this salon between

Philadelphia and New York, but I said 'No, I can't.' I got on the plane and went home to Peter, and at the airport he told me it was all over.

I arrived back, and it wasn't the fact that I'd been away for so many months, it was like coming home, but to be told that when you're at the airport? Or driving between the airport as you go home, that it's all over and he's found somebody else. He wanted me to move out that day, the day I arrived back. It was so devastating. So I moved out and into another story.

My life has never seemed so boring.

I admit I was spellbound throughout his tales. Steve is a consummate storyteller and I felt as though I was living it with him; pretty unusual, considering the experiences and topics dealt with. I wonder why we find these stories so fascinating, and yet rush morally to condemn those that have lived them? I don't particularly yearn to become a rent boy, not that it's really a choice, but wild horses could not have dragged me away from hearing all of the sordid, fantastic details. We're all voyeurs in some fashion, perhaps because we don't want to 'lower' ourselves, but still thrill to the idea. Because it's living, *and perhaps also because it allows us to feel virtuous in turn.*

I can't condemn Steve's activities, firstly because I don't think that is an appropriate gesture of gratitude for taking me into his confidence, but more importantly because I admire him. He's a funny, energetic, warm person, which flies in the face of all of our preconceived notions about hardened people 'like that'. As he has illustrated, rent is a market transaction; it can doubtless screw up the buyers as much as the sellers. It all depends on personal strength, which Steve, compared with Teddi's stories of fifteen-year-olds, managed to turn to his advantage. I'm fairly certain that I would fall into the 'screwed-up' category; I don't think I have that sort of toughness. Perversely, it makes me respect Steve all the more.

Sunday, 22nd November

Steve has got it together with his now out-of-the-closet admirer, ironically also named Pete. He seems enchanting and sane, at least until it comes to his choice of worship-worthy objects and then he falls head over heels for our tart with a heart. What an induction. At least it means that Steve and his ex-lover will stop trying to beat the hell out of each other at the club, although Steve claims that *he* is the one being constantly ambushed, drifting around in an Ophelia-like haze only to be repeatedly mauled by the Big Bad Wolf.

Video-taped the show this week, although I think we may cut out the segment where a snockered Jason momentarily steps off the stage during 'Land of Make Believe'. Although every air molecule was causing our inebriated unicorn to wobble slightly, you'd probably miss it, as some poor man seated on a barstool ended up involuntarily offering his thigh as an alternative floorboard for Jason's piercing stiletto.

Carla has apparently actually seen Pablo's videotape of *Back to Havana* and has declared it 'brilliant'; no doubt she was referring to her own numbers. Either way, the chance of our being granted a viewing looks incredibly remote, much less getting our hands on a copy. Surprise, surprise.

Latest developments include Ruby's negotiations with some charity doyenne in Hong Kong for us to come out and do a season, feted by all and paid astronomical amounts. Why can I not see this coming off? The big picture is always very appealing but we inevitably seem to get entangled in too many practicalities en route. Sometimes I do feel like we are permanently floating around in some kind of fantasy bubble.

For now a winter wonderland is going to be our next stop. We have to amend the second half of the show to incorporate a Christmas section, which means a rehash of old tapes and costumes all at Ruby's expense. I think the office gives her something like £500 for the whole brouhaha, which just about covers changes to the sound tape.

She also decorates the entire club out of her own pocket, while Jason and I sit and marvel at her own peculiar brand of madness and the extreme good fortune of the office to have found someone who actually views the club sentimentally as opposed to in her own financial terms.

Sunday, 13th December

My whirlwind radio tour is over, thank God. It's been a crazed week, doing alternative Christmas brunches by day and generally burning the wick at both ends. Have developed a vicious cold, which is unpleasant enough during broadcasts but especially a joy when trying to sing and dance without blowing your nose. I remember attempting this intricate manoeuvre for the first time, only to be rewarded with a Kleenex covered in glitter and a face that looked like I'd been dipped in a vat of Hawaiian Punch. Experience has taught me to keep sniffling, even if it means that I resemble a demented coke fiend.

My broadcasting employers have expressed a desire to extend my temporary contract for another year, which is a nice, reaffirming feeling; I must be doing this well after all. We've also added LBC performances every other week, although what a straight news station wants with me is still a mystery. I'm happy though, and I can certainly use the money. At £100 per day, the compensations for working day-times are far more apparent than my nightly club work.

Add to this the fact that Alexander is only now, at my insistence, exploring decent job options. The honeymoon's over, and I can't keep carrying the bulk of the financial burden for ever. To be fair, however, he has encouraged me to drop the club and focus on broadcasting, saying that we can manage with less money if it means that I'm happy and my career progresses. If I'm really honest, I suppose I'm too much a creature of comfort – the radio tours are great, but they are only once every six weeks and do not supply a steady enough income.

Car journeys allowed me to re-learn the lyrics of our Christmas show songs, ones that I've only hummed since throwing out my Fisher Price tape recorder. The really beautiful thing is that all my songs are in a completely different range from my own, belonging as they did to other people. Now I'm performing 'Jingle Bells' as a passable impersonation of Alvin and the Chipmunks. Ho, ho, ho. And I may as well start putting away the money that I've just been informed we will not be earning during our Christmas break towards impending larynx surgery.

Performed a gig at Hamilton Place with Ruby for a very chichi group, beautifully done. Any organisation that plies me with champagne from the minute I arrive goes right up in my estimation – I'm so easily won over. Ruby brought along an old friend to help both of us with our costume changes. This took on a rather different interpretation for 'Baby', as Ruby affectionately refers to this hulking man, who proceeded to unzip me every time I'd miraculously managed to get into a complicated outfit. We were changing in the wine cellar, which with its sub-zero temperatures was right up Ruby's alley. Seriously, she must have been a penguin in a former life if her bedroom is anything to go by. You could forget a sandwich in there and find it perfectly preserved three years later. She's always complaining about the club being too hot which, while I can agree in mid-July, does not make me run for the fan in December. As Jason pointed out, 'gale force winds could be blowing through here and you'd think it was warm.'

Add to this all the waiters peeking through regularly and it was like changing outside on Park Lane. Having said that, however, it was fun, I earned a lot of money and, according to Ruby, we had the chance for some good 'mother-daughter' bonding.

Tuesday, 22nd December

Bonding has been extended to a family of six for our last two engagements – Ruby, Misha, Jason, Steve, Marcia and myself. We performed for some huge Christmas party at Thorpe Park, which was downright surreal – walking in the dark, rain pelting on us and our costume bin-liners, past these gigantic plastic cartoon animals. In a totally empty amusement park.

This changed once we got inside the packed main tent. We were nowhere near as spoiled as at our previous function, but they did supply us with a case of wine to celebrate Steve's permanently on-going twenty-ninth birthday. The most hysterical part of the evening were our two bus drivers. I had been the first to meet them and whereas the younger one welcomed the whole idea as quite a laugh, the older one seemed disapprovingly distant. They ended up staying with us in the dressing-room, helping us change and being the campest twosome I could have ever expected. I'm sure I was not the only amazed one, although Ruby was calling them Gladys and Blanche from the minute she got on the bus.

Did our final Christmas function tonight at the Park Lane Hotel, again with non-existent dressing-room facilities, and were forced to reflect upon the fact that PR agencies really haven't got a clue. Except on how to delay paying you, where they come into their own. Merry Christmas.

Sunday, 3rd January 1993

Fantastic New Year, and now barbettes appear to be the catchword of 1993. Or lack of, I should say. Our turnover rate seems to be escalating, not least of all thanks to Pepper's and Tevita's departure. The former is apparently working day-times in a bakery now and Tevita informed me of her intention to get some office temping work.

I'm really proud of them. This has got to be one of the hardest steps. Once the change has occurred it's no great shakes to go around thinking of yourself as a woman and consequently being accepted as such, but they are still in that no-man's-limbo-land. Their boyfriends are a case in point as well – Pepper's is 100 per cent behind her, which is good since she's due for the operation in the very near future. Tevita's seems to be swinging to and fro and making her decision all the more difficult. What a nightmare.

So we've had a barbette conveyor belt set up. Without much success, it has to be said. I never fully appreciated how extraordinarily beautiful and tasteful our queens were until I saw the influx of Elvira lookalikes that have responded to our ads. And those were the convincing ones.

Now we've ended up with two new ones, Nicki and Holly. Nicki being the first and only black barbette besides our past, Detroit-born Kim. Maybe Misha was on to something – there does seem to be a definite lack of black transvestites and drag queens, and perhaps it is a cultural thing.

George was, as always, tremendously helpful, by pawning the decision-making onto Ruby and popping back with helpful warnings along the lines of 'look out, this one has a face like a dog's ass messed up with a brick.' A master of descriptive imagery.

Interview With Mitzi
On Barbettes and JoJo's:
Past and Present

Mitzi is head barbette, so I asked her what she thought of our turnover and what lay behind it.

Generally, I've worked with better. I've worked with a *lot* better.

In what sense, drag or attitude?

Attitude. A lot of the people who come down and work here now, think they can come down, get pissed, have a laugh and get on with it. Well, that's all wrong. You've still got a job to do.

For instance, someone came to work a couple of weeks ago, really, really pissed, and they did the show. Yet on stage they were very scared, because they came back and said 'Oh, I very nearly bumped into Bea, and just an inch off, Bea would have been in the bar.' So I said, 'Well you think about it, you come and you get pissed. We're not allowed these nights off. So if the management see you in that state on your nights off, then they'll stop our nights off. And it's unfair to us.' A lot of people that work here think it's just easy money.

So it is used as a stepping stone?

Slightly. At the moment there's no one here that I feel is using it as a stepping stone – I mean everyone that works here enjoys working here, although we have trouble with a few.

So why do I hear some people talking nostalgically of the days when JoJo was still hostess with the mostest?

Everyone was scared of Jo. Jo was the boss. What Jo said, went. If we came out on the floor and Jo didn't like what we were wearing, she'd send us back to change. And if that meant two or three times . . .

That's the problem with this place now. We haven't got anyone to look up to in drag. I mean, we can look up to Ruby, but Ruby isn't in authority to tell us to go and change.

Because of this political power struggle going on?

Exactly. George has made me head barbette; what I say goes and I'm like, 'So you're telling me that if I don't like what they're wearing I can tell them to go and change?' And he says, 'Well . . . no.' And I'm like, 'Well then why are you giving me this? You're not giving me anything, just another snigger, someone to put the blame on.' Which is fine, it doesn't bother me. I'm very strong in that sense. If someone throws something at me I can usually take it.

I'm always here. If anyone rings me at home, they can always catch me here, no matter what time of the day it is, because I'm always here doing something. Something always needs doing, and no one else will do it except me. If I say to someone 'Would you come in and do something,' they'd be like 'It's not my job, no,' and I'd be like 'Fine, I can't be bothered to argue with you, I'll come in and do it.' I tell you, if I come in and do it and it gets messed up again, there'll be hell to pay, because I'm taking my spare time to do it.

When George ordered everything up off the floor I was the only one that came in every Saturday and scrubbed and mopped the floor. They've got the attitude of 'it's not my job.' Well we've all got to muck in together. That's it, those are the problems I have. I've got no co-operation at all.

I'm not saying there is bad management now because it is being managed really well, but the thing is Jo kept her distance. Jo knew when to say 'Right that's it, this is a business now not a charity, you're here to work for me and if you don't like it you're out.'

The good thing with Jo was that if anyone was giving you hassle, you used to send them to Jo and say 'Look, Mum wants to speak to you,' and then she'd be like 'Now, now, now, don't play with the girls, they've got a job to do. If you want to play with the girls, make arrangements for afterwards.' Whereas now, they just get thrown out, which I think is very unfair.

The trannie-fuckers are on their own, they stand at the bar, and they just stare. Just stare and stare and stare. We do have a laugh with them, but you've got to make it known that you are only there to entertain them and nothing else. I mean if you wanted to, that's fine that's up to you, but with me I always tell them that it's a laugh, let's have a giggle, it's a night out, you've paid so let's have a laugh. Usually we can have a laugh, and it's OK, but if anyone gets out of hand it's 'Call a doorman, let's have them thrown out.' And I think that's unfair, because they just want to have a good time; they're lonely, they've come down here, they like what they see, and they want to be part of it. But the girls we've got down here at the moment are so frigging frigid, they just totally clam up and put barriers up. That's what I mean by taking it too seriously.

So how do your boyfriends deal with this attitude?

Lovers don't like it. If you're going out with someone, they think your attention should be towards them all the time. So if I go up to a customer, bend over and be all camp and flirty with them, he gets wound up. And I explain, 'Well I'm doing my job. That's all I'm doing. I'm going home with you, don't worry.' And he says, 'But how do I know that? How do I know that when I'm not down there . . .?' And I say, 'Well you should trust me.' I'm a terrible flirt, I am. I'm awful.

Have any women ever come down to the club and fallen for you?

Yes, a black girl. We went out on a double date with two black girls. Ha! She wanted me in make-up and stockings.

How about men?

They come down, and we've got legs up to our armpits, hair out to here, good figures, and it's a lot of men's fantasies. Because we all look like models, we've got the perfect shape that a man looks for. Yet he comes down with his girlfriend and we can have a laugh with him *and* we can have a laugh with her. The women ask questions, whereas the men won't. The women will walk up to you, poke you and, when you sort of slap their hands and say 'What do you think you're doing?', they whisper 'I just think you're fab.' They like asking questions, just silly little questions, especially about 'the face'. It's a form of art if you like to call it that. It's my way of expressing myself. If I'm depressed, I could put on such a grim face that people will know I'm not exactly up to par. Yet if I do big eyebrows, big white highlighter, lips out to here, glitter everywhere, I'm in a good mood. You can change your face to reflect the way you feel.

When I first started working here I didn't know a thing about make-up. At all. Pandora did all my make-up the first night I worked here, and it was brilliant. I just couldn't believe it was me! The next night I had to do it myself and I looked a bastard. I did green eyeshadow, I did a little round socket line, and eyebrows up to here which smudged because I didn't do them properly. Since then I've just got better and better.

But it has completely changed since I first started here. For the worse. I would say it's just hanging in there. The novelty's worn off. I mean, I love the place. If it closed down tomorrow, I would cry, I would be so upset. But it hasn't got the appeal that it once had. It's the people who are here, a lot of them take it too seriously.

Do you think that was reflected by all the transsexuals that we suddenly acquired?

Yes. I mean, a lot of people thought 'Oh great, a drag club, I want to be a woman' and use it as a stepping stone. Now they can do that for two years, come and go as a girl, and that's fine; but it's not so good for the club, because the club is primarily a drag club.

So what do you think the audience want when they come down here?

Comedy. They want a laugh. A lot of people are shocked, because I asked someone last week, 'So how did you know what sort of place this is?' They said, 'Oh we just walked in, saw a queue and thought what's happening down there?' And I thought, 'Oh great, so you didn't know it was a drag show?' and they're like 'No we didn't' and I said 'Didn't they tell you on the door?' and they said 'No.' There's no publicity. They look on the billboard outside and they see all these names, girls' names . . . they could be girls.

And this in the middle of a seedy peep show strip. Small wonder they're confused.

Mitzi expressed a sentiment that I've shared for some time now: the club is changing and possibly not for the better. I can't speak for the halcyon 'JoJo' days, having arrived shortly after her departure, but I would agree that we are becoming too commercial and in the worst possible way. We are becoming our image, without the depth to support it; we are providing the glitzy service our undemanding clientele expect, but on a superficial level. The outrageousness, the fun, the excitement, have been subdued, and I still can't, for the life of me, put my finger on the reason why.

I can certainly understand the barbettes' lackadaisical approach towards work. I'm only in the club between three and four hours a night and I feel fed up; if I earned as little as they do, and got twice as much grief, I'd probably have exactly the same attitude. In my case, I only answer to the office and Ruby; the barbettes also have to contend with being full-time employees, compared to our self-employed status, and having George constantly breathing down their necks.

George is a good overseer, but I think the office may have miscalculated in not installing another hostess to replace JoJo. People expect to see the eponymous Madame and I think Mitzi has a valid point in suggesting that the barbettes need this Mother-type figure. One with more power in the running of the club than Ruby, whose domain, despite her close ties to the office, really does not extend beyond the stage.

Sunday, 24th January

We've started rehearsals for our next show, appropriately entitled *Far From Reality*, which life is increasingly starting to feel like.

At least this title won't muck up any exhibitions, like *40 Years a Queen* did. I gather this was the planned name for Her Majesty's exhibition at the Albert Hall, cancelled at the last minute due to 'an identical show currently running with conflicting interests'. I can only assume they were referring to ours, in which case this comment is testament to the great British art of understatement.

We've got in two new barbettes, a beautiful Filipino called Angel and the roughest, toughest Scotsman, delicately christened Amber. Also two new boys, replacing Zach and Marcia. Zach plans to finally take the stunt world by storm; perhaps stealth and surprise may be more effective. Marcia similarly plans to embark upon a dramatic career, and has enrolled in college acting classes. It's interesting to note that these are two of the very few cast members in my experience, besides the Manchester crowd, that have left JoJo's of their own volition.

So now we have Jake, who used to be in the show fifty million years ago and refers to himself as an 'Actooor' – give me a break – and Ada, who is in the company of *Miss Saigon* and in possession of a stunning voice, which he will be putting to good use in our *Joseph* medley. The whole show wrapped up in three-and-a-half minutes.

Ada, campest thing in Christendom but with a body to die for, was listening with great interest as Steve recounted his first exposure to being a G-stringed boy.

'I arrived, and suddenly I had two days' rehearsal for a whole show . . . and me never having been on stage, never having been on stage in NO clothes, G-string, the lot, flabby assed. In those days I was in the show with a boy named Rocky and Jake, who's in the show now. And there were these two gorgeous, stunning boys. Like drop dead gorgeous. And me. So I was slightly intimidated by them and the fact that they'd rehearsed, and they'd done it all. I was staying with Marcia, and it was like "I can't do this, I can't possibly go up in a G-string, blah blah blah . . ." You have to know you are basically there for the girls. And the gay men. The opening night, I remember, I went and did the first half and the second day we rehearsed the second half, and went in.

'And the first night I went in, and I'll always remember, "Hold Tight", that finale number, and they said "down, DOWN!" I had to go on my knees and I went down too early, so that everybody just fell over me into this big pile up, darling. There was me on the floor, and everybody on top of me in this *huge* pile up. That's all I can remember, and that opening night was so camp. The first few months I was really finding my feet, and then I began to realise that it was, you know – faaab.'

Ada looked reassured. I think.

IV

Far From Reality

Typically boring production weekend. Our last night was quite a joy, Claire moping around because she's been replaced by Michael, dresser back in the days of *Continental Capers*. A completely adorable pisshead, whose one advantage over Claire is that he will be capable of propping up Ruby and her duvet-esque Sumo wrestler costume for 'If you like Sushi, like I like Sushi'. Claire's attempts to deal with a sozzled Ruby tended to result in a flattened dresser, squashed somewhere between the costume rails and the empty brandy-bottle-laden bin.

This show really is the most aptly named one to date. Ruby's inspired opening had us situated in the middle of a, wait for it, *farmyard*. We look suitably naff in our drag-queen-down-on-the-farm garb, although Misha and I are let off lightly in our white satin, little-girl dresses, with lace bandana and blonde pig-tail wigs. The white stilettos were the hardest part to accept, although Jason has to hoedown in a blue satin overall, glittered combat boots and a straw hat. Compared to him and Ruby, similarly attired, Misha and I look like fashion plates.

Bizarre opening songs include 'Down on the Farm' (surprise, surprise), 'Old Miss Ruby' and 'Out of Town', all accompanied by a dancing pantomime cow. We really earned our wages learning these ditties, only to be followed by Ruby and Steve, the latter posing as an amazingly convincing piece of poultry in 'Chick, Chick, Chicken, Lay a Little Egg for Me'. This number *is* an egg, if you ask me, and I think Steve is the hands-down winner of the 'Bastard Costume' award for this show.

It's a close call, though, in 'The Ugly Bug Ball'. Jason has given us the most impossible steps to do, considering the types of costumes we're in. Actually, I tell a lie: everybody else's are semi-manageable, only Steve's and mine threaten to dislocate parts of our anatomy. In Steve's case, it's more of a sweat-a-thon issue: he is bundled up as a furry caterpillar, covered with little baby-socked feet. I get to be the spider, which initially sounded very sexy but now sees me strapped into an eight-legged hoola-hoop – and here was I thinking I'd seen the last of those plastic monsters when *Forty Years* ended.

Jason is the horse-fly and Misha, a ladybug. The prospect of being a comparatively cute insect had the trannie excited, until she discovered that we had maliciously designed her a crash helmet as a headpiece, with two little spring-suspended skulls as antennae. She immediately tied bows on them, but the reaction was hysterical.

We move into a rain theme next, and of course *I* get the STUPIDEST number in the whole bloody show: 'Pit, Pat, Pit, Little April Showers', in sixties sequinned mini-dress, transparent plastic Mac, umbrella and hat. The finishing touch, however, has got to be the huge white Wellies, which force the four barbettes and me to shuffle through our tap routine while trying not to smash the stage lights with our umbrella tips.

The fairness of our set-up is illustrated by giving Jason and Misha drop dead, sex goddess, black and silver 'chuj' (read glamour) outfits and a post-1970 song, 'It's Raining Men'. Mother then slinks on in similar, albeit more, costume material, with a matching boa wrapped around her head and trailing down her back, for 'Stormy Weather'.

In a mad dash for 'modern material', we zoom into our *Grease* sequence. I enter first in a red satin bikini bra and matching slitted skirt, with red chiffon jacket and Rizzo-style black wig. Biker girl from hell, my alter ego. The boys and I launch into a raunchy 'Greased Lightning', surprising in light of my naff songs so far, after which the remaining cast enters for Jason and Ruby's 'Summer Lovin''. Our romantic lovers are decked out in leopard print and green lapelled material; Ruby's blonde wig flies everywhere, as does her bikini top/skirt combo, but these are remarkably well ordered compared to her lyrics. Misha pierces a few new eardrums in 'Look at Me, I'm Sandra Dee' and, for once, has lines she can relate to: 'I don't drink, I don't swear, I don't rat my hair, I get ill from one cigarette'. She's tried to have smoking banned from backstage on health and safety grounds which, logical though it is, meant a head-on collision with the bulk of the smoking (and now fuming) cast. I see Misha's point and hear his on-going hacking cough, but I'm not overjoyed by this edict myself. We can't leave backstage during the show and it is especially during the interval that you want to unwind with a cigarette. This move is making Misha a bit unpopular at the moment.

Back to the show and our finale, 'Elegance', followed by Ruby buzzing around us glorious sunflowers in her furry bee costume.

We wear these floral explosions on our heads and they are sizeable enough to repeatedly knock us senseless when trying to shimmy through low doorways. Our stems consist of long, green, shiny, slitted halter dresses, which are replaced by UV-lit skeleton costumes for the beginning of the second act. From there we gallop through Jason's 'Ushka Dara', which bears no semblance to any Turkish I have ever heard, and my Arabian dancing-girl 'Baubles, Bangles and Beads', with the barbettes. Lovely song, but so flat that I've decided to make it a surreal drug song and dispense Smarties around the audience.

On to a stupendous 'Sand Dance', with Ruby, Jason and Misha in stripey old-fashioned swimming trunks, sporting Turkish hats and hopping around in a sandbox. Then the spectacular 'Joseph' and 'One Night in Bangkok', followed by a cretinous 'We are Siamese'. Misha and Bea with gold-painted, upside-down funnels on their heads. As Jason quipped, 'You look like the tin man in drag.' Next we're in Japan for the slickest visual number of the show: Jason, Ada and Steve, in red and black, whirling gymnastic twirlers (long sticks with a long material strip for twirling) to 'Made in Japan'.

I get to follow a heaving Ruby and four barbettes, onto what remains of the stage after their rousing, Sumo-style 'If You Like Sushi', with my manic 'Supermarket in Old Peking'. A *very* devious, if not downright nasty, device to keep me sober until the end of the show, by putting in a song that redefines fast-forward. Ruby:1, Bea:0.

Misha and Jason lust after their 'Japanese Boy', in the three-foot high Japanese headdresses that we've already had to start sellotaping onto our heads to keep in place. In transparent blue kimonos that would make a Geisha girl blush, Ruby leads us all through 'Chinese Laundry Blues' and into 'Chop Suey'. I reckon this show's title was chosen for the simple reason that it allowed Ruby and Jason to throw together any and every screwball idea they ever wanted to do and create one chaotic whole.

Wednesday, 10th February

We are quickly discovering that dancer Jake, and I use this expression very loosely, is completely tone-deaf. A real pleasure to stand next to in company numbers. Then again he starts off at a disadvantage, in the shape of an incomprehensible sound system. For example, we've only now discovered that the real title of the song played non-stop in the club last autumn, tentatively christened 'Cruise with the Wildebeast' or alternatively 'Fucking the

Aubergine', is in fact 'Be what you want to be'. Says it all really.

Despite that raging defence, Jake does appear quite hopeless. Being the back half to Ada's front in the pantomime cow routine doesn't give him too much opportunity to balls up the moves, and it was decided that Ada should teach him harmony for the 'Joseph' section. When he still hadn't mastered 'It was red and yellow and green' ad nauseam, Jason commented on the failed mission, to which Ada snapped that it was like 'teaching the Pope to be a Protestant'. Jake announced that he was going to mimic my moves like a parrot and Mitzi responded 'Why not? You sing like one.' The poor guy's confidence has been systematically shattered.

This is not entirely true, actually, as it would take a small tank to make even a dent in that boy's ego. If I thought Zach laid it on heavily, I have since had an opportunity to revise that opinion with Jake's non-stop pick-up attempts on anything with a pulse, including myself, as token fellow heterosexual. I think a coma might approximate my reaction to his sexual allure, although God knows he does very well with all the women that come down. I think our little stud must average at least four a week.

Saturday, 13th February

Did an AIDS benefit at the Limelight last night with Ruby, Jason, Misha and myself tottering along, schlepping bin-bags down an applauding Old Compton Street thanks to a lack of taxis.

Fairly successful, typically sozzled, and vaguely recall meeting Tony Hall. Or so I was informed by Misha afterwards. I was having way too much fun watching Jason try to extricate himself from mad woman Angie's clutches. Angie, ex-backing singer to Nina Hagen and complete mental case, comes over regularly from Germany to visit her 'husband'. That is to say, an unmarried Jason. Her usual party trick is to arrive at least once during each run in a wedding gown – and with her flaming fuschia hair and six-inch platforms we ain't talkin' Laura Ashley.

She cruised off with Erasure on their Canadian tour last August when she decided that Jason didn't appreciate her enough. The man is gay, what do you want? According to Jason, she pays for his toys, he lets her sleep in the same bed, and that's the extent of it. Sex does not even come into it, which, as a good unmarried daughter-in-law, she probably discussed with Jason's mother when she came down on her birthday last year. I hope Angie enjoyed her responsibilities – 'I haf to kum for my mudder-in-law' – as she was paying for everything: the hotel, the dinner, most of her presents.

Apparently she's even been to Jason's home to stay and I can just imagine her fitting into a small village. It is her misfortune to have had several operations for breast cancer and we animatedly discuss this in German every time she comes down. I have to say, I think she's great. A complete scream. Jason's decided she'll probably outlive him anyway, although that's not her argument. 'You haf a rich voman, who's *kraaazy* fur you, doesn't care zat you're not, even zat you're a poof, und vill soon die und leaf you everysing – vat more could you vant?' she yells.

As Jason has glumly informed me, 'The truth is that Angie has declared that when she dies of cancer she will shoot me and we'll be buried side by side, for all eternity, in our own red glittered coffin.'

Now there's a thought to take into Valentine's Day.

Sunday, 21st February

One person whose *volte face* is continuing to surprise us is Steve's. He and Pete seem to have settled into domestic bliss remarkably well and, joint sexual escapades aside, appear totally fixated upon one another. This commitment has astounded everybody, but I attribute a lot of it to Pete who is an incredible person. Also quite a successful career man.

A casual comment by Steve the other night made me decide to interview Pete. He and Ada were discussing some character they'd cruised while out clubbing, called Pepe, and described him glowingly to me as 'the handsomest man in the world – straight in Italy, gay over here.' I had to laugh at this glorious bisexual contradiction and decided that, as I've been getting to know Pete very well, I really should get an angle on what coming out of the closet and being launched into this unreal world is like.

Interview With Pete
On Coming Out

Pete began by explaining his background.

Very straight, I think, very *proper*. Bit middle-of-the-road, middle-class, quite work-orientated. Work dominated my life. I always had a very big circle of friends but I never really had any long-term relationships; the longest was three months.

What was this due to?

Incredible intolerance. I mean, as soon as a relationship started to involve any compromise from my side, I'd end it. Normally in a very cowardly way; I'd run away. But that was fundamentally because I wasn't really very interested in having a relationship, I was far too . . . on my own. The strange thing is I don't really feel now that I'm in a relationship with a capital R; it's just something that has evolved. I don't see the same pressures, responsibilities and obligations in this relationship that I always felt I ought to have in a straight relationship beforehand. Those relationships, in a straight sense, were always almost like marriage. There were so many rules.

Because it was stereotypical?

Yes, very stereotypical, especially from where I came from. Going out with someone, and conforming to that, was a huge sacrifice to my personal life, which I was, repeatedly, never really able or willing to make.

But I don't see this now. The benefits patently outweigh the down side, otherwise I wouldn't still be doing it.

So when did it suddenly strike you that maybe this was not a bad idea? How did that come about?

I went out to dinner with a friend of mine and we had a very pissed evening, talking about both coming up to being thirty. We both decided we'd done this, we'd done that, we'd done the other, and we were feeling quite smug; it was a very self-satisfied conversation. This woman's quite a successful career woman and she's getting married next year. So we'd decided we'd done all these things, but there was this thing ticking away at the back of my mind, that there is this whole area of my personality I've never really explored. And because it was a very late and pissy evening, I put her in a taxi, sent her home to her boyfriend, and went out to explore the other side. Which is the night I met Steve.

It was hideous, absolutely hideous. I put her in a cab on Old Compton Street and went off to the Village. I got a flier for whichever club was opening that night – at the time there was a new gay club happening all the time. I was always very familiar with the gay scene because so many of the people I work with are gay and so many of the bars we go to are gay bars because there's a nicer atmosphere there than in the straight bars, especially in Soho. So I was very comfortable about it, picked up a flier and got in a cab and went to this club which opened at about midnight. It was called 'Dick' and it was a turner, a Tuesday nighter.

I stood there in this queue to get in with people that even in my most distracted moment I couldn't have found physically attractive, and thought 'Why am I doing this?' I stayed there for what must have been a good three hours and I was ready to leave.

There were a couple of people there who I'd seen who were quite interesting, but I didn't do anything and I must have looked like a fish out of water. I mean I was looking very straight, I'd come straight from work; I wasn't in a baggy cable-knit sweater and beige corduroy slacks but I might as well have been in terms of the gay scene. Very conspicuous and felt it.

I carried on drinking and just as I was about to leave, was cruised by this blond body-builder across the room, scantily clad, and that was Steven. He'd just finished at JoJo's. And we had this incredibly macabre dance of the seven veils across the room, where we moved a bit closer and carried on staring, and moved a bit closer, and eventually we were standing next to each other. It took about half an hour for us to actually make physical contact. I think I brushed his arm or something and he turned around and there were these physical fireworks. I mean it was absolutely *electric*, the most amazing physical experience I've ever had. Spontaneously. In the middle of this nightclub – ghastly nightclub as well, I hate it.

I was living with Suzie, my flatmate, and he was living with his then boyfriend, so neither venue was particularly appropriate to consummate the evening. So we ended up going back to my old office and shagging on the floor.

I was sitting absolutely spellbound at this stage, and voyeuristically asked him what it felt like the first time, especially being accustomed to women.

Very exciting. I mean, there was a huge amount of naughtiness involved as well. It was very illicit and naughty and exciting. I was *desperate* to tell someone about it and I couldn't. I didn't tell anyone for a while, I think.

Why? Because you had primarily straight friends?

Well, not primarily straight friends but 100 per cent friends who thought *I* was straight. So there was no one I could go to and say 'You won't *believe* what happened.' Eventually I got in touch with an old friend, a freelance designer, who's a woman and who is just such good fun, and we got pissed on a Friday night a couple of weeks following it all. I told her, and she thought it was the most excitingly naughty story she'd ever heard.

And you felt that she would understand?

No, it wasn't a question of her understanding. The biggest barrier I think I found in coming out is that as soon as you become gay, you become 'the gay one'. And all other aspects of your personality, of your life, and anything interesting about you, becomes sublimated by being gay.

Is that how you had viewed gay people previously?

Probably, yes. I think I was as guilty of that as anyone else. Instead of someone being the brown-haired one, or the tall one, or the good-looking one, or the clever one, or the nuclear physicist one, they're the gay one. And you always become the gay one first. I wasn't interested or excited enough by the gay scene or gay issues or gay anything else to suddenly become a flag bearer for that. So I was very keen that it shouldn't change anyone's perception of me, and I sort of trickled it out over the next couple of months.

To a certain extent, being gay means a lot of things to a lot of different people. To me it's a purely sexual orientation. It's not a political way of life, and it's not a cultural thing. It's just who you go to bed with. By preference.

This came as news to me, having always thought that there must be a psychological change in how you approach daily life.

No you don't. I don't think so. I'd *strive* to attempt not to. I'd resent it if the fact was that I was doing so. But in terms of what gay is and how it happens, I'm fairly sure it's something that's acquired. There's a latency in every individual, and then if something in their life happens that pushes them one way or the other . . . Although I'm from a very Darwinian school of scientific training, I don't subscribe to the fact that you're either born one way or the other and there are so many more chromosomes or a chemical in your brain. It just doesn't add up to me.

So how does the background fit in?

Very, very close, by a lot of standards quite puritanical middle-class. Father worked for a bank, my mother was a teacher. We lived in a suburb near Hampstead and I went to a boys' day school, did exams and went to university. Really quite prosaic middle-class background, relatively methodist. It wasn't what I'd call a liberal background.

So I take this to mean that you haven't yet told your parents?

Definitely not. There is no point in telling them about people they don't know. The way I'd rather do it is to introduce them to Steve, like they've got to know André and people at work, and for the relationship to sort of dawn upon them. Because the concept of gay that they have in their minds is very different from the reality and I'm not really the person to educate them. They can find that reality, although I think they're very conditioned in their views on that sort of thing.

Are your parents flexible enough to accept this eventually?

Their concept of a gay man is a cross between Danny La Rue and a dirty Mac flasher on Hampstead Heath. They see it as something that's very perverse and quite disgusting physically; but also something synonymous with sadness, loneliness, early death, danger and rejection, and as parents they wouldn't be chuffed about that kind of lifestyle. Also because of AIDS. My parents would dearly love grandchildren and there's only one way they're going to get them and it's not going to be from Steve. So yes, that will prey quite heavily on their minds.

They are quite self-sacrificing people. They sacrificed a lot to put me through school, they sacrificed a lot for my education and they are now at an age where they are starting to put things away for me to inherit. My mother buys jewellery to give to my wife-to-be. When they're refurbishing their cottage down in Wales, they have a bedroom for me and my wife and a nursery-style bedroom for children – for Christmases and things like that. That is an 'agenda', if you like, that it would take a fairly big shake to change their minds about.

But I find that sexuality is such a plastic and motile thing that I've not pinned my flag to a pillar. I may change my mind later on. I'm very deliberately and aggressively independent about how I'm classified. I'd rather not be classified and to be classified as gay or straight I'm very uncomfortable with.

What concepts of gays had you grown up with before that fateful night?

Early on, a schoolboy concept of gay was a dirty old man, basically. That was what gay was and I was probably as aggressive a queer-basher as everyone else. It's funny – one of the guys at school came out when he was about six years old and is now still incredibly gay, very out. I gave him a very hard time at school. He's now a very good mate of mine and I go out with him a lot, although we've got relatively little else in common. He was knocked over, I mean *gutted*, totally bowled over. It was a surprise for a lot of people, because I don't conform to a lot of gay stereotypes. Well I didn't then, although I probably do now.

I think once the seed had been sown in my mind that it was something I needed to do; it becomes silly to refer to a night as 'that night', because it was a process. It was something that had occurred to me, there was a worm nibbling at my brain if you like. As soon as that happened it was relatively easy and I think that the reason most people don't that have such inclinations or inquisitive feelings is fear. I had nothing really to fear. I was confident about my social life, about the company, about the people who I was close to, to know that it would make as little difference as it has made.

As somebody who has had a foot in both camps, how would you begin to compare a homosexual relationship with a heterosexual relationship? Is it the same thing?

No. It couldn't be more different. I mean there's almost no grounds on which you can compare them. I almost have a Pavlovian response to straight relationships because I find them so hide-bound, and gay relationships . . . Well, talking of gay relationships, I have a lot of gay friends, I have a gay lover, but it's almost that the gayness is different. It's so hard to articulate. Because of the nature of me being straight before I met Steve, and I'm now having a relationship with Steve, the relationship makes its own rules.

I'm fairly certain that we are not in a classical gay relationship. It's certainly not based on anything like any heterosexual relationships I know of or have heard of, and certainly not been in. But it's nice because it's a relationship where the terms are made along the way; he hasn't brought his preconceptions from the gay world and I haven't brought any from the straight world. Although we probably did in the beginning, but knocked them out.

So define a classical gay relationship by your standards.

They tend to ape heterosexual relationships. They tend to be relatively monogamous, husband and wife; there'll be a top and a bottom, there'll be a joint mortgage, living south of the river, go to the gay club twice a month, drink in gay bars, subscribe to gay papers, go on gay holidays. But otherwise slot into a relatively straight world.

How is your relationship different?

Well, we're by no means monogamous. We live together spasmodically, we go out almost every night. I suppose the most fundamental thing is that we're not faithful to each other sexually. That places a lot of burden on the other sides of the relationship in terms of commitment.

So we're talking about friendship in many ways. A lot of people would argue, and maybe that's a preconception, that gay individuals tend to be promiscuous. Would you agree with that?

Individuals? Yes, definitely. Far more so than heterosexuals. I mean I've probably slept with more people in the last month than I've slept with in my life to date. And that's been true ever since I met Steve.

Is that through choice? Because you wanted to or because of the nature of the relationship?

Yes. I mean, every now and then Steve will bring someone home, and I'm expected to perform with this person. I enjoy myself, but I couldn't claim that it was my choice. But yes, I suppose ultimately it's my choice.

So what was it like, having sex for the first time with a man?

A bit tricky. It was wonderful, in a number of different ways. It was wonderful having sex with someone of your own sex. Just *that* as a pure conceptual thing and knowing which bits of the body to touch, because you knew *exactly* what *you* liked, and therefore you had a fairly good idea, although with variations, of what the right thing to do to someone else was. Some of the physical dynamics were a little hard to get my head around at first. Certainly having sex with someone who was turned on by the same things that you were turned on by is wild and very different.

Having sex with someone of your own strength or even stronger, because Steve was a lot stronger than I was then, is quite erotic. It enables you to explore fantasies and do things that you probably wouldn't dare to do on a first date with a woman, because you're being much more careful, and less brutal really. And the rough physical side to sex I enjoy, which is something that you can't do to someone who is a lot weaker than you. So that as well. Funnily enough, a lot of people I know find the concept of gay sex just impossible to understand because the fear of AIDS is so great.

I had to point out that 'we' heterosexuals were not exactly laughing all the way to the condom counter either.

Yes, but the fear isn't as great. It's not as conditioned. Most straight men would consider gay sex to be terribly, terribly dangerous. It's Russian Roulette sex. Which I suppose some people, on the other hand, might find exciting. But that's never occurred to me at all. Or not *not* occurred to me, but it's never affected me sexually.

So how does this whole domination scene work?

We tried once, very early on, with him taking the dominant role. It's not something that Steve enjoys at all. Not at all. He finds it almost impossible to be dominant, although very recently in the last fortnight or so, he has been dominant with other people, which he actually shocked himself by. We went to Amsterdam the other weekend and he even toyed with the idea of going with a female prostitute, which I nearly passed out at.

I was someone who'd just opened this new cookie jar and I didn't even know how to put my hand *in*, let alone know my way around. Talk about diving in off the deep end; in a way it was a real baptism of fire and I went from zero knowledge to a hundred per cent. Then it took a couple of months actually to rationalise . . . It's very strange, because for the past ten to fifteen years I've always been the elder brother, the dominant one, the one in charge. I'm always the one who looks after the passports and the traveller's cheques. I've always been the relatively responsible one: I was managing director of a small company and had a lot of responsibility that way.

Then suddenly to have to totally abrogate that and effectively to be an accessory to somebody else, and that's what I was, basically Steven's handbag for several months, that was a huge, huge change. Once I was actually seduced by it, it was a relief not to be in charge. That was very interesting but that has changed now. I mean that has changed back. I'm now feeling again a bit like Daddy, which isn't great.

Are you happy?

Mostly, yes. I'm not happy with some things, happy with others. I feel that our relationship has got to a stage where we've sort of grown into each other. We co-exist. Considering I couldn't ever have conceived living with a woman, Steve moved in after two weeks and has lived there perfectly naturally, normally, and without impinging on me or pissing me off any more than I piss myself off, which is incredibly easily. We co-exist very well. We're not in that dizzy 'in love' stage any more; I don't know if we should be or not. I'm certainly very fond of him. He drives me mad but I'm certainly not tempted to look elsewhere for a relationship.

So, I don't know if that's happy or not. Most of the time yes, some of the time no; it's a relationship. I don't think anyone goes around with their head in the clouds. There are some things that I want that he can't give me, and there are a lot of things that maybe I don't place enough value on and he does. I don't know. It's become very cosy and easy and sort of . . . settled. It's not a question I ask myself really. But yes. On balance, I'd say yes.

So many women have met Pete and groaned about yet another gorgeous man 'defecting', as though this was some mortal battle we women were locked into with our gay male counterparts. 'Fight to keep men straight': a possible slogan for the new generation of women for the first time confronting open defiance to the conventional chains that have bound men who, for whatever reason, prefer their own kind to ours.

I think an important part of our dismay goes beyond biology and straight into vanity. 'How could he not find me attractive? What about the natural order of things?' must race through many women's minds. We're told from adolescence onwards that the male species is ruled by its libido and that we have to ward them off with crowbars to keep ourselves safe. Suddenly all this counts for nothing when confronted by total lack of sexual interest and our confused pride is smarting.

Yes, it is 'a waste' for us to have Pete join the gay ranks, but our loss is Steve's gain. And Pete's, judging by the sound of it, who has found longer lasting happiness than he's ever experienced with a woman to date.

I've heard it argued that homosexuality should be viewed from a less genderised perspective, that is to say, a case of falling in love with another person *as opposed to a man or a woman. This is fine in the abstract, but most gays I know, even if their goal is love as versus pure sex, subscribe to the motto of 'You've got to kiss a lot of frogs to find your prince'. Ergo, how can you separate physical lust from gender choice?*

In my experience, gay men particularly are exceedingly promiscuous. Having given it some thought, I assume it's linked to the aforementioned libido; generally, men have a higher sex-drive and women are the ones slamming on the brakes. Gay male encounters encourage unbridled romping precisely because it involves only men.

The one thing I am rotating over and over in my head is the way Pete didn't question his outlook more, if at all, while involved in stifling heterosexual relationships. Maybe he started recognising slowly that these women were not for him, but I would have thought that somewhere en route he would have found some man attractive? It must have been very strong denial indeed not to have even looked at another man with the faintest glimmer of desire. And yet, as he has said, perhaps it was simply a sudden dawning.

I'd hate to be one of his exes, in some ways; you must always have a little question mark in the back of your mind, 'Did I help

push him in that direction? Did he enjoy any of our relationship?'
Then again, I know of enough cases where the situation has been
reversed. I clearly recall when I was twelve years old that the moth-
er of a childhood acquaintance, who had been married fifteen years,
scandalised the community by leaving her husband to set up house
with a lesbian lover. I suppose we should remember these similarly
increasing incidences when we feel singularly hard done by as a sex.

Sunday, 28th February

Received another concerned letter from my parents yesterday. Although they try to butt out, they can't stifle their mounting worry that I will one day be buried a drag queen, maybe because my career pace indicates to them that I'll never leave the club, and because they see my health deteriorating as a direct result of my crazed working conditions. Alex seems to agree with them, but is currently working three unchallenging jobs simultaneously himself and is hardly in a position to support even one of us should I move into a job transition. So, for now, I'll continue the increasingly predictable routine.

Oh, nearly forgot. We had Jonathan Ross down the other night. It transpired that he was there to accompany a friend of his who, at some stage in the past, had apparently become very infatuated with me. While this is not an uncommon occurrence for many performers, and I have certainly been the object of irrational love impulses from many a guest (interestingly enough, all except two have pegged me as a woman from the start), it always remains a slightly surreal experience. To meet someone who professes unrequited love for you based on a performance is both flattering and pitiful. Also embarrassing since, more often than not, they are actually unrecognisable to you; the nature of the game dictates that the admirer has the unfair advantage, because with blinding stage lights in your eyes you've never actually *seen* them before.

My reaction to all of this, barring God-like Adonises of course, is, 'You don't even *know* me, how can you claim to love *everything* about me?' Usually, there is no arguing with them; they'll remain 'in love' with you until they either give up or find someone else to focus their undivided attention upon. Certainly they become your staunchest groupies. For a while.

One element I find extremely disconcerting is the way many of them have partners who know all about you and, according to your dewy-eyed admirer, are jealous but accepting of your singular role in their lover's life. I would have a very hard time with that one, although I wonder what any of these types would do if I actually swung around and jumped their bones? Probably faint.

Returning to this particular evening, said gentleman proceeded to tell me afterwards that his pregnant girlfriend knew all about me and could he take me to dinner and make my life easier in any way? The weirdest coincidence revealed itself the following evening, when I first had the chance to tell Alex about the entire scenario, only to discover that he'd been at the offices of Jonathon Ross's Channel X that day, trying to flog a script idea. He laughed and feigned disappointment, moaning about his missed blackmailing opportunities.

The whole thing made me reflect. How sad to feel that you have to bring down your celebrity friends to guarantee an introduction. I would have been happy to talk to him anyway and really didn't need to stand around making idle chit chat with Jonathan. As it was, I informed him that I had serious reservations about his latest *Americana* programme and we discovered that we'd both studied Modern History at university. Talk about a wild and wacky interchange.

Sunday, 7th March

Dresser Michael is managing to be endearing and infuriating in appropriately equal doses. I wonder what his dressing at *Miss Saigon* is like, although I can imagine that being earlier in the drinking day they probably get marginally more competence.

God knows we give him enough abuse in return and he does make the most wonderful human punching bag. I think Ruby put it pretty neatly when Michael went into an unusual speed-athon the other night, and she told us to 'just put half a bottle of tranquillisers into his drink and he'll be back to normal'. A typical example of Michael's awareness was last night's attempt to send Ruby on during her UV-light skeleton number without one of her bone socks; as Jason sarcastically remarked, 'What are you going to do, tie her legs together?' Or alternatively putting an outfit over Ruby's unamused face, who snapped 'Not over my face, I'm NOT Lola LaPlant.'

At least he makes us laugh, especially when compared to Carla, who was down the other night drunk as a skunk and professing undying love for us all. Not to mention regularly perforating my eardrums by shouting these endearments at a two-inch range. Unlike Teddi and Becka, Carla's route post-JoJo's seems to have more in common with Jay's 'don't know where to go now' approach. Even Jamie seems to have found his niche – I bumped into him and his latest boyfriend a few weeks ago in the Camden Sainsbury's, buying enough avocados to potentially start a small guacamole business and looking totally content.

I sweetly dumped Carla on Teddi, currently appearing as the dragged up torture object on the *James Whale Show* in addition to his regular slots at the Piano Bar. He shot me a look of pure venom, and proceeded to try and disentangle himself from Carla's 'adore you' clutches.

Meanwhile, Ruby was downstairs giving an interview to some Italian student who had decided to transform himself into a dragologist. Needless to say, citing the club generally and Ruby in particular as the pinnacle of the genre did not hurt his chances of an in-depth conversation with Mama. He complained about the unoriginality of what little Italian drag there was and I was amazed that it even existed over there. I would have thought these artists would be lynched, especially in such a macho society and had to shake my head in wonder at this growing fascination of the Italia squad with such a blasphemous, 'evil' activity. If the Catholic Church frowns on homosexuality, then you are definitely going to fry in hell for this one guys. Then again, we were hearing about the huge influx of Brazilian transsexuals into Italy and the attendent 'surprise' that may or may not be revealed after a darkened encounter. Probably makes our drag look comfortably obvious and comparatively permissible.

I would love to interview la Ruby myself, but I know that her autobiography will be out one day and don't want to take any wind out of those proverbial sails. Having been in on at least nine reporter sessions with her myself, it promises to be absolutely spellbinding.

Sunday, 21st March

I cannot fault this show for amusement value, even if it is countered by Becka, now singing upstairs at the Piano Bar, dribbling all over Stanley Kubrick during the show. Having said that, she is doing fantastically well for herself, having just completed filming a drama series with Hale and Pace as some sort of 'matronly dominatrix'. Sounds promising.

Backstage has seen a new addition, in the form of Gerard. A colleague of Ada's from *Miss Saigon* – we are being inundated – he is equally talented, Australian, and replacing Steve who has decided to understudy Ruby's drag act. Now there's a mental picture for you. If nothing else it means that we are getting back some of the theatre crowds. In this case, the Saigoners might as well consider opening a permanent alcove.

We had a nice cross section down other nights as well, including Tony Slattery and company from *Radio Times*. Then of course there was always the *Joseph* crowd, although Jason Donavan never seemed to pluck up the courage to make it over.

Sunday, 28th March

I am not coping all that well with my double lifestyle. I think two years at this club are starting to take their toll, in that I just don't have the energy anymore. My radio tours are getting longer, my patience shorter. I think I may have to start looking for some alternatives, maybe even State-side. I am encouraged by Alex in this ambition, whose film career is still going nowhere fast. This is in part attributable to the deplorable lack of film financing in this country, and my would-be Martin Scorsese would no doubt benefit from relocating to the US.

Furthermore, I think Alex is getting rather fed up with my drag work. He's been so supportive and understanding that I guess I figured it wouldn't ever be an issue. Yet as he very rightly pointed out, he left the club over nine months ago, physically *and* psychologically.

Being the type who likes to finish an experience and move on, my job ends up serving as a constant reminder of the past, which must be very frustrating for Alex; he can't completely make the break until I do. He also watches my mounting boredom and restlessness and views my leaving as a positive step for me, in which he is probably right. On a daily level, however, it boils down to this recent, simple outburst: 'It's 3am and I don't want to be lying awake in bed hearing about bickering feuds and gay men's sex lives.' Can I blame him?

I'm feeling increasingly tired and I appreciate that I don't assist my case any by maintaining the raucous party life that I've grown accustomed to. Ada and I went out the other night after work to The Maltese Club, increasingly popular with JoJo employees since they allowed bar tabs. A frightening prospect for our livers and bone structure, as Ada joked. We've met some prize characters, a few of whom have come down to see us and were promptly thrown out.

Ada and I claimed impending nuptials to avoid hassle the other night. While this worked at the Maltese, I was to encounter hurricane Alex when I got home who suspiciously questioned me as to just how gay Ada was. The thought was laughable until I was forced to sleep on the couch. Role reversal, or what. I don't know what he's so worried about. Ada and I were shown Jeff Striker's centrefold in *BoyZ*, to which Ada marvelled at what a big boy he was and likened him to Alex, informing me that Alexander's monogamy was really a waste, it being 'like Quality Street, all that should be shared, not kept to one woman.' I'm never letting Alex backstage alone again.

The amusing, or scary, thing, depending on your perspective, is that although the show may be Far from Reality, I can never really escape. Even walking into a stationers or watching TV, I see the postal advertising characters drawn by Beryl Cook. These are apparently based on Ruby, who was her next-door neighbour, and whom Beryl and husband accidentally discovered on a night out at the club with the astonished 'Look, it's BRIAN.'

Otherwise, insecurities are the order of the day at present. Jake was getting abuse from Ruby for wearing his opening scarf as a daywear bandana, which says a lot for his fashion sense or lack thereof. Ruby shouted for Gerard to come in, ostensibly to compare the state of their scarves, and Gerard entered flapping, 'Oh nooo, we're not comparing BODIES again' and exited, throwing a Garbo and screaming 'leave me alone!'

Misha has taken this a step further by announcing that 'you'll be calling me pigeon penis next.' Which I would hardly think worrying for him, in light of the fact that he is now well and truly inhaling female hormones. It's crazy, especially as he is recklessly endangering his only source of income besides the trannie dressing service. Future unemployment is a dreadful thing to have to add to this sort of mental crisis.

But it's nice to see that, in spite of Misha's confusion, there is still a very strong sense of humour at play, demonstrated last night when some girl admiring Misha's hair suddenly found the wig in her drink. I think we're all gradually coming unhinged.

Sunday, 11th April

I've just seen our latest review, ripped out of some magazine by George. Under the segment 'Night Owls: After Dark', it read as follows (with my admittedly cynical reactions included):

'If you're looking for a completely different fun night out, why not sample the discreet decadence' *discreet, are you serious?* 'at Madame JoJo's self-proclaimed "Club Extraordinaire" at 8–10 Brewer Street. Since Paul Raymond opened the doors seven years ago, "Jo's" has become one of the most popular and enjoyable late-night venues in London's West End.

'Their "extravaganza" Far From Reality is the current highlight of this theatrical and slightly louche' *what, is this a selling point?* 'club which is open from 10.00pm until 3.00am, Monday to Saturday. Admission is £8 Monday to Thursday,' *overpriced for our punters* 'and £10 on the extremely popular Friday and Saturday nights.' *Ditto.*

'Included in the price of admission is the over the top floor-show/ cabaret performed in two distinct halves' *one drunk, one paralytic* '12.15am–12.45, and 1.15am–1.45am. On two levels there are three bars,' *each packed, impossible to get a drink* 'a dance floor,' *crammed herd-like* 'comfortable banquets,' *what, are you nuts?* 'and tables which can be booked in advance. Food is also available.' *Inedible, except for the sandwiches – you have obviously never eaten here.*

'Although the flamboyant bar staff and artistes are drag queens' *this'll thrill our macho bar guys in shorts, especially sexy, masculine Roger* '(or fellas in frocks)' *nicely put* 'this is not a gay club.' *I'll say. I think we've established that one.* 'There are often more women than men.' *Shrieking drunken hen nights.* 'It is high camp in the true British tradition of Danny La Rue' *wait til the guys read this* 'and pantomime. What's more it is comfortable and classy, as opposed to sordid and sleazy. Madame JoJo's welcomes one of the most diverse and colourful clientele in London. You may find yourself rubbing shoulders with minor royalty,' *Major Ferguson* 'a politician,' *not one with a future* 'someone's Mum,' *ours* 'or a six-foot Marilyn Monroe.

'Extremely popular with people in all aspects of showbiz, the chances are that the cast of the West End show you've just seen will be sitting at the next table.' *Hell, the chances are they'll be in the show.* 'It's the only place I've seen an eminent theatre critic laughing over a drink with a director he had coolly demolished in print earlier the same day.' *Only if they were planning on sleeping together afterwards.*

'From the moment your coat is taken by a very respectable lady' *now there's a first* 'you are in for a relaxed if theatrical experience. The "star" of the show is the flamboyant and funny Ruby

Venezuela, who is responsible for devising, directing and starring in the cabaret Far From Reality.

'More pantomime dame than Divine,' *good you mentioned that, or she'd have a contract out on your head* 'he is ably supported by the assorted drag artistes and scantly clad hunky male dancers. This is not your pub drag show, there is no mime or coarse quips.' *Really? Misha must not have offered to sit on your face that night.*

'It is both spectacle and satire. They have a large performance area,' *these reviewers really should go for an eye check* 'and with camp humour, theatrical imagination and energy create a witty and truly spectacular extravaganaza.

'There is ample opportunity to get down and dance,' *as long as you only need a guiding bass rhythm* 'and the music is both nostalgic and contemporary.' *Maybe in the mid-eighties it was.* 'The bar staff, handsome young men, and Barbettes – outrageously made-up and coiffured young men – are courteous and efficient.' *You must have caught them on a really good day.* 'This is not a perverse or seedy establishment but great fun, and extremely popular with all walks of life from London and abroad.

Inshallah.

Sunday, 18th April

Hong Kong is still on Ruby's mind, if not on paper. Although she was talking of doing a trip via Riyadh last night.

Apparently some rich 26-year-old Arab down at the club suggested she join his nine wives in domestic tranquillity, Saudi-style. Ruby has always fancied the idea of becoming a concubine and when Jason and I pointed out how jealous the wives would be we practically had to tie her down to keep her with us. She's already been looking around for a tax exile, with Her Majesty's collectors breathing heavily down her neck for years of backlogged Inland Revenue debts, and our calculation that she would probably only have to sleep with him twice a week was enough to make her prepared to throw caution to the wind.

Especially as she won't have to deal with her boyfriend's Pink Panther costume for a 'P' party in Cambridge. Jason's already told her to just dress him in a tampon, dipped and framed, and call it a 'Period Painting', but she's still indignant over lover boy's recent criticism of her drinking. I do think becoming a tenth wife is taking false outrage a bit far, however, particularly when she and Jason have a marvellous offer to cruise off to the Cannes Film Festival late May and host a huge wing-dinger party. Then attend one thrown by Elizabeth Taylor. Every queen's wet dream. They talked of taking me along but decided that the office would never allow three of us to go for a weekend. I am, of course, totally mollified, knowing how many sacrifices the office has made on our behalf. Blech.

Then again, we need as many hands on board as possible with dresser Michael constantly inflicting damage upon himself. His most recent escapade involved attempting to swim across a street in a post-pub session, swearing all the while that it was a pool. When he came in still hobbling two nights later, I suggested that 'one more night and we put her down.' This was met with resounding agreement and had Michael worried enough to modify his previous insistence to Jason and myself that he was not on drugs to swearing separately to Ruby that he hadn't even been drinking. This would be much more worrying if it were true.

As it stands, we try and laugh it off. When Michael managed to misplace one of my shoes, which we have to pay for ourselves incidentally, Ruby helpfully suggested 'just use the other one as a brooch.' A quick smack and Michael miraculously uncovered the missing heel.

Speaking of missing heels, Marcie is encountering her own private drama with a too-good-to-be-true international photographer, who has disappeared for a month to verify Marcie's commitment to him. He also came out of the closet for her. This is starting to become an epidemic . . . In their case the story is much more complicated, involving as it does a miscarrying wife and rocky marriage. Poor Marcie.

Interview With Marcie
On Homosexuality, JoJo's and
Breaking Down Barriers

She began by reminiscing about her first encounter with Enrico.

Enrico met me in drag and he didn't even think about me being out of drag. When he saw me the next morning, I was de-wigged, de-make-uped and everything, but he didn't even take much notice. He took the wig off in the morning, when I went to take my make-up off, and he didn't even take any notice of it; he was just looking at my face and thinking about what had happened. We didn't have sex or anything like that, but he was just thinking of what was going on. He couldn't even remember what my hair looked like the following night – the fact that I had none.

When I was out of make-up, it freaked him a bit, he didn't like it that much. But now that's changed, now it doesn't matter if I've got hair on, or make-up on, because he's got to know *me*. But at first, it was really uncomfortable, because he saw a boy there: a complete, skinhead boy.

How does this compare to your last boyfriend?

The last boyfriend had a complete aversion to drag on me. I'd wear make-up: mascara, a bit of foundation, ultra glow, and he didn't care about that. But dragwise, while he knew I'd done it (and I never really told him about everything), he still wondered why everyone kept calling me Marcie.

It started off as a camp nickname; everyone calls me Marcie, whether I've got make-up on or not. He ended up being the last gay boyfriend as such, because he couldn't cope with it at all.

When we split up, and he started seeing me out in drag, it used to really embarrass him if I went over to him. He'd say 'Oh you look really good'; but if he was with a friend he wouldn't say 'Oh that was who I used to go out with', he'd say 'That's my friend'. And that's as far as it went.

This is what impresses me even more about Enrico: that someone who was recently still straight could be so open-minded about going out with you in drag.

He doesn't give a damn, basically. Being an artist himself, he's completely arty-farty, and anything that he sees looking good or that he's proud of, he'll show to everyone. As far as he can do it, without being in danger to himself. And the fact of him being a punk when he was young – I mean he's been a hippy, he's been a punk, he's been this and that, so he's pretty cool about things like that.

Obviously, being a photographer, he mixes with the strangest people, and living in New York and working at *Vogue*, he's met everyone there is to meet. And the artists that he knows! There's this schizoid artist who really is mad, completely gone, and Enrico loves it! Anything perverse, anything different, he loves. He loves JoJo's. Enrico knows Jo from New York and he used to come to JoJo's years ago and send bottles of champagne over to her. He just likes being there, not to turn him on but to stimulate him mentally.

So what were the biggest problems initially?

At first he was a bit apprehensive, but then he knew it was happening, and why. Everything has gone so smoothly, and yet we've come through so much shit, like with his wife and the miscarried kids. What he thought he was has been chucked out the window, forget it.

So he doesn't see me as a boy or a girl, he just sees me as me. There have been problems, like jealousy, but we're divinely happy. It sounds so sickly sweet, but that's the way it is. I never thought it was possible. We literally talk all the time, saying neither of us can believe it, it is unbelievable. He's only had one person he can talk to, his friend G; all of his other friends were straight, and he didn't want everyone at work knowing what was going on. He needed someone to talk to, but it's only been G, and nothing shocks *him*. He said 'Don't do anything about it at all yet'; he's known Enrico for about twenty years and nothing like this has ever happened to him.

So being his friend, I suppose G was worried about his marriage and that this could just be a fling. Enrico said 'This is not just a fling that is happening, it has lasted too long. This is nearly four months we've been together, not just two weeks.' Enrico's had twelve affairs during his marriage and they've all been covered up; well not all covered up, quite a few of them his wife has known about. But they've all been a short time, just sex and a bit of fun.

This is completely different, there's so much happening. Like I've said, my past boyfriends have had a problem with the drag element. I used to be in gay relationships although most of them have been bisexual men. But then that's being sexist again, because their sexuality's a release; they wanted to sleep with a man but they needed to keep their girlfriends. They needed to keep their hetero-sexuality there, so they could never really have a proper relationship with me. The fact was that if they stuck with me for a commitment, they'd still go out and meet a girl. What's the point? And they seem to think that because it's a girl it doesn't count. That's the 'normal' bit of them, so it doesn't count. But I think it also works the other way. If their relationship is with a woman, the fact that they're cheating with a guy doesn't count, because it's with a *guy*.

They can't go and get them pregnant. Men seem to think that men don't have feelings, although everybody knows we all do. But it's the fact that you're a guy, or you're a gay guy, and it's this whole thing about gay men. Everyone seems to think that gay men don't have feelings as such; they think that because people do have sex in toilets, they do go and have sex in parks, it's all raw sex, so if you want to have sex with a man you go and have sex with a man. Which may be the case with some people, but there are ones around who are like me, who *do* have feelings, who *do* want to settle down; well, not settle down but have some kind of permanence. I don't need to go out to a gay club and score for one night.

I do flirt, that's part of me; he does the same, he flirts as well. Not with guys, but with drag queens and transsexuals. But it is harmless flirting because he knows at the end of the night he'll come back to me.

The thing is, we know we look good. I know I look good, he knows he's attractive. He gets offers at work every night to have threesomes, to do this and that; even the barman comes over to him saying 'Enrico, take off your jeans, I'm dying to give you a blow job.' He just stands there and laughs in his face. But people always come up to us at some club, and say 'You look fab', which I love. It's very big-headed, but I love it, and he loves that. He always asks me at the end of the night 'How many people came over to you?' Even now someone will come up to us at the bar and say 'Weren't you at that rave at King's Cross? You two looked brilliant.'

He's proud of it, and he's proud of me. And it's a good thing to have someone proud of you. It's the first time in my whole life that someone's actually turned around to me and said 'I love you, I'm proud of you.' He wakes up with me and I look a complete bastard, with my beard hanging out, my hair is looking a complete twat as it's growing, and he'll take the piss but he couldn't give a damn.

The only thing that he does find hard, but laughs at, is when we'll walk down the street and he'll be dying to throw his arm around me, or give me a kiss or something. You know like when you have a laugh, and you just do. At first he used to be really funny about it; well not funny, but 'Don't touch, don't touch'. Now, in the past three weeks, he just grabs hold of me. Right in front of everyone walking down the high street! In North London he grabbed hold of me and gave me a kiss. Broad daylight, people walking around, and it was like 'My God.' Do you know what I mean? It's like, gay guys don't *do* this. Everyone is really paranoid about it. He's new to the whole thing and doesn't understand; he just did it. Doesn't even think about it, just carries on walking down the road.

This is one area where I really do sympathise. I can have every-thing short of sex on the street whereas even holding hands is taboo territory outside of gay hangouts. How do you feel about this?

It bothers me to a degree, but then it's not something I get hung up about. It's not something I'm going to change. No one is going to change it until the government change, but that's political. I don't bother with it; it's always been there, it's the old you-don't-miss-what-you've-never-had.

In the States, they always used to quote the Kinsey report that ten per cent of the male population was gay, and now they've done a new report finding only one per cent is gay. What is your impression of this?

Everyone is born bisexual. I would say everyone's potentially gay. How many people do you know, honest people, that are straight, who can actually turn around and say to you 'Yes I've thought about it, or I had a period in my life where I thought maybe that's me, maybe it isn't?'

All it takes is for one experience to be at the right time. It's all to do with timing, in that if it's the right time, the right place and the right situation, that someone is going to try it. At the end of the day that's going to determine whether it's right for them or not. You find out. But it is about finding out; whether you are or not, you've still got the potential there.

There are a lot more gay men . . . They can take surveys on how many people they know are gay because their lifestyle is out there in front, and maybe, yes, it could come out to 1% somehow. But everyone that's gay doesn't turn around and say 'Yes I am gay'. They don't want every Tom, Dick and Harry to know, to become part of a statistic. And how many men that are married are gay? A disgustingly huge amount. I know that, you know that, from persons that appear at the nightclub. And it's not just the nightclub – what about those that won't even come out?

When did you come out?

It started when I was really small. When I grew up, my cousins were all girls; there was never any male environment as such, always at my mum's side. I had strong brothers and a strong father at that time but it never stuck in my head, they never made an influence on my life. I've said to my Dad before, which really hurt him, that I can only remember him from about the age of eight or nine. Before that, I don't remember. I mean, my mum I can remember from the time I fell down the stairs, and that was when I was about two. I have a picture in my head of seeing my mum on the sofa as I'm running around.

But besides that, I always saw myself as a girl in my head; that's what I thought I was, that's how I seemed to be. At that age you don't really analyse. I see the little girls I'm playing with, as a kid, and you had dolls and little flouncy numbers, everything was really short and girly; you know, girls' things. So that's what I thought I should have. That was me. That was the stuff that was around me in my childhood. And I would go on 'I want to be a girl, I want to be a girl', and went on until I started getting stick for it. Pre-school it went on, and then I used to say it at another school. And you know when you start dressing yourself as a kid, I'd put on the most feminine things I could find. Also, my nails were quite long and I used to get hassle for it all the time.

The family used to just let me get on with it. My mum just thought I was a very gentle little boy, she knew I was very feminine. My family knew that. I was the baby of the family, I could get away with what I wanted to do. So it was a case of 'Don't be whatever, be more like a boy, get in trouble *please*.' But I had an aversion to football; anything acutely masculine, or what a boy should do, it was like, forget it. I'm sorry, I want to play netball and wear a nice little skirt. I feel now, if you look at the (I think) seventeen strains of transsexuality, that there is a strain I would fit into.

So how did this tie in with doing drag here at the club? Was this performance inclination always apparent?

Everyone's always known, my parents have always known I'd end up doing that. I used to be really into drama and I've always shown off by dressing up. In primary school, teachers would always say to my mum 'Get him into a school with drama.' And then auditions with the National Youth Theatre, things like that, but I never actually did it though. I always knew I'd end up going somewhere, somehow.

How did you venture down JoJo's scarlet staircase for the first time?

I used to go down with Tanya. When I first met her, I used to be very Boy Georgie: wear hats, a bit of make-up, long coats and that sort of thing. Through Tanya I met Jay and we used to go down to Jo's. That's the first time I did trannie-drag properly and I looked like a prostitute from hell. Then we just used to go to Jo's now and again, and go with Jay to Fidenzi's after work.

Then Tanya started working at Jo's, and I started going down more regularly. They asked me to do the bar one night, then six nights a week, working with Roger and Brian. One night, Eddie (the assistant manager) said to me, 'Marcie you look fab in drag, would you like to cover the loos one night?' Pandora and everyone else were trying to get me to be a barbette, and I thought 'Fab, go for it.'

In those days, it obviously seemed a lot more glammy and much more fun than it is now. It was different, completely different. Everyone was much more into it then, there was much more enthusiasm there. Everyone would make the effort. We would go out and spend the day shopping for make-up and earrings.

Unfortunately, Jo had just left. George hadn't become very dominant in the club at that time, so you could be glammy-fem. The thing that ruined it was when he turned around and said 'Right, you can't wear black, you can't wear tit-pads'; he just wanted it more outrageous, and we had to wear more glitter and bigger and bigger make-up.

So the glam bit started to get a bit muddled, although Kim carried on. Then Pepper would come out in tiger make-up, Tanya came as 'Hi, I'm your drag queen from hell', and it just turned. I think that was the downfall, because they tried to get too much back of what was there before but people weren't being what they were, and it just started changing. Attitudes changed because of the management, because of resentment.

What does drag mean to you personally? Is it a self-expression?

My drag reflects how I feel. Completely. I don't think of drag as 'I want to get up there, go and put my make-up on, do my job.' For me it's not so much of a release, because that's verging on transvestism for me, which is very different.

Misha, to me, is your classic transvestite. 'Was' rather, because he's not doing it now, so make that before, when he started, up until recently. The only way to explain it, to me, is really a fantasy release, whereas my drag is part of my life, I'm actually much more comfortable like that. Being a feminine person, or how I am, and I'm not saying a woman, but a feminine person – it's like putting the icing on the cake, although that sounds like a crap cliché. That's how I feel best, because I know I can attract people like that.

So when you take it outside the club and you deal with everyday people, how do you find they react to you?

You get different amounts. It depends to what extreme you take it. Heterosexuals, the ones who live in and around London, are more interested, they look without scorn. Some of them admire, and people that come down to the club are more relaxed about it anyway. If you're talking of taking it outside of London, then there is a complete major freakout because they just don't know how to deal with it, they just don't want to know it's there. They don't want to believe that.

How about your parents? Have they come to grips with the whole thing?

190

The only time I actually thought I'd better tell them was when we had done the first photocall for the *Daily Star*. And I thought 'They're going to see it, so I do have to tell them.' Not because they'd recognise me, but I never knew how far I was going to be taken. I just thought, 'I need to tell them'; that I was gay, actually. I never told them at the time. They didn't know anything.

I just thought 'Sod it', and they said fine, they still loved me and everything; they always knew I was gay. Both parents knew, but they never spoke about it. They had their suspicions but they never joined them together, they kept it from each other. They didn't accept it; basically they didn't want to.

I mentioned that I'd discussed this with Teddi and how my original belief had been that parents somehow assumed it reflected upon them.

I think it's a lot deeper than that. I think it's a lot more to do with the fact that it's always happening to someone else's kid, you know what I mean? It's *their* family. There is that element of blame, of 'What did we do wrong?' That's going to be the first one, that happens all the time. Every family. But I think parents on the whole have an idea of where they think they'd like to see their children go, not in fact where they're *wanting* to go, but where *they'd* like to see them go. Especially if you're doing well for yourself. I mean I had a really good job hairdressing, I was making something of myself in the salon and I had a good reputation around the area. It was really great, I was doing really, really well. I had my flat in Beckenham, money in my pocket, and everything was fab. I was doing competitions and work at photo sessions. And then I landed all this on them.

Just the fact of being gay, even saying the word 'gay', goes BANG! It's like your life is going to now fall apart, you're going to become this toilet-hugging, wanking machine. They've seen this thing on Quentin Crisp, and they suddenly think you're going to turn up with painted nails and lipstick on and your hair dyed red. With your boyfriend on your arm, trying to be a happily married heterosexual couple in their living room. And it scares the shit out of them basically.

It's like, 'What are we going to do about the family?' And I come from a massive family: my dad's from a family that's got six children, there are five kids in our family, and each family's got five kids. And it's all close-knit.

So how many were boys and girls in your five?

Three boys and two girls, including me. No, three girls and two boys. I was going to say two-and-a-half girls and two-and-a-half boys.

I'm happy for Marcie, or rather, for her happiness. I have some serious reservations about Enrico's possessiveness and Latino passions, especially in light of Marcie's now-unconditional devotion; Desdemona keeps flashing through my mind, although I would hardly classify Enrico on a par with the Moor. I find it hard to believe that a heterosexual man can make the leap from married life to boyfriend of a drag queen with such apparent ease. If Marcie were a transsexual, it would be a different story . . .

I suppose one could argue that Pete has also managed the transition to homosexuality fairly smoothly, but he's involved with a gay man who looks like a gay man. Also, my suspicious mind questions why a man like Enrico, supposedly with predominantly straight friends and no previous homosexual experience, would be working in an ultra-gay bar? It would be as if upon commencing at JoJo's I had suddenly become a lesbian. To be boringly fair, though, Marcie and Enrico's scenario is an all-time first for me, and perhaps I'm so sceptical simply because I don't understand it.

Saturday, 1st May

Did Pete's (of Steve fame) office promotion party last night. I don't know exactly who they were planning on impressing with a 'Leather' theme, but God knows our nightmare tape scene could have only been counter-productive. We felt like the proverbial spouse brought in to wow the boss, only to get drunk and throw up over his lapels.

Ruby had put together some kind of a mish-mash for her, Jason, Misha and myself, only for us go into a magnificently dramatic opening and promptly have the tape decelerate into the equivalent of a 33 record played on 16. Beautiful. Talk about anti-climactic. Off ran Steve to the club to pick up an alternative, which we then had to re-tape backstage. By the time we went on even teetotaller Misha had downed copious champagne cocktails and my lungs felt tar-incarcerated from smoking a small tobacco plantation worth of Marlboro Lights.

Fortunately my gig a few days ago with pianist Nigel at The Blue Elephant went memorably better. In fact, by comparison we were Albert Hall worthy. We did have to lounge around for a while, trying to look inconspicuous with boa feathers flying everywhere, but Nigel managed to keep me amused with his latest sexual exploits. The guy is incredible. So quiet and demure by day, and suddenly this crazed wild man in the sheets.

He proceeded to relate a story of going back with some guy, only to have him announce that they had to first feed his Amazonian frogs. OK, figures Nigel, a couple of flies in the tank and we're off. They go into a room covered with the slimers, and this guy decides that this is the perfect aphrodisiac. I was totally absorbed in all of his recollections, but not so much as the gay guys on a whole are with one another's exploits; there is a real vicariousness to story-telling here.

Although even they can be amazed. Witness Nigel's tale of Teddi's shock upon arriving last weekend at his house to do some demo work. Even though they've known each other for ages, I gather that Teddi was not quite expecting to march into a den of naked skinheads lolling around the flat and casually strolling in and out of the studio. Which is another case in point – the number of open affairs and group orgies carried out by committed gay partners still astounds me. Makes me feel terribly prudish and narrow-minded.

These feelings were banished when Alexander and I went to see comedian Eddie Izzard's show and laughed riotously throughout, especially at his highly entertaining transvestite sketches. This man will go far and I was relieved to see that he was most emphatically out of the closet with regards to his own cross-dressing. With more role models like this, perhaps the stigma surrounding transvestism will gradually diminish and disappear one day.

I recommended the performance to Misha, who went along the next night and, in his inimitably shy fashion, managed to plough through to Eddie's dressing-room. According to Misha, they had a frank and enjoyable ten minute conversation, with Misha leaving him an open invitation to visit the club any time. I don't know whether this offer will be taken up, but Misha returned happy and heartened by the encounter.

Sunday, 2nd May

I have had enough of the tragic nature of my career prospects at JoJo's, especially as it has now been revealed nationwide that PR is Britain's richest man, ousting the Duke of Westminster from the Number One slot.

Misha's and my wrangles with Schnitzel over a wage increase, one-and-a-half years later, resulted in a £5 weekly rise for this show. We found this such an insult that we ended up laughing it off and regularly informed one another how we had blown this week's huge bonus. I mean admittedly, PR doesn't have to spread the wealth around just because he has it. I appreciate that we are mere employees, but it would be nice to be made to feel this, rather than being treated as simply necessary evils.

I think I'd better re-energise my efforts towards the US television stations, or I'll still be dragging up on a zimmer frame.

Sunday, 9th May

Ironically enough, in light of my current escapist inclinations, drag appears to be the latest fad. Put more precisely, as with all fashion, it is the latest re-release. I was reading a book review today about the mafia's blackmailing of J Edgar Hoover, during his FBI years, for dressing in drag at homosexual parties.

Otherwise, everywhere I turn I see the beaming face of New

York drag queen RuPaul. She sang a by now very familiar tune, stating that 'Eleven years ago I learned the true meaning of power dressing . . . Everybody was hypnotised by me, I was this object of desire. I mean, honey, we all wear drag . . . It's just that becoming this goddess, which is how I think of myself, enabled me to tap into my true potential. Now I encompass yin and yang, night and day. I am a microcosm of the universe.' Let me take that back. I don't think I've ever heard anyone at the club, besides an extremely drunk and dramatic Steve, come up with that last pearl.

Steve went on for Ruby last Friday, as the Russian émigrée Natasha Nicaragua. It was frightening: in Ruby's make-up and dresses Steve looked like her younger sister. Although I guess going from G-string to drag is more than a superficial transformation, he was fantastic and for the first time we actually caught the tune and lyrics of Momma's songs. Then he went out on the floor and two seconds later came back screaming about 'these bloody heels' and crippled feet. This in Ruby's poxy two-inch pumps. You wimp.

Steve, Jason and I sat afterwards discussing this 'natural' evolution, which Jason claimed he had always known would occur, ever since 'we had the Christmas Silver Ball, in the Garden, which was like THE big event before Kinky's. The Silver Ball at the Garden was *the* party to go to. And suddenly Steve asked to borrow one of my frocks. Then, Stephanie arose . . .' Well, I suppose if any occasion was going to provide the turning point for Steve's feminine, dramatic alter ego to emerge, this was it. Even Jason, Mr Androgynous-don't-even-*think*-of-putting-me-in-a-dress, admitted 'I actually had a frock in those days. All in silver, with a big collar and black feathers, which he wore to the party.'

I remarked at how far he'd come and how this transition had happened. Steve grandly claimed it as 'a natural progression, I think, darling.' Jason shrewdly quipped 'there's more money in drag than being a dumb boy.'

Steve nodded animatedly, adding 'let me tell you, that is *true*. Although I've done four years as a boy and can go out there now and just be a boy and know exactly what to do, the really strange thing for me was the Monday night when we went to Kinky's. It's that transformation when I suddenly felt that there was this *creature* coming out, that was there underneath.'

Nostalgically, Jason decided that 'Steve also did a lot for the boys at JoJo's as well, because before we had Steve it was always not straight theatrical but wanting to do theatrical work. Before Steve arrived here and wanted to do more, wanted to learn more, wanted to sing songs, it was always a place where you had model boys who wanted an easy way to get an Equity card. The first show I did here, your boys walked on, flexed their muscles, smiled and went off at the end. Apart from being prop movers and holding you up or holding your hand, that's all you could do with them. Steve wanted to lift me, and we did more dancing, and now we've got Ada and more singing. I really do believe that if it wasn't for Steve coming here, the boys wouldn't be as big a part of the show as they are now.'

I asked Steve what he was planning on doing now, become a full-time understudy or perhaps do some drag on his own? Steve seemed uncertain, this having 'hit me out of the blue and all that.' His lover Pete was down and amazingly supportive. I talked to him later about the experience, and he laughed 'I didn't recognise him! I was with Marc, his ex-boyfriend, in Compton's, and I knew he was going to do drag because he was going to stand in for Ruby in the first act. He and Ruby came in drag into Compton's and I said hello to Ruby and gave him a kiss and I wondered who the queen was next to him. And I didn't recognise him! It was fun, I thought it was fab.'

Pete proudly added 'He did it extremely well, I mean, it does impress me. He has an enormous amount of talent and he's very, very professional about things he chooses to be, but he has such incredibly low self-esteem. I never expected him to be anything less than very good at it. And he is. So, I wasn't shocked. People asked "How do you feel about Steve being in drag; is that disgusting, does that affect you sexually, does that affect you?" Not at all,' he concluded. 'It's a role like any actor plays, and it's something he's good at and he enjoys doing.'

Very open-minded, in fact far more so than an article I've just been reading debating the joys of a lesbian family, where the writer articulates the fears of lesbians actively promoting homosexuality and children consequently receiving a distorted view of the world. The rebuttal of this was that these same children can still have positive male role models outside of the family structure, all the while gaining the important aspects of family life – someone to listen, provide for needs, food, warmth and security.

I paid particular attention to this write-up because Jason is in exactly such a situation. His best friend Scrubber, ex-drag queen and now AIDS deceased, had a child with a very close lesbian friend. The little boy is named Josh, to whom Jason is the godfather. We get up-dates on everything, from where they spent the day to how Jason had to be brought in to teach Josh to pee 'male-style', and I think Josh sounds extremely loved and lucky.

Unlike Ruby, who has just been informed that only one principal will be given the weekend off to go to Cannes. As it is Jason's contact, he will be going and take Teddi with him instead. Look out unsuspecting world.

Monday, 17th May

Glory, glory, hallelujah, reality may yet prevail. I have just been informed of my trial acceptance with a US television station. The only hitch in my rosy picture is that I have to be out of here in three weeks' time and I, for one, do not revel in the prospect of breaking this to Ruby and the gang.

Herein lies the irony of the whole situation, or perhaps the truth. I will miss the club immensely and my colleagues even more. All my regret and guilt are directed towards them. But as for the office, I couldn't care less.

I guess what it boils down to, having heard similar sentiments from the cast, is that the world JoJo's encapsulates and the people it contains are the only reason any of us are still there. I used to marvel at the change in attitude from the 'old days', and yet I think the office brought that upon themselves. There is precious little loyalty left towards the organisation now.

Tuesday, 18th May

I feel even sadder about leaving after last night's reaction.

Telling Ruby and Jason about my imminent departure provoked misty eyes on their parts, but a wonderfully generous gesture of happiness for me. They feel even more like family now and announced that, given the chance, they would do exactly the same thing. In fact the entire club voiced unhappiness at seeing me leave but were fully supportive of my good fortune. All in all, not so much a revelation as a happy confirmation of my faith in their characters.

Mitzi touchingly took me backstage after the show and presented me with a parting gift. Her only engagement ring to date, given to her by a 'straight man' many moons ago who then bottled out at the last minute. It's a very pretty sapphire and diamond cluster and she made me promise to wear it and remember her every time I looked at it. She looked genuinely unhappy and whispered that she wanted

197

to change her life and scenario. The management would be fools if they lost her; all she wants is to be put on the licence and she'd be as happy as a pig in mud.

The office was less pleased for me. Quelle surprise. Schnitzel rang me at home and repeated no less than five times that I was lucky, not because of my future, but 'because we are releasing you'. From what, I asked myself. It was like announcing that you had decided to open the stable door long after the horse had bolted.

Sunday, 23rd May

Just received a good luck letter from ex-barman Brian in Cornwall, not to mention the pleasantest shock of my life.

He has just discovered that he is not HIV positive after all, in one of the most surprise developments of a long twisted saga. It transpires that Brian's deceased ex-lover discovered his illness on holiday in France and, insisting on Brian being tested, mis-translated the results to an exclusively English-speaking Brian. Who carried this burden around with a heavy sense of doom for the next two years. Can you believe it? By committing suicide, Brian's lover effectively took his secret and two years of Brian's life to the grave with him. As Brian writes, perversely, the hardest thing is to come back to life now . . .

Wednesday, 26th May

Had Gunter Sachs, la Bardot's ex-husband and Germany's supposed richest man, down. He only stayed for the first half as he was recognised and beat a hasty retreat. Otherwise, the place was crawling with *Prime Suspect* producers and casting agents. They're planning on filming a drag scene and were scouting for talent.

Speaking of stellar opportunities, Jason's off to the lights of Cannes tomorrow, so I seized the chance to interview him yesterday.

Interview With Jason
On Drag, JoJo's, Stardom and Spawning Children

We started off by simply discussing Jason's unique style of androgy-nous drag.

My drag has never been girly. I've never been into drag on the feminine side. The word that comes up time and time again is 'androgynous', but it's not even androgynous. The reason I started was through Jeff, 'Poison Ivy'. There was Poison Ivy, Scrubber as 'Bette Noir' and Black Kenny as 'Praying Mantis', and we used to go out. But it was the early days of the Men's Club, it was when fashion was still fun; you'd been through the New Romantics, you'd been through male fashion being exciting. Male fashion then got very staid and it's still staid now. I mean, it's getting better, there is a very good look for men, but it's not outrageous as it was in those days.

Basically, you'll get people like Tim, Darina, and Michael from Kinky; all that era of people were used to, when they first started clubbing, being able to wear something funny and outrageous. Not necessarily for a laugh, but fun. It all stopped because fashion no longer did that. And you'll find that a lot of people from those club days then transferred it into drag, because that was the other way of dressing up. Therefore it was never on a female impersonator level.

So yours is as much a fashion expression or statement?

Well yes, I think as far as drag goes I'm one of the more fashionable drag queens on the circuit because my looks do relate to fashion. More so than any Hollywood idol.

Which Hollywood idols do you find worthy of admiration?

I was always a Marilyn Monroe freak and, of course, Bette Davis. Joan Crawford is another one . . . It's that whole image. It's definitely most of your late thirties up to late forties Hollywood idols.

It was that era, and it's more than because of the glamour. It was your first era of power women, women that took the control.

199

Where did you start?

I trained as a professional dancer. I've done major works, but always as someone else's backing. Even when I was at college, I had Paul Jenna and Errol Hinklen, both of which are now principals, one with the Royal, one with the London Festival; in school I was always a good pupil, but there was always someone better than me.

I trained at the Royal Ballet School and then the Ballet Rambert. I was a student member of the Rambert Company, which basically means they use you as a dogsbody. You're a student but you understudy the whole company; it's like 'Well, I'm sorry – pay me', and then no real chance of a contract afterwards. So I got very disillusioned with contemporary dance. I saw an advert in *The Stage* for a job in Cannes, tits and feathers work, and went out and did it.

It was hysterical, it was like six months' paid holiday. I was getting £200 a week, tax free, to work in the South of France for forty-five minutes a day, and then go out partying the rest of the night.

Then, to top it all, Eartha Kitt was there, and suddenly you're working with one of your all-time idols, you're on stage with them, shaking like shit. All I'd do is walk her down a set of stairs and drink a bottle of champagne with her on stage, but when you think you've known this woman all your life and suddenly you're on the stage with her, it was quite a bizarre feeling.

I came back and didn't work here, but it did a lot of good to get out of that serious, one-channeled view of 'Dance is the real art, all the rest are just second-rate careers'. Then I did some more commercial work over here, all going back to your original question of how it all started, when I was at Metropolis. Because I've been a patron of this club since it opened, I was always a regular, I knew all the people here. When Ruby was asked to take over as director of the show, she asked me to come in as a choreographer and be in the show, because she wanted what she called a 'Creole'-type character, sort of like the black guy in *Live and Let Die*.

The first show was very Joel Grey, all my costumes were tailcoats, and it was very much 'a dancer in the midst', being this bizarre creature and dancing around the other people. I had very little to do in the first show and Ruby trying to get me to sing 'Chim-chiminey' will be my absolute most hated song in the whole world! That was my big number in the first show. Tell me about it. I'd done various looks that they knew me as, like an outrageous drag persona from the scene, as I dressed up to go into clubs. Then Ruby asked me to come in with her, and I had to think of one of my characters that worked. Up until then, I'd always done something different.

Because Ruby's warm, fat and friendly, I had to be tall, lean and hard. I had a basic face that I worked: keep the eyes very draggy, to fit in with the drag make-up here, but not lashy and feminine and eye-shadowy, so that there was a difference between my make-up and their make-up. I then looked at Ruby's face as well, so it was a cross between the drag side, the Ruby side and a male side, and I tried to combine the three. I think what I came up with worked and through working with Ruby I became the masculine side to her feminine side, and we started doing things together. I still feel now I should almost get hissed and booed as I come on, not clapped and cheered. I am more the villain.

It has changed, because people know me now. I remember Christmas, when I first started going out on the floor, people would avoid me. OK, I had the image and the presence there, and they were scared by it. It must have been two or three months after I started working here, when one of the regulars who used to buy me drinks every night actually turned around to me and said 'I bought you drinks because I was terrified *not* to.'

I still have it with other regulars but there again, you become Jason when you talk to customers you know now, whereas then, because you didn't really know any of the customers and it was a much more different clientele, it was The Image. It's the same with Ruby. The two of us go out on the floor now and we're ourselves, we might as well not be in make-up now. Whereas in those days, because of the sort of clientele we had, the people didn't know you; they were fascinated by your being and you stayed in character so much longer.

Do you think that was better?

I wouldn't say better or worse. We're getting better again now. We went through a very slack period here, but this is one thing I've said to the office: when the club got successful, instead of becoming exclusive they became commercial. It's too small a club for it to be commercial.

When we were busy in those days, it's *then* that they should have stuck the rules down and it's *then*, when people called for a table, that they should have said 'Well sorry, we haven't got one tonight, but you can book for next Thursday.' We could have done it and we could have now been a club where people have to wait two weeks before they get in, a feat to get through the door. They had it within their grasp and lost it.

When you're a money man, and when you're running a place, it must be a very hard decision to make. But you know, is a place taking more money when you've got the tables full and you've got good spenders on them, or are you making more money when you pack it out and they're like sardines? The thing is only Sharon and Tracy will put up without comfort and, therefore, at the end of the day you lose your good spenders because they're not going to put up with an atmosphere like that. They want their comfort. It's like on a Friday or Saturday, it's pointless for the barbettes to be on the floor half the time. It's too busy. It's OK saying our club prices are reasonable; yes, reasonable if you're getting a service. But when they're three deep at the bar and the barbettes can't get through to the table, what service are you offering?

Where do you see the club going?

Well, you see, it's going to be very hard for them to get it back to the clientele we had. We're no longer going to be an exclusive venue. Unless the office kick themselves in the ass and make it more commercial, get more tourists in, then who knows if we're going to be here in a couple of years' time? It could quite easily continue, you know – we're quiet in the week at the moment but that could change, but it will take a lot more work from the office, a lot more incentive from people that have the power to do things about this.

I've heard them saying 'Well, the Fridge had so and so many in last week'; yes, they're comparing us to a one-nighter, a venue which is a gay one-nighter. How can they compare a gay one-nighter to what we're doing here? Yes we are a mixed club clientele-wise, but at the end of the day we're a commercial, tourist and straight crowd. We rely on our weekends now to pay our wages.

Moving into how drag affects him personally, I mentioned what I now refer to as 'The Torch Song Trilogy dilemma', and asked whether drag interfered with his chances of a lasting gay relationship.

I don't let that bother me. Unlike a lot of drag queens, I do have a very full life as myself.

I find it very sad when certain drag queens can only go out to clubs as them . . . Yes, occasionally I go to clubs as Venus, but I go out to tenfold more as myself. It's when you let the image overtake your life and don't think you can have a life without being a character, without being recognised by people knowing who you are, then you've got a problem. It's a job. It's like any other job I've had. You come in to work, you put your face on, you do it. It's like any of the theatrical jobs I've done except I wear high heels and more make-up.

Would you ever take it to the extent of somebody like RuPaul, writing her book, her exercise video, running around doing this, that and the other?

I met her in New York and she's a wonderful person, but again that is the new angle. Yes, I could take it further, but there's no *need* to. There is no niche for me on that level at the moment. It annoys me when people like Lily Savage and Regina Fong get fabulous breaks on TV, and both of them do brilliant work, but the minute they do anything they get the tabloids comparing them to a Julian Clary rip-off. And like, who is Julian Clary? I mean, what *is* he? He is the epitome of what a Northern housewife would like to think every gay male is like.

But at the same time, he got the break, he got the contract. Now, if I was offered that contract and was told, not necessarily to sell-out but 'We like what you do, but we'd like you to do it this way, and we'd like you to do that script and here's your pay cheque . . .' You know, how far do your morals go? It's very easy to say when you've not done it. He has publications now and a production company; he's done well for himself.

As the token gay?

It's the way that they are portraying him; they're so easy and so fickle with judging other talent, and it's like 'Oh my God, we've got this new outrageous person to talk about, oh class him with Julian Clary. It's *that* group, *that* category.' I have laughed at his shows, I have seen him do some good work, so I'm not ripping him off as a performer. He has a talent. I'm just annoyed that in future, when other people are coming up, they're going to be classed as a rip-off of him. That's all I'm saying.

On a different note, what do your parents think of you being here?

They are fabulous. I am so lucky with my parents, in the fact that I was always brought up to be very open.

Although I did have a bad patch when I was younger, now they are the most fabulous parents. They come down and they love it here. Ever since my first job in France . . . My dad, when I was at college, always got on at me and my funny clothes and the reason we didn't get on was that he was paying for me to go to college; he was convinced I would never work. One day, coming home from school, I stood there at the train station and he drove away without me. I had to phone my brother and say 'Come and pick me up'. But underneath, my mother always said that he did appreciate what I did, because he was always a frustrated artist, my father, but never got the chance to do it.

Now they come down and they're proud of me. My mum and dad came over to France and suddenly I was working. I had paid for them to come to the South of France, to Cannes. Dad was surrounded by topless female showgirls, which he still carries around photos of in his wallet. These two topless lead girls next to him, and he was fabulous. And they love it here.

You know we have our ups and downs, but they've made me the way I am, and I'm happy with what I am now. I understand why people have problems with parents but I cannot relate to it, because I never had that. I never had a day of having to come out.

I did have one experience, though. My dad's very old-fashioned and my brothers were never allowed to sleep with their girlfriends. Yet suddenly I brought a guy home with me and he was in the spare room. My dad works in the same town where John lives and John slept in the spare room. In the morning, we woke up in my bed with my dad tapping us on the shoulder to wake us up. I wasn't sure whether he was going to hit me or what. And he just casually said 'Would you like a coffee?', went and made us coffees, brought it up to us in bed and was fine with John all the way home. I could have picked my dad up then and kissed him.

Because, going back to sexuality, my dad never really wanted to talk about it. We still don't really talk about sexuality but, in his house, I blatantly threw it in his face which was wrong of me to do. Especially knowing that my brothers weren't allowed to sleep with their girlfriends at home, for me to do that was out of order. And he accepted it just like that. But, at the same time, the only reason he's old-fashioned is the fact that my elder brother has to do it first.

I was always the one that wanted to be first, but I would always have to push my brother, you know 'For God's sake get your ear pierced, I want mine pierced.' Things like that. And eventually it happened: I got my ear pierced because my mum and dad had an argument. And she thought 'Fuck it', she'd lost the argument, she took me into town and got my ear pierced, and then went 'Ha ha ha, *I* paid for it, you can't blame Jason, *I* did it.' That explains my mother.

One situation that has always intrigued me is the fact that, despite his long-term gayness, Jason has fathered two children. I asked him whether this was just a temporary lapse.

Well, no. I discovered male sexuality long before I discovered female sexuality. Sexually, things don't really happen to me with women; physically it doesn't work, and it's fucked me up a lot of times in my past. I've got a lot of female friends that I have been in love with: I love women, but sexually, men are for me. I was only fourteen with the first one, and I can't call it a stage I was going through, it was just a fabulous woman that I met. She was thirty-two and married, but I was hanging around with people a lot older than me. It was just a fling, a wild thing that happened. I was doing a lot more drugs in those days and it was part of the wacky, surrealistic world I was living in.

The second one, I still don't know whether it's mine or not. I'm not really that bothered, because she turned out to be a complete bitch. That was arranged, because I always had the first one working on my mind. There is that fatherly instinct in me, I do love children.

This was a girl who had had one ovary removed and apparently she was having the other one removed in four months' time. So if she was ever going to get pregnant, she was told, she had to have a kid then.

It was a feat and a half trying to keep it erect for that sexual session, because by then I was definitely a confirmed gay man. I didn't hear from her at all until I got a 'phone call at Metropolis just saying 'I've had the baby.' I'd heard so many lies about her since then, I asked her to go to the hospital to have tests to prove it was mine and have heard nothing from her since. I know people that have seen her around; she still insists that I'm the father and she's called it Jasmine, of all bloody names.

Yes, in a way I'd like later on in my life to think that the women would be sensible enough to let the kids find me, if they want to find me. But who knows? And now that I've got little Josh, I don't care. Josh is my kid. He's far more special to me than any biological kid I could ever have myself now. Because he's from two friends that are so dear to me. And, you know, with Scrubber not being here anymore, it is more like being a father than being a godfather. That kid is mine. It's one thing I can do for Scrubber: I can tell Josh what his father was like. Which isn't an easy job. But I'm very proud to have that opportunity. That's my baby.

What a lot of roles to play. How do you feel about your public persona?

I always feel quite embarrassed about it, I feel embarrassed if I'm out with the guys and someone says 'You're Venus, aren't you?' I actually almost feel uncomfortable.

It's like at the clubs: you go to all the clubs, and you get in free and everything else and it's really nice, but if I go to the door as a guy, not dressed up, and they don't recognise me, I'll pay to go in. I cannot say 'Hi, I'm Venus ManTrap from Madame JoJo's, surely you're going to let me in?' Yes, if I was in make-up, fair enough, because obviously the only reason they ever let anyone that's known – celebrity status, club status, or whatever – in, is because you're a known face and people say 'Oh, look who it is.' If I'm there as a man, I'm not giving them the image that they want, so why should they let me in free?

It's like this Cannes thing. I just think it's hysterical that I'm being paid to go to Cannes to do nothing apart from get pissed. I'm being flown out and hosting the Moving Pictures UK Party, where all I have to do is say 'We're here courtesy of Moving Pictures UK', and then go to a final night party, which Liz Taylor's hosting, as guests of honour. You know, guest of honour, courtesy of Liz Taylor. I'm like 'Hello, hello, who am I to deserve this?' I wear a bit of glittered lipstick, I walk around in high heels, and suddenly I am of the class to be introduced to Liz Taylor at *the* Cannes Film Festival party.

But that is my life in general. I mean *so far* that is my life. My life is black and white; I'm either at a fabulous party or I'm at the dole office signing on. It's never in between with me, I've never necessarily worked up through a ladder and I've either had brilliant jobs or I've had shit jobs. No in between. I love that, it keeps you in reality. I can go there for that weekend, have a fabulous time, mix with God knows who and do God knows what and the next day, I'll be back in Shepherd's Bush in a little tiny flat, thinking 'Well, you know'.

I do enjoy that liberal life, being an absolute nobody one minute and the next minute, being treated like royalty. And to have that within your life without being of that celebrity star status, where you can't do anything, being, just a couple of times a year, treated on that level and the rest of the time being able to go back into obscurity, I find fabulous.

I wouldn't want to be known as Venus that well, I don't think . . . or anyone. It's that soap opera status – I would hate to be thought of as anybody else, as a character, like a soap star is. Yes, I would like people to know who *I* was, but my definition of being successful, of making it in whatever career I'm doing is to have someone of major importance say 'I've created this part for you.' Or, you do a part, when you know you've had that part created for you, and whoever does that play afterwards, whatever, they're casting you. That is what I want from my professional career. Either as Jason or as Venus. But at the end of the day, it *is* Jason. Because Jason's created Venus.

For someone who, in his drunken moments, can give the impression of being a total headcase, Jason is probably the most well-adjusted person working here. Of everyone in this club he is certainly my vote for 'Most Likely to Succeed'. He has a healthy sense of self and a clear vision of which direction he's headed in, which in this environment makes him a rare species indeed.

I still find it incredible to think of two little female Jasons wandering the planet, let alone visualise their daddy in bed with a woman. Jason is one of the least bisexual people I know; I always assumed that he already knew he was gay prenatally. Must have been one hell of a 'surreal', druggie phase.

The androgynous one's parting words were to enjoy our relative obscurity and that he'd give Liz a kiss for us. Who, he is certain, will be an absolute blast. After all, he announced, 'Old stars never dry out, they just get better PR agents.' Better tell Ruby.

Sunday, 30th May

Checked out an *Arena* programme on Lou Reed's 'Walk on the Wild Side', a masochistic move, it turned out, with regards to getting a break from work. All very familiar stuff by now. Drag has always sold, and especially now during its very public 'revival'.

Lee 'Black' Childers, a friend of Candy, Jackie and Holly's, put Andy Warhol's films into a fairly accurate perspective, saying that 'He was creating stars. I don't think he really had a full grasp of it himself, of what he was doing to these people's lives. He created these people, who then could walk the streets of New York with a certain elevation above the rest of the scum.' He laughed and added, 'because they were suddenly *staaars*. They were still lowlife street people, panhandling; you didn't get much money, you know, for it. He would pay you, but not much.' Well, at least some things never change.

Warhol's attitude was considerably less understanding, stating that 'Those drag queens carry on and complain about all their problems and stuff. They don't really know what girls go through. I mean, they've never had a period.' The interviewer pointed out that 'they take those pills', which Andy dismissed, repeating, 'they've never had a period. They can't really tell.'

Speaking of not being able to tell, trannie Annie had a fantastic stroke of 'luck' the other night. She came in all shaken, having been mugged first on her council estate and then en route to the club. The guy held a knife to her throat, she gave him her things and thanked God that he hadn't tried to feel her. She probably would have been dead.

Did a final video-taping of the show early last week, in honour of my imminent departure. They are replacing me with a queen called Seana, who used to work at JoJo's fifty million odd years ago. Very nice, very relaxed, very *male*; obviously, the last fact also being the most important in my eyes. Call me insecure or egotistical, but I'm quite happy not to be replaced by another woman. Ruby overrode policy with her choice and it looks like a good one; Seana may not have the voice, but she has a lethal sense of humour and will bring an acidity to the show that I was not as capable of supplying. This situation is marvellous, because it avoids comparisons; also jealousy, from my point of view. If someone is going to take my place, I don't want it to be in the same way.

Tuesday, 1st June

Jason, star to the stars, is back. A tour de force, no less.

He was a huge hit, not only self-proclaimed but also pictured in all the major newspapers, TV broadcasts and MTV worldwide. Never one to let sudden fame go to his head, the ManTrap's unique blend of charisma and bitchiness was then extended to all major producers and directors who approached him, enquiring why they were important enough to waste his time on. I don't believe it.

Meanwhile, Teddi was vomiting in the foyer. What a delightful pair of ambassadors. To be fair, though, they apparently hosted the party with great aplomb, and delivered 'much more than was expected'. I just bet.

Wednesday, 2nd June

A very sweet, teary-eyed Teddi came down to the club last night and presented me with his parting gift, a book by Philip Core, called *Camp: The Lie That Tells the Truth*. Teddi's inscription was already enough to make me lose it and start bawling. It read: 'To my dear Queenie, "Once I was a little boy, With nasty thoughts inside my head, With friends and help and life and love, I've overcome those things I dread." I thank you, for your help over the last one-and-a-half years. I wish you every success. There are few talents out there. It's nice to know I worked with one. All my love, Teddi.'

The club as a whole has spoiled me shamelessly, and Ruby and Co pooled their resources, or an hour's drinking money, to buy me a beautiful gold necklace. Jokes aside, I now have a lump in my throat as well as around it.

Friday, 4th June

Just when you thought nothing could surprise you anymore, you get a drunk mad woman running on stage, trying to join in and hug all the performers. This was Wednesday night's drama, to which Jason grabbed her by the hair and half flung her down the stairs. Always the gentleman. We all just stood there amazed, never having had this experience at the club before. As did our beloved bouncers, who then got an earful backstage.

George assured us that this 'would NEVER occur again', which of course it promptly did the next night and with precisely the same results. Except this time it was a male, completely starkers, who ran drunkenly onto centre stage during Jason and Misha's 'It's Raining Men'. I'll say. We figured he must have undressed in the bathroom, as there was no way he could have done it in the club without somebody seeing. Which means he had to jog the entire length of the club and still no bouncer intercepted him. Absolutely pathetic, I thought. Ada agreed, although for a different reason, announcing 'I've seen more meat on a dirty fork.' Well, there you go.

Tomorrow is my last night and I already have well-wishers galore filtering in on my guest list as of tonight. The oddest part is that I don't think it has really sunk in yet. Everybody is getting all tearful and upset and I find myself having to play-act a sadness that I haven't had to come to grips with so far. Right now all I really feel is a mixture of exhaustion and numbness. With a small dose of anticipation.

Sunday, 6th June

It's 6am and Jason has just dropped me off. It seemed somehow right that he should be the last person to end up with, since I have developed a genuine, understated love for him. Which I know is reciprocated, even though we both acknowledged that there was no point to exchanging addresses since we're both terrible correspondents. Both of us knew intrinsically that we would not lose touch and, as Jason promised, 'whenever we're in the same town, we'll find each other.'

Ruby was red-eyed for the last three nights and declined coming out with us after the last show, deciding that it was too much like having to give up a baby for adoption.

I'm going to miss them so much. Primarily because I left in time. Much longer and I probably would have started to resent them as a natural consequence of feeling trapped in a dead-end job. I can't say world, because I very much doubt that I can ever leave it behind. Somehow, as much as I became a part of it, it has become a part of me. I realised this last night, when everybody was showering me with love and gifts and asking whether I'd ever conceive of doing drag again. My immediate response was 'Not a chance, I've had enough,' but I know that to be a lie. Drag gave me a freedom that I'd never encountered before and I'm left wondering whether I will ever be able to recapture it in any other way again.

210

Andy, one of the barmen, wrote on my show poster that they presented me with on stage, 'The End of An Era'. Yes and no. The career side of it is over for me, at least for now, and certainly with regards to JoJo's. But I cannot guarantee that if Ruby got together a fantastic club . . . well, let's just say that Queen Bea is still alive and tap dancing 'Pit Pat Pit Little April Showers' in galoshes somewhere deep in my soul. As The Eagles sang, 'You can check out anytime you like, but you can never leave'.

Epilogue

Dear Alex,

One whole week chalked up so far, since my return to a very grey, bleak London town. Look me straight in the eye and tell me you still wish you lived here . . .

Perhaps this is being unfair to what is, in the immortal words of Johnson, only a boring town when one is bored of life. Put in that light, I don't know whether I am merely offering an accurate weather report or wallowing in the depressing readjustment to a new, somehow emptier, reality. It is quite disheartening to be pounding the well-worn turf and feeling out of place, temporarily without a London identity. Suffice it to say, even the same old streets seem different and, in my own eyes, I have grown a million light years removed from the person I was nine months ago.

Fortunately not, however, from the people that helped define my self-image and daily existence. Have been out with a fair bulk and vive la difference! Careers derailing and re-routeing all over the shop, not to mention personal lives. Makes my becoming a Country and Western DJ of the US airwaves look par for the course, really.

The interesting thing, or sad (depending on perspective) is that precious little is being played out against the backdrop of JoJo's. The entire cast was sacked last September, shockingly enough, so I suppose my agonised departure was a stroke of good fortune in the final analysis. At least that is what a number of the gang told me, adding that they wished they'd left simultaneously and avoided this disillusioning embarrassment.

I gather that the constant reminder of Debbie Raymond became too much for the Chief to bear; well, that is my overly romanticised view of what is probably simple and sound financial reasoning. Either way, PR decided to lease the club to another management. They, in turn, offered jobs on the basis of re-auditioning, which the trannie informed me 'of course went down like a bucket of cold sick.' I can just picture it.

Doing this to Ruby was a calculated insult. On a par with the tale of Shelley Winters being requested to audition for a part and, upon arrival, being asked for her CV. Legend has it that she opened her handbag and slammed two Oscars on the table before calmly walking out. I imagine Ruby's version may have been considerably less eloquent.

Needless to say, the cast declined and are now doing independent work throughout London, although of varying natures. Starting on a happy note, Jason is currently on tenterhooks awaiting the go-ahead for the budgeting of his late-night gay chat show. This is alternated with his rocketing European cabaret career, so the Venus ManTrap cohabits a curious existence with his Mr Media, Junior Gaultier alter ego. His ability to combine the two makes me marvel as I find my desire to perform on stage decreasing in direct proportion to my advances in broadcasting. Call it ego, but I find the thrill of variety and intellectual challenge a total contrast to the usual drag routine, and the knowledge that I can affect more people in one broadcast than I could squeeze into JoJo's throughout an entire year, totally addictive.

Steve has also managed to remain true to his love of the stage, to the extent that he even briefly contemplated a return to the club before being rescued and hurled into the artistic big time. So far, brushes have included a cameo appearance as – shock, surprise – a stripper in *Bhaji on the Beach*, but we gasped last night at his brilliant rendition of Macheath in *The Threepenny Opera*. Our boy has moved ahead in leaps and bounds, and is displaying all signs of being the Midas of the career scene; latest developments include a screen test as Zeffirelli's potential *Siegfried*.

Day-times see him charging about as co-owner of Rox, the Old Compton Street hairdressing salon established by him and Pete, which has so far featured in all the leading magazines. Plans include opening a branch in NYC, so maybe Steve's dreams of working State-side will come true after all. Pete has just completed his very successful gay map of London, and New York will no doubt afford him an excellent opportunity to expand his fledgling cartography empire. Their friendship has, remarkably, persevered despite their recent split, which is sadly more than can be said of Ruby and Jason's.

I am still not entirely sure what went wrong, as there have been so many different versions and whispers, but the gist appears to be that Ruby is smarting from some imagined wrong-doing at Jason's hands. Jason retorted privately that it was absurd and she was merely feeling guilt pangs and paranoia about another issue, but whatever it was, she has not been seen or heard from since Christmas. Rumours are flying that she has finally escaped to her long discussed tax exile in the sun, but I can't really see it.

Mitzi, happily, is a positive development, and one of the few still at the club: she proudly showed me her name on the licence outside the Piano Bar. Presumably printed over George's, who was flung out of the club along with most of the staff. These managed to find employment at Rox, with Steve, and at Base, where George now works. Stories circulate about George running around asking people whether they were enjoying the music, which in a venue like this is about as appropriate as distributing canapés and kirs. The extent of his discomfort can probably best be gauged by his decision to try and start his own place; word has it that he is negotiating with Schnitzel for some premises around the corner from JoJo's, trying to model it on the golden days of yore and possibly having Venus front the entire shebang. Look out, unsuspecting world.

The one to whom my heart really goes out is Misha. He was the only person to submit to the humbling position of re-auditioning, just to be 'granted' a part as a backing barbette. True to form, he managed to work his way up, partly thanks to the sacking of the chosen choreographer and the director's subsequent resignation. Three weeks later, Misha had taken over both jobs *and* the star role at the club. Sadly, the final result was nowhere near its previous calibre; this from Misha's mouth, I hasten to add, not a bitchy after-gripe of my own. To give credit where it's due, Misha actually blossomed, to the extent that upon hearing his fantastic version of 'Rough and Ready Man', Jason turned to me and shrieked, 'That bitch never sang like that for us! Where did this *voice* come from?' Now he's been informed that his services are no longer required, and that he is being replaced by Terri Fox and – wait for it – Teddi, whom Misha had recruited back. This has got to be about the only plus for the new show, to be directed by our favourite visionary, Pablo, and entirely mimed.

Darling, I can't tell you the disappointment that provokes in me. Even the Piano Bar is being transformed into a hostess bar and the Dream Boys are being shipped into Jo's to perform every Monday and Tuesday. As Jason quietly echoed, 'This really is the end of an era.'

I met up with Misha for dinner the other night and finally felt in the position to offer some sisterly insight: 'We've all been there, we've all had to leave and forge new lives for ourselves. As great as the loss is, you can't wish it back; it just wouldn't be the same.' I think this outlook may have added implications for Misha, whose latest surprise tactic consisted of grabbing both my hands in the middle of Café Casbah, and thrusting them upon his new silicone breast implants. Dressed as two women, this of course raised a few eyebrows and was certainly a great deal more amusing than the prospect of Misha's impending trip home to the ancestral pile. I still don't know what to make of it all: why have your tits done if you don't necessarily plan to have the full operation? He talks of having reconciled himself to eternal solitary living, but what if he does fall in love? Furthermore, Misha still doesn't concede any elements of gayness in himself, and is talking of performing in Las Vegas now . . . Good luck.

Speaking of which, word has hit my royal ear that Marcie has finally leaped in the deep end while holidaying in sunny Mexico and become Enrico's ideal, *real* woman. That one really floored me. Ditto for trannie Annie, who is taking the whole thing a step further and sealing it with a wedding band. Which, of course, brings me to you.

I can finally, and in all honesty, say 'Congratulations' on your surprise marriage. Although I don't think either of us ever really understood the reason for our split-up last summer, I know it was for the best. Unexpected, certainly, to have the very freedom from the club that we longed for help bring about our undoing; I suppose we just wanted very different things. Nevertheless, and clichéd as it may sound, I'm glad that you were a part of my life.

I sat chewing the cud with Jason the other night and we both decided that, for all the griping and groaning, every one of us left Madame JoJo's richer. Certainly not financially – Schnitzel saw to that – but better and wiser for the experience. With hindsight, I can even bring myself to acknowledge a debt to the Paul Raymond Organisation; without them and their club, a lot of magic would never have happened. We were just lucky to be part of a pretty transient world while it lasted.

For all the annoyances, insecurities and chaos, our lives at JoJo's were never dull. I don't think many people can say that.

Bea, a.k.a Queenie.

215